REFRAMING
HOLOCAUST
TESTIMONY

THE MODERN JEWISH EXPERIENCE

Deborah Dash Moore and Marsha L. Rozenblit, editors

Paula Hyman, founding coeditor

REFRAMING
HOLOCAUST
TESTIMONY

NOAH SHENKER

Indiana University Press
Bloomington and Indianapolis

This book is a publication of

INDIANA UNIVERSITY PRESS
Office of Scholarly Publishing
Herman B Wells Library 350
1320 East 10th Street
Bloomington, Indiana 47405 USA

iupress.indiana.edu

The paper used in this publication meets the minimum requirements of the
American National Standard for Information Sciences—Permanence of Paper
for Printed Library Materials, ANSI Z39.48-1992.

Manufactured in the United States of America

Library of Congress Cataloging-in-Publication Data

Shenker, Noah [date] author.
Reframing Holocaust testimony / Noah Shenker.
    pages cm. – (The modern Jewish experience)
  Includes bibliographical references and index.
  ISBN 978-0-253-01709-3 (cloth : alkaline paper) — 978-0-253-01713-0 (paperback :
alkaline paper) — ISBN 978-0-253-01717-8 (ebook) 1. Holocaust, Jewish (1939-1945)—
Influence. 2. Holocaust, Jewish (1939-1945)—Study and teaching—Audio-visual
aids. 3. Holocaust, Jewish (1939-1945)—Social aspects. 4. Oral history—Audio-visual
aids. 5. Video recording—Influence. 6. Interviewing—Technique. I. Title.
  D804.3 .S557 2015
  940.53/18075
                                                                    2015004496

1 2 3 4 5 20 19 18 17 16 15

In Loving Memory of David M. Shenker, MD

1942–2012

CONTENTS

Preface   ix

Acknowledgments   xiii

Introduction: Testimonial Literacy   1

1. Testimonies from the Grassroots: The Fortunoff
    Video Archive for Holocaust Testimonies   19

2. Centralizing Holocaust Testimony: The United States
    Holocaust Memorial Museum   56

3. The Cinematic Origins and the Digital Future
    of the Shoah Foundation   112

4. Telling and Retelling Holocaust Testimonies   151

    Conclusion: Documenting Genocide through
    the Lens of the Holocaust   192

Notes   199

References   229

Index   239

PREFACE

In February of 2007 I accompanied Joan Ringelheim, then the director of the United States Holocaust Memorial Museum's oral history department, as she set out by car from Washington, D.C., to a quiet residential neighborhood in Virginia. There, at the home of a cameraman with whom she had worked several times before, Ringelheim prepared to interview Sarah Z., a Polish Jewish survivor of the Holocaust.[1] The comfortable domestic space appeared to put Sarah at ease immediately upon her arrival. The living room had been set up as a recording studio, complete with sound padding and a black backdrop. The basement den housed a monitor for Ringelheim's assistant, Elizabeth Hedlund, who took notes that would later be used for cataloguing the testimony. As the video camera ran, Sarah was composed in recounting stories of having grown up in a small apartment in Warsaw and describing her family life and the celebration of Jewish holidays, all of which were disrupted by Germany's invasion of Poland.

In the midst of watching her recount her wartime events, we paused for coffee and pastries. During that intermission, Sarah spoke with much more animation about her personal history and her experiences recording the interview with Ringelheim, me, and the crew members, remarking that her memories "stay with you all the time." Her recollections of the Holocaust were not compartmentalized, only to be revealed at the start of the recorded testimony, but were entangled elements of her life. Later that day we took another break, this time for lunch. Gathered around the table, Sarah recounted in fuller detail, compared to her video testimony account, her son's car accident as a young man, his subsequent paralysis and eventual death a decade after the incident, and the unbearable pain of burying her own child. Her fluent on-camera performance of the relatively insulated experiences of her wartime childhood contrasted with her less polished and more destabilized expressions of grief off-camera as she recounted to us the story of her son's death. For Sarah, her process of giving testimony not only concerned reconstructing events taking place during the Holocaust, but also engaged with her own personal forms of remembering that went beyond the wartime era. Whereas she was controlled and confident on-camera, she lost her composure when facing, off-camera, the challenges of her postwar family history.

I set this scene, as it were, in order to underscore the extent to which the interview with Sarah extended beyond what was captured on the archived tape; it was conducted across a continuum where the interview flowed into the preparation and downtime, the coffees and the lunches, that marked the recording process. The interruptions, tape changes, and other intermissions illuminated the ways in which the Holocaust did not necessarily entail the most traumatic events of Sarah's biography—the loss of one of her sons *after* the Shoah was perhaps equally if not more central. Ultimately, the documentation of Sarah's testimony reflects the dynamics that are fundamental to this book—the potentially contested and collaborative, though always mediated and layered interrelationships between witnesses and the archives and interviewers that collect their stories.

From Living to Testimonial Memory

Although audio and audiovisual interviews with Holocaust survivors have been recorded since the end of World War II, the period between the late 1970s and the early 1990s saw a proliferation of video Holocaust testimony archives in the United States, constituting a combined collection of more than 60,000 interviews.[2] They emerged in anticipation of the passing of the survivor community—a development that underscores the challenges of preserving experientially charged testimonies of the Holocaust in the absence of living witnesses. That is not to suggest that testimonies of living survivors delivered in person at museums, archives, and other spaces are raw accounts in contrast to their framed audiovisual versions. Rather, it is notable that archives and museums mediate both of those forms of witnessing.

With these concerns in the foreground, *Reframing Holocaust Testimony* focuses on three archives and memorial sites in the United States: the Fortunoff Video Archive for Holocaust Testimonies (or Fortunoff Archive) at Yale University; the United States Holocaust Memorial Museum (the Holocaust Museum, USHMM, or simply the museum) in Washington, D.C.; and the USC Shoah Foundation (or Shoah Foundation) in Los Angeles. These three institutions represent quite distinct yet at times intersecting institutional histories and approaches to the collection and dissemination of testimonies. However, the archival structures of these sites do not determine the potential meanings and uses of their respective holdings. While certain infrastructures serve to advance a particular archive's representational and institutional cultures and aims, the spontaneous and fragmentary dimensions of personal memory are not always easily integrated with or subordinated to those preferences. An examination of specific interviews in relation to particular institutional frameworks can demonstrate the dynamic and often contested performances of testimonies, as well as how the traumatic registers of memories often disrupt or transcend archival attempts to contain and instrumentalize stories of the Holocaust.

The Americanization of the Holocaust

Reframing Holocaust Testimony focuses exclusively on archives based within the United States (though these archives house testimonies recorded worldwide, in dozens of languages) in order to explore how audiovisual testimonies of witnesses have in part facilitated the Americanization of the Holocaust. That entails a process by which the events of a defining European event have been imported by, and adapted to, the cultural narratives, institutions, and political contexts of the United States.[3] Although filmmakers and educators have played key roles in this process, this book pays particular attention to the influence of museums and testimonial archives within the United States. Since the end of World War II, tension between particularistic and more universalizing notions of representing and mobilizing the Holocaust in America has assumed an integral role in a debate about how the nation's Jewish community frames its collective identity.

The geographic, as well as temporal, distance of the Nazi Holocaust—what James Young refers to as the absence of a "topography of terror" in the United States—has enabled survivors to acquire central roles in constructing an interpersonal bridge to the events, allowing their experiences of genocide to be integrated into the collective memory of a country far removed from the catastrophe.[4] Young has described a process by which survivors "reinscrib[ed] these [Holocaust] memorials with the memory of their own origins."[5] So too, it is possible to reinscribe testimony archives with the memory of their development, including their integration of the Holocaust into an "experiential mode" of exhibition that has become common at sites such as the United States Holocaust Memorial Museum. This institutionalization of the Holocaust also serves the effort to narrow the spatial and temporal chasm between present American memorializations of the Holocaust and the historical events they commemorate.

As this book focuses exclusively on American archives, the witnesses whose testimonies are examined deliver their accounts in English, rather than in their native tongues, and include primarily those who resettled in North America after the war. The use of English in the surveyed testimonies is crucial, as language is itself a mediating factor in shaping how witnesses recall the past, with varying implications.[6] Nonetheless, because many of these recordings circulate beyond North America and speak to issues in testimony that transcend national borders (including the documentation of contemporary genocides and human rights crises across the globe), much broader implications can be gleaned from this study. Finally, although the three archives featured in this book are not the only institutions of their kind that have value, they are foregrounded because each site represents distinct, yet also intersecting approaches to, and cultures of, testimony; they range from what were originally more local, grassroots efforts to those that were conceived as centralized projects with national and global ambitions.

Institutional Cultures of Testimony

Testimonies of the Holocaust are co-constituted through distinctive archival approaches working in dialogue with the individual witnesses, and are not simply captured as "raw" accounts. Therefore, this book examines testimonies within the larger contexts of their diverse institutional creation rather than limiting analysis to recorded interviews. It is based on comprehensive research and writing conducted over the course of a decade, with three years combined working on-site with the institutional archives of each of the three case studies, in addition to conducting a close examination of over two hundred video interviews in their entirety. That work draws from a wide array of sources including internal institutional files, interviews with archive and museum staff and faculty, combined with close analysis of archived audiovisual testimonies and their editing for use in documentary films, interactive programming, museum displays, educational programs, and other exhibition formats. Working from this broad constellation of sources from each of the three institutions, I was able to develop new comparative analytical frameworks for examining the productive tensions between archives and witnesses. Although each archive adopted its own unique cultures and methodologies to mediating testimonies, survivors have their own authorial voices that often exceed archival preferences. Those voices are essential to this book.

ACKNOWLEDGMENTS

There are several people who I would like to thank for their indelible influence on this book. The condensed format of these acknowledgements limits my ability to convey the full extent of my thanks, but I hope that the following words will in some small way express the depth of my gratitude.

I want to thank Michael Renov, whose patient, generous, and insightful guidance over these many years has shaped this book. In his own scholarship and in his consultation on this project, he has always reminded me to keep my eyes and ears trained on the ethical aspects of any mediated exchange and to always be sensitive to the texture of individual experience when analyzing the institutional landscapes of testimony. I would also like to thank Janet Walker, whose eloquent work on issues of trauma has had a formative influence on my own scholarship, particularly as I grapple with questions of maintaining a historical investment in Holocaust testimonies without jettisoning a concern for the vicissitudes and subjectivities of individual memory. Furthermore, her personal guidance and advocacy for this project have been instrumental to helping me maintain my footing when my confidence seemed depleted. To Paul Lerner, I extend my sincere thanks for his warm encouragement and for setting such a wonderful example in both his scholarship and teaching. While he and I work in different fields, his influence on this book transcends disciplinary lines. I am also grateful to Henry Greenspan, who taught one of my first university classes and who has illuminated through both his research and pedagogy the ways in which Holocaust testimonies emerge through labor and dialogue. As I remind my students, titles always matter, and I am immensely grateful to Cathy Caruth in suggesting the one that finally made it to the cover of this book. I also extend my warm gratitude to Amy Hackett, who provided valuable observations and much-needed bluntness as I confronted the editorial process.

There are several friends and peers who provided instrumental communities of support. In particular, I would like to thank Chris Cooling, who has always been there to help me step back from my work and remain anchored and focused on my obligations to the world outside of this book. I am also indebted to Dan Leopard, David Bressler, Lauren Kaminsky, Michelle Standley, Dan Lurie, Lesleigh Cushing, Ben Stahlberg, Rick Stapleton, Jeff Trzeciak, Elliott Shore, and David McCabe, along with others, who have provided much-needed warmth and encouragement in addition to rich intellectual discussions. Moreover, this project would never have taken its final form without the intellectual exchanges and friendships cultivated during my fellowships from McMaster University, the Council on Library and Information Resources, the Holocaust Educational Foundation, and the United States Holocaust Memorial Museum. At the latter I was particularly privileged to forge enduring personal and professional relationships with Daniella Doron, Paul Jaskot, and Eran Neuman.

This book was made possible in part by funds granted to the author through a Charles H. Revson Fellowship at the Jack, Joseph and Morton Mandel Center for Advanced Holocaust Studies of the United States Holocaust Memorial Museum. The statements made and views expressed, however, are solely the responsibility of the author. I am also grateful to the Emerging Scholars Program at the Mandel Center for Advanced Holocaust Studies for its support in the preparation of the manuscript and of the book proposal. The Revson Foundation Fellowship provided me with access to the resources of the United States Holocaust Memorial Museum, including not only the institutional archives and other holdings of that institution, but also its wonderful staff members and administrators who went above and beyond in taking the time to meet with me and discuss my research.

With that in mind, I would also like to extend my sincere gratitude to the faculty and staff of each of the three institutions examined in my book: the USC Shoah Foundation, the Fortunoff Video Archive for Holocaust Testimonies, and the United States Holocaust Memorial Museum. I owe much of my work in this book to the time, resources, and input provided to me by the people who are passionately committed to the work of testimony carried out by those institutions. Those archivists, staff and faculty members, and administrators include (though are not limited to) Stephen Naron, Debra Bush, Joan Ringelheim, Elizabeth Hedlund, Raye Farr, Lisa Yavnai, Avi Patt, Jeff Carter, Edna Friedberg, Ann Millen, Bridget Conley-Zilkic, Ellen Blalock, Leah Wolfson, Susan Bachrach, Steven Feldman, Michael Gelb, Douglas Greenberg, Stephen Smith, Douglas Ballman, Crispin Brooks, Karen Jungblut, and Ari Zev. I am most indebted to the archivist of the Fortunoff Archive, Joanne Ruduof, who has been tremendously generous with her time and keen insights, as well her frank and incisive comments on this project. I have also greatly benefited from the perspectives generated in vibrant conversations with Lawrence Langer, Marion Kaplan, Atina Grossmann, Dawn Skorczewski, Oren Baruch Stier, Laura Levitt, and Selma Leydesdorff.

The completion of this book would not have been possible without the immense support of the Modern Jewish Experience editors, Deborah Dash Moore and Marsha L. Rozenblit, and the remarkable work of Indiana University Press, particularly on the part of Dee Mortensen, Janet Rabinowitch, Nancy Lightfoot,

Sarah Jacobi, and Joyce Rappaport, among others working as part of the IUP team. Their dedication to this project has been unstinting. And I would be remiss if I did not thank Edward Linenthal and Avi Patt for going above and beyond in their incredibly close reading of the book manuscript.

I am immensely fortunate to be on the faculty of the Australian Centre for Jewish Civilisation (ACJC) and the larger Faculty of Arts at Monash University, an institution that serves as my academic home in the most genuine sense of the term. It has provided me with a vibrant community of scholars from whom to learn and with whom to shape this book and my professional development at large. I am thankful to my colleagues within the School of Philosophical, Historical and International Studies, particularly those members of my research group who have given generously of their time and effort in reading and commenting on various portions of the book. I am most grateful to my wonderful ACJC colleagues, including Mark Baker, Andrew Markus, Leah Garrett, Daniella Doron, Nathan Wolski, Andrew Benjamin, and Helen Midler, and for the generous support provided by Naomi Milgrom, Ricci Swart, and their families.

I would like to conclude these acknowledgements by thanking those who have been particularly privy to the challenges and rewards that have manifested throughout the course of this project. I earlier mentioned Daniella Doron, to whom I am eternally grateful for our immersing conversations held in the lounge chairs of our shared office space at the Holocaust Museum. It is during those discussions that not only my book, but also our close relationship, were cemented. She has been an unending source of support, scholarly example, and joy—not to mention very careful and close reading—and has sustained me throughout this very difficult process. Eldad and Marsha Doron have also provided much comfort along the way.

I am also indebted to my loving family, including my resourceful and loving mother Judy Shenker, and my supportive sisters Abby Nimberg and Amy Shenker. They have always availed themselves under very difficult circumstances and continue to provide me with the foundation upon which this work, my future scholarship, and my personal development will continue to rest. I am also guided by the beloved memory of my grandparents Rabbi David and Aviva Polish, who instilled in me a passion for intellectual inquiry and intense ideological and political debate forged at their Shabbat dinner table.

Finally, this book is dedicated in loving, devoted memory of my father, David M. Shenker, MD. As I consider those who contributed to this book, I cannot help but think of endless hours as a child, sitting with him in his study as he combed over my writing on yellow legal pads, ensuring that each word and sentence was carefully considered. Both that experience and my father's tireless work ethic and exemplary character continue to shape not simply my scholarship but also my larger life.

Acknowledgments   *xv*

REFRAMING
HOLOCAUST
TESTIMONY

Introduction

Testimonial Literacy

We are transitioning into an era in which survivors of the Holocaust will no longer be alive, leaving behind only documented traces of their testimonies. To preserve the individual and historical textures of those experiences, it is imperative to cultivate infrastructures for and approaches to testimonies that train our sensitivity to their lived, physical origins as well as to the institutional practices that shaped them. Fundamental to inheriting Holocaust survivor memories is the recognition that the faces, bodies, and voices of testimonial subjects not only provide necessary interpersonal and ethical underpinnings for attending to the suffering of others, but that they also work in conversation with an array of archival infrastructures. Testimonies emerge from an individually and institutionally embedded practice framed by a diverse range of aims that cannot be reduced to their empirical historical content or visceral impact. In that sense, post-Holocaust generations receive testimonies not as enclosed capsules of memory but as constantly mediated, contested, and fragile acts of remembering. Not only are testimonies molded by institutional and technical interventions at the moment of their recording, but they are also shaped as they migrate across various media platforms and as archivists develop new forms of digital preservation.

Examining Holocaust testimonies involves looking at these infrastructures and the labor of the interview process, extending to moments that never make it to the video screen. Analysis presents the challenge of addressing the media specificities of testimonies—of examining them not as raw sources but as processes mediated by the encounter between witnesses and the interviewers and technologies employed by an archive. Those include the roles of institutional protocols, those that are not always apparent on screen (e.g., pre-interview questioning, internal ratings of testimonies, and staff debates about the usability of testimony), that impact the production and reception of testimony. On-screen issues ranging from the depth and nature of interview questions, the lighting setup, and the placement of interviewees within the camera frame also influence how testimony is delivered at the moment of production and transmitted to future generations. Furthermore, some moments in testimonies emphasize how witnesses express themselves through tone of voice, physical gestures, and frequent silences. The meanings generated from those expressions emerge through careful listening and viewing by audiences, and hence an examination of testimonies is inexorably linked to a consideration of the debates and choices that shape how testimony is delivered and filtered.

The proliferation of archives that collect and disseminate testimonies of the Holocaust has been matched by diverse and expansive efforts to teach, research, and theorize about those sources. *Reframing Holocaust Testimony* illuminates those practices and discourses by examining audiovisual testimonies of the Holocaust with the aim of cultivating what I term *testimonial literacy,* or an eye and ear for sensing the layers, ruptures, and tensions that mark the processes of giving and receiving accounts of the Shoah. That literacy also entails an awareness of the messier, more unplanned moments that emerge throughout the testimony process but do not necessarily make their way into exhibited or officially transcribed testimonies. These include exchanges caught between takes, as the camera continues to roll but the interviewer is unaware of that fact. And it extends to the sighs and screams that are withheld from the transcript for fear of suggesting emotion at the expense of sobriety.

Such moments that capture a sense of the mutual labor involved in testimony are often consigned to the periphery rather than the center of the archival process. And in relegating them to the margins, archives often obscure the preferences and approaches that interviewers and archivists bring to the work of testimony. However, video testimonies can also exceed the intentions and methodologies of their respective archives. Analytical approaches developed within film and media studies are central to this book as they help to draw attention to the fleeting, ephemeral, seemingly marginal elements that flicker across media screens or are left on the cutting-room floor, but that nonetheless represent unexpected and essential traces of meaning. It is crucial to first become familiar with the various architectures and media forms of remembrance that shape interviews before analyzing the extent to which video testimonies can transcend their framing and leave behind illuminating fragments.

Reframing Holocaust Testimony moves beyond an exploration of the relationship between interviewers and interviewees in order to develop a systematic and comprehensive approach to locating the institutional voices of Holocaust testimonies.[1] Whether in the case of the Fortunoff Archive, the Holocaust Museum, or the Shoah Foundation, an archive's interview methods are never neutral; rather, they are embedded in particular sets of institutional histories and methodologies. In calling attention to those mediating factors, Geoffrey Hartman has noted the following: "While the video testimonies have an unusually direct emotional impact, they are mediated by frame conditions."[2] Hartman includes in this category having survivors speak in languages other than their mother tongue and being interviewed at a time and place that is far removed from the historical events.[3] This book expands upon Hartman's concept of frame conditions to analyze how testimonies are created by the particular institutional cultures and media practices of the three archives under examination, working in conversation and often in conflict with individual witnesses.[4]

Marianne Hirsch has eloquently reflected on the ways that the Holocaust is becoming "multiply mediated."[5] Her examination of the ethical and empathetic dimensions of confronting and teaching the Holocaust in the "face of extremity" conceives of future generations as inheritors of Holocaust memory.[6] By proposing the term *postmemory* to describe the movement away from a living connection to the Holocaust, Hirsch describes how subsequent generations who engage images of the Shoah can be "fully cognizant of the mediated and media-driven source of representation that shapes both knowledge and meaning of the Holocaust."[7] As she contends, the emergence of postmemory has the potential to facilitate a process of "retrospective witnessing by adoption" or "adopting the traumatic experiences—and thus also the memories of others—as experiences one might oneself have had."[8] Rather than constituting an act of appropriation, Hirsch contends that "on the contrary, compulsive and traumatic repetition connects the second generation to the first, producing rather than screening out the effect of trauma that was lived so much more directly as compulsive repetition by survivors and contemporary witnesses."[9]

The concept of postmemory has potentially strong purchase in regards to audiovisual testimonies, even though it was originally developed in response to photographs and other still images of the Holocaust. More specifically, the "embodied knowledge" that is being transferred to postmemory generations is increasingly manifest in the form of video testimonies across a multitude of venues including museums, archives, and online communities.[10] Certain formative scholarship on audiovisual Holocaust testimonies has not comprehensively addressed those multiple mediations, including issues of institutional and archival practices.[11] That influential body of work often emphasizes the one-to-one transferential dynamic between the interviewer and the interviewee, usually at the expense of examining how formal practices and institutional infrastructures shape not only the production of testimony, but also its dissemination and reception across multiple archives and interviews.[12] Nevertheless, there has been a growing group of scholars directing their work toward issues of archival reception and technical mediation, thereby expanding on the established canon of testimony scholarship.[13]

This book falls within that latter group by salvaging the archival voices of testimonies, but is still equally concerned with identifying and preserving the traces of what Michael Renov describes as "embodied memory" within testimony archives, that is, the individual expressions of witnesses that can often work against the more universalizing and instrumentalizing dimensions of interview protocols.[14] The archives featured in this book do not necessarily approach the production and prospective reception of testimonies with the same degree of investment. Certainly it is crucial to acknowledge that each of the three selected sites adopts its own set of expectations concerning how testimonies will be developed, conducted, and accessed. At the same time, this book does not lose sight of the signatures of individual expressions in testimonies. The performances of individual testimonies underscore how witnesses can represent a form of embodied history that cannot be relegated to institutional and depersonalized discourses of knowledge and power.[15] In other words, some poetic expressions of testimonies evade positivistic categorization and segmentation. Yet at the same time, those poetic aspects of testimony are subjected to several mediating factors.[16]

One of the challenges presented by this project has been the task of analyzing the archives in question as potential venues for generating a "counter-cinematic form" that will resist the historical amnesia associated with mass media.[17] As Geoffrey Hartman argues, testimonies can serve that counter-cinematic function as sources for training our eyes and ears to the textures of individual expression rather than as impositions of narrative closure and coherence. As central as it is for archives to create spaces where witnesses freely express themselves and where audiences can be "trained to hear" (as well as see) those testimonies, there is also the challenge of archives drawing attention to other voices that enter into the conversation—including the presence of the interviewer (or interviewers) and the epistemological preferences of institutions.[18] An archive's holdings provide a window into the infrastructures that help frame the lived quality of testimonies, rather than positioning them as part of a "living monument of retrieved voices" uttered by witnesses.[19]

Certain scholars have advocated that archives openly, perhaps even self-reflexively, acknowledge the processes and limits that shape their collection of testimonies.[20] However, in the absence of that deliberate, critically aware turn in institutional authorship, users and critics of more conventional testimony projects can nonetheless listen and watch closely for unintended and revealing ruptures that express the frictions and layers of memory work, thus complicating the imposition of false closure and its accompanying narrative pleasures. Testimonies can thus embody the notion of "received history," one that "interweaves both events of the Holocaust and the ways they are passed down to us." That concept can be extended to archives, often by reading against the grain of their respective institutional preferences.[21]

The Dynamics of Testimony

The three case studies that constitute the core of this book describe how memorial sites and archives attempt to structure the encounter between witnesses and interviewers, and subsequently that between recorded testimonies and audiences, in ways that have profound analytical, affective, and ethical implications. The institutions being examined give varying degrees of agency to witnesses during the process of collecting their testimonies, and each approach shapes the process of reenacting the past. Therefore, by exploring the architectures of the interview process, this book can shed light on the spaces where both archives and witnesses assert their respective agency. That exploration can honor the individual textures of witnesses' memories, while also calling attention to how archives can be both midwives and obstacles to the creation of testimonial memories.

Given the highly mediated quality of Holocaust testimony, the compelling conceptions of deep and common memory explored by Lawrence Langer, Saul Friedländer, and Charlotte Delbo should be wedded with an analysis of the archival methods that help elicit them. Expanding on Delbo's conceptualization of Holocaust memories, Langer differentiates common memory from deep memory, showing how a witness can move from the chronologically grounded and more removed nature of the former, only to find him- or herself thrown out of sequence by the destabilizing and often anti-redemptive grip of the latter.[22] That has often been evident in my own research as I observe how certain archives and interviewers are invested in developing more easily accessible, often chronologically charted testimonies (that is, common memory), only to meet resistance from subjects who are thrown back into the past, unable to move forward with a particular account as they are immersed in deep memory. In that sense, while testimony archives do not simply capture or record common and deep memory, they do influence how they emerge and take shape. Friedländer has expressed a particular concern that the traces of deep memory will fade from the scene after survivors pass away, leaving in their place a more redemptive, restorative common memory. *Reframing Holocaust Testimony* engages that prospect, examining the possibilities of preserving the recorded traces of survivor's stories and then transmitting them "beyond individual recall," perhaps by maintaining deep memory through particular modes of archival production and testimonial interpretation in lieu of living carriers.[23]

The challenge remains for archivists, scholars, and users of testimonies to avoid reducing witnesses to particular archival expectations. Langer's perspectives on testimony tend to emphasize its anti-redemptive nature, working against cathartic interpersonal exchanges by presenting "frozen moments of anguish."[24] Patricia Yaeger has noted precisely this kind of dynamic, describing moments in testimony that "refute our compassion and constitute zones of experience that may be sympathy-secluded, empathy-unfriendly: that jar the act of compassion."[25] As my analysis of particular testimonies will show, there are moments that personify Yaeger's description of "when something uncontrolled and uncontrollable about the speaking body disrupts careful listening by creating an abrupt change in scale: a moment when body and speech seem to move in opposite directions."[26] These points, Yaeger observes, often arise when the listener wants to receive and open her- or himself to the pain of the other, but is inhibited from doing so by a performed act of estrangement. This estrangement can be ethically charged by forcing us to recognize our inability to fully comprehend traumatic memories.[27]

Reframing Holocaust Testimony calls attention to both the formations and ruptures of intimacy that occur throughout the process of collecting Holocaust testimonies. The work of video testimony can never be reduced to a typed transcript—it is an audiovisual form of historiography that renders history legible in embodied form. It draws from voices, faces, and other expressive elements that work not only in concert, but also in conflict with one another, revealing a more complicated picture of a witness's experiences and how he or she grapples with its aftermath. And yet by focusing exclusively on the fragmenting aspects of the interview process, there is the potential for scholars to miss those moments in interviews that can also be coherent and even affirming expressions on the part of the witnesses. In an attempt to focus attention on the agency of survivors and other witnesses—an effort that is of great importance—there has been a tendency in some scholarship on Holocaust testimonies by those such as Yaeger and Langer to engage the anti-redemptive aspects of testimony at the expense of more fully considering the redemptive elements with which they seem locked in opposition. While an anti-redemptive line of analysis serves as a means of countering the cathartic frameworks preferred by certain archives, it still represents its own form of preferences for how testimony should be practiced and interpreted.

The work of Aleida Assmann, for instance, describes how video testimony represents an integration of history and memory: "It renders accounts of the ways in which the historical event of the Holocaust has deformed and shattered the patterns of an individual life."[28] Yet without an extensive analysis of particular testimonies, Assmann's claim that testimony "unsettles" the storytelling process and narrative coherence, and ultimately "shatter[s] the biographical frame" of witnesses seems limited.[29] *Reframing Holocaust Testimony* not only highlights individual performances of testimony but also the methods and practices that help shape them, and in so doing discerns some semblance of structure and coherence in the frameworks of testimonies. Never perfectly enacted, testimonies are contingent upon the specific dialogue fostered among interviewees, interviewers, and the institutions the latter represent. In other words, testimony is marked by *both* shattering and unifying impulses, each represented by the tendencies and preferences of the respective testimonial parties. Video testimonies can offer moments of cogent analysis rather than or in addition to bursts of raw emotion. Assmann, like Langer and Yaeger, contends that video testimony blocks attempts to frame traumatic memory in a redemptive way. While that is often the case, there are moments when testimonies, depending on the particular personal and institutional voices that frame them, do in fact suggest some form of closure, if not redemption.

Although Assmann draws our attention to the mediated aspects of video testimonies—that is, to the ways in which they depend on moral and technical support and the guidance of an interlocutor—she focuses on how they are "mediated and refracted through a specific personality," rather than on the influence of institutional and media practices.[30] In her words:

> An archive is not a museum; it is not designed for public access and popular presentations. . . . There is, of course, some order and arrangement in the digital archive, too, but it is one that ensures only the retrieval of information, not an intellectually or emotionally effective display. The archive, in other words, is not a form of presentation but of preservation; it collects and stores information, it does not arrange, exhibit, process, or interpret it.[31]

As I argue, however, the boundaries between archives and their exhibition contexts are much more permeable and subject to intersecting narrative structures. The methods for selecting interviewees, conducting training sessions, and producing interviews are developed alongside considerations of transmission and access. I will show that the "order and arrangement in the digital archive" not only provide access to information; they also attempt to calibrate the intellectual and emotional representation of testimony. The archives that I examine in this book are always engaged on some level with entangled considerations of preservation and transmission, intellectual engagement and affective responses.[32]

Testimony and Popular Representations of the Holocaust

Tracing the development of testimonial archives intersects with histories of Holocaust survivor identity. Several scholars have pointed to 1978 as a critical moment in the emergence of survivors as bearers of expertise, authenticity, and moral authority in Holocaust commemorations in the United States. They often cite President Jimmy Carter's establishment of the President's Commission on the Holocaust, which mandated the creation of the U.S. Holocaust Memorial Museum and converged with the airing that year of the popular NBC miniseries *Holocaust*, which reached 120 million viewers.[33]

Annette Wieviorka has traced this development in an international context, historicizing the official (as opposed to individual and communal) invocation of survivor identity back further to the development of Holocaust survivor culture two decades after World War II. She contends that survivors did not form coherent social groups in the public spheres of the United States, Europe, or Israel until the trial of Adolf Eichmann in 1961–1962, an event that allowed the discourse of Holocaust witnessing to take hold at an even deeper, more public level.[34] While Wieviorka's historical scope is limited and does not account for the development of survivor identities and Holocaust commemorations both during and immediately after the war, she rightly underscores the trial's momentous pedagogical impact: "For the first time, a trial explicitly set out to provide a lesson in history. For the first time, the Holocaust was linked to the themes of pedagogy and transmission . . . but above all, the Eichmann trial marks the advent of the witness."[35] In contrast to the Nuremberg trials, the Eichmann case was based heavily on both written documents and oral evidence from victims—with the testimonies providing a living immediacy and embodied charge that could not be captured in documents. This living valence is what, in Wieviorka's view, represents the potential of Holocaust testimony: the "immediacy of these first-person accounts burns through the 'cold storage of history.'"[36]

That sense of immediacy is, however, always framed, not only at the interpersonal level, but also in terms of archival and institutional practices. Scholars who address the institutional cultures of Holocaust testimony archives have often reinforced hierarchical distinctions between high and low (or popular) forms of representation. For example, Wieviorka compares the development of the Fortunoff Archive at Yale in 1978, following the NBC *Holocaust* miniseries, with that of the Survivors of the Shoah Visual History Foundation, established in 1994 by Steven Spielberg after the release of his critically acclaimed film *Schindler's List* (1993). More specifically, she found the influence of Spielberg's film on the development of the Shoah Foundation particularly distressing in that she

Reframing Holocaust Testimony

asserts that the foundation, in contrast to the Fortunoff Archive, privileges redemptive and accessible narratives over anti-redemptive, impenetrable accounts. She states: "Whereas the founders of the Yale archive insisted on focusing on the survivor's sense of having lived on 'another planet' . . . the Spielberg project is based, to the contrary, on the desire to show 'ordinary people,' people who have returned to 'normal.'"[37]

This position reflects a certain strain of scholarly commentary on the intersections between audiovisual Holocaust testimony and popular culture, one that reinforces distinctions between more rarefied and more widely accessible collections. It also speaks to a broader scholarly aversion to the Americanization of the Holocaust. Wieviorka and others have expressed concern about loss of the specificity of survivor experience and do not adequately acknowledge the social and pedagogical potential of testimonies circulating across broader venues. As the argument goes, the popularization of survivor identity through film and television, while leading to the increased presence of the Holocaust in American life, has not increased knowledge of the events, but rather imbues the historical experiences with simplified lessons of redemption, hope, and tolerance.[38] Yet while there is reason for concern regarding the potential for homogenizing Holocaust memory, this book demonstrates that even some of the most institutionally centralized and popularized sites of Holocaust testimony do not present a monolithic embodiment of Holocaust representation.[39]

Debates on the popularization of Holocaust remembrance reveal a strong current of anxiety regarding the relativization of events through media saturation. Geoffrey Hartman has expressed some skepticism about the proliferation of Holocaust representations, remarking: "Our sense of what is real is mediated by the media, by electronic phantoms that extend the confusion of reality and propaganda, or place events on the same level."[40] For Hartman the implications of that leveling effect are profound in terms of how future generations are bound—absent first-person encounters—to receive historical memory in mediated forms. He recognizes that educators will play an increasingly crucial role in "replacing eyewitness transmission" of historical events, but he urges them to guard against what he terms "anti-memory"—or the trivialization of the Holocaust and the fostering of forgetfulness through sentimentality.[41] However, we cannot ignore the vast wealth of audiovisual testimonies already housed in archives, even if some of them have adopted strategies that scholars such as Hartman consider problematic. This book demonstrates that it is possible and essential to engage these testimonies—whether in more popular or rarefied archives—in ways that call attention to their complexities, including those not intended by these sites.

History, Memory, and the Performance of Testimony

The contours of the debates concerning the mediation of Holocaust testimony are additionally shaped by deep frictions between contested notions of history and memory, performativity and authenticity, and cognition and affect. The film and media scholar Janet Walker has convincingly argued that in order to begin grappling with those tensions, it is critical to engage closely with both the rhetorical and performed aspects of Holocaust testimonies. In doing so, it is possible to move away from a conception of traumatic memory that asserts that either a trauma occurred and its subsequent recollections are true, or that it did not occur and the recollections are false.[42] We can thus maintain an investment in historical truth without jettisoning matters of subjectivity or imposing false notions of closure on events. With that in mind, Walker makes a powerful case that it is imperative to adopt a position that extends beyond the limiting binary of "literalist" versus "social constructivist" approaches.[43] In a similar vein, Allesandro Portelli refers to the "dialogic discourse" at the heart of oral (and video) testimony—a position that does not compartmentalize historical "fidelity" from "subjectivity" but rather addresses their necessarily intertwined relationship.[44]

This more inclusive position would develop strategies to "triangulate" memories—to examine testimonies, for instance, alongside other sources such as historical commentary and original documents.[45] The scholarship of Holocaust historian Christopher Browning reflects such an approach. He provides an incisive critique of the manner in which historians of the Holocaust have traditionally been averse to integrating postwar testimony into their work, preferring instead to deal with documents contemporaneous to the events. Browning acknowledges some of the limitations to using testimonies as historical evidence, but nonetheless presents a powerful argument that they can be used in a rigorous and responsible fashion, particularly considering that the lack of archival evidence for many aspects of Holocaust history demands careful examination of testimonies in their stead. In order to be used effectively, however, he argues that testimonies cannot be interpreted as homogenous expressions of collective experience, but rather must be seen as more fragmented collections of frequently conflicting personal accounts. It is in that regard that Browning's work has substantially informed my own, in particular his examination of the ways in which personal accounts often complicate institutional attempts to unify memories of the Holocaust. As he suggests, the relegation of testimonies to their *collective* (as opposed to *collected*) status is not only ethically problematic, but also counter-historical. Browning powerfully demonstrates that historians can approach Holocaust testimonies as more than discourses of uniqueness or universalism.

Browning's important methodological contributions have thus advanced discussion of how scholars can incorporate an understanding of interview and archival practices into their use of testimonies.[46] To be sure, testimonies need to be vetted and cross-checked with the same kind of care used for more conventional sources. Nonetheless, video testimonies are mediated and performed in unique ways, and can be revealing even when they are not completely accurate in terms of historical content; they can still shed light on the ways in which witnesses perceive themselves and labor through their stories. Thus, audiovisual testimonies should be analyzed carefully, both in terms of their narrative and performative elements, but also for their evidentiary functions. In the case of video testimonies, archives often attempt to mitigate and even efface what they perceive as the tensions that mark the intersection between historical investigation and the subjective, experiential aspects of testimony. In that sense, I engage Dori Laub's powerful contention that the listener to trauma is a "party to the creation of knowledge *de novo*" and "a guide and an explorer" in the testimony process.[47] However, the creation of knowledge and the map that helps navigate the paths of memory do not only involve the dyadic relationship between the survivor and those who bear witness to the process of witnessing. They are also part of a broader constellation of technical, archival, and epistemological frameworks as well as a diverse range of audiences and users. While Browning has played a pivotal role in demonstrating the historical usefulness of testimonies, it remains for scholars of the Holocaust to examine the archival and media specificities of those sources. Those specificities not only impact their accessibility, but also shape them as texts of history and memory.

A Mosaic of Testimonies

In writing this book, my first—and most daunting—task was to develop an approach for choosing which testimonies to analyze. The sheer number of testimonies compiled by the three archives was itself overwhelming, constituting a vast mosaic of testimonies that together exceeded 60,000 interviews. Any select sample of those testimonies necessarily excludes most of the individual witnesses recorded by these archives. Therefore, in the same way that the Fortunoff Archive, Holocaust Museum, and Shoah Foundation had to devise their own approaches for collecting and transmitting testimonies, I too had to create a methodology for choosing and then analyzing those archives' collections.

With that in mind, I developed three separate yet often intersecting categories of witnesses—a designation I will interchange with the terms *survivor, subject, witness,* and *interviewee.* Most of the individuals whose testimonies I examine fall under the category of Jewish survivorship, thus delineating the parameters of this study. While the Holocaust was experienced in different ways by individuals who embodied a diverse range of religious, ethnic, racial, sexual, political, and other identities, most of the witnesses who are recorded and prominently featured by the three archives in question are Jewish survivors. Although such terms as *witness, survivor,* and *interviewee* all have limitations and biases, particularly in obscuring the collaborative aspects of testimony, they still reveal how these archives position those whom they record.[48]

I divided my sample of survivors into three categories. The largest group comprises witnesses who gave testimony at each of the three archives. Chapter 4 is reserved for these "comparative" witnesses. The other samples include survivors whose testimonies frequently circulate within and beyond the archives for exhibition or pedagogical purposes and witnesses who are deemed by archives to be exemplary in terms of projecting or embodying the particular preferences of their respective archive or memorial sites.[49] These classifications are not necessarily exclusive of one another in that some witnesses fall under more than one category. For example, certain exemplary subjects are more likely to have their testimonies placed into circulation or may be more inclined to give testimonies on several occasions and at more than one archive. Nevertheless, these three categories allow me to better isolate how each institution attempts to project its preferences on the process of creating testimonies, elucidating what archives perceive as compelling Holocaust stories.

The most difficult yet crucial category that I had to locate and research comprises "comparative" witnesses: those subjects who gave testimony at each of the three sites. Cross-referencing catalogues of interviewees in each of the three archives, I was able to generate a sample of at least fourteen of these subjects.[50] Their interviews do not fully represent the multivocal quality of testimony archives. Because only a relative handful of witnesses recorded interviews with all three archives, they are exceptional cases. Nonetheless, they represent an invaluable trove of testimonies, allowing me to compare and contrast across each of the three sites how witnesses are positioned, and in turn position themselves in the context of different institutional practices across different time periods.

Testimonies that circulate within and beyond the institutional confines of archives and museums, including such forms as documentary films, museum exhibitions, and pedagogical programming, can be called exemplary in that they represent or embody an archive's idealized, selective vision of its approach to recording testimony. Because not every exemplary testimony is put into circulation, my second category of testimonies draws only from interviews that were edited for wider distribution within new formats. Exemplary witnesses are designated as such through internal assessment and ratings protocols, while the circulating witnesses are subject to further curatorial processes that determine which subjects to highlight, and in turn, which segments of their stories to feature in distributed materials.

A number of considerations determined my third group of exemplary witnesses. Each of the three archives developed its own institutional methodology—some more formal and standardized than others—for rating or otherwise assessing the testimonies in its collection. These institutional criteria ranged from dramatic effectiveness, narrative coherence, or psychological complexity, to a witness's ability to balance the emotive or cognitive demands of testimony or to his or her inclination to glean lessons from an experience. In other instances, archives identified exemplary subjects not only by the quality of their videotaped testimonies, but also by how well they delivered their accounts in person to live audiences. In some other cases, an archive designated a testimony as aberrational among its holdings. However, it is vital to underscore that while archives may characterize these testimonies as "exemplary," those descriptions speak more to the preferences of archives rather than to the ways witnesses often deliver their testimonies against the grain. Not only do "exemplary" survivors often challenge the instrumentalization of their testimonies, but there are also the interviews of more "ordinary" witnesses—explored in this book—who often fall through the cracks of archives.

Frames of Interpretation

In order to pinpoint some of the processes fundamental to the production and dissemination of testimonies, I have categorized the interviews in each archive and each of my three group types according to various frames of interpretation. Those include, among other things: the methods interviewers use to engage witnesses in discussions on how they became aware of the events they describe on tape; the kinds of narrative outlines the archive uses to attempt to structure testimonies, often into coherent, sequential units; and the degree to which subjects are given adequate space in which to assert their own agency in delivering their stories. Those preferences shape, in conversation and often in conflict with interviewees, the conditions of possibility for giving and receiving testimonies, rather than providing the final say. And they cannot account for the diverse backgrounds, experiences, and identities—including those of gender (among other considerations)—that impact witnesses' experiences throughout their lives, including those of giving testimony.[51]

My first interpretative framework covers the labor of testimony, by which I mean those moments in interviews that capture a witness's physical gestures, vocal expressions, reenactments, and general performance of memory, both in dialogue with the interviewer and framed through the modes of production. These moments include instances when witnesses struggle with translating deeply interior reflections into terms that might be externally legible through linguistic, physical, and other forms of expression. This process represents a form of reenactment in which the aural, physical, and visual performances of memory, which are themselves products of (interior) mediation in their own right, encounter the archive's external mediating demands.

I also analyze the interplay of common and deep memory. In the process of collecting testimonies, the demands of interviewers and the archive can attempt to shape how witnesses negotiate the terrain of their remembering, often imposing coherent narrative sequences only to see them uprooted by an interviewee's immersion in the past. Interviews often reflect an archive's effort to enact the more unified and narratively coherent experiences of common memory at the expense of exploring the shards of deep memory. Other testimonies reveal an attempt by interviewers to extract that deep memory without first attending to the narrative devices that would allow it to emerge. In other words, deep memory and common memory are entangled—and exist in dialogue—with one another, and thus they require careful attention from those bearing witness. It is often when interviewers attempt to sequester common memory from deep memory that the frictions between institutional itineraries and individual memories come to light.

Another frame of interpretation includes what I refer to as the "off-camera dimensions of testimony." Those are moments that seem to reside near the periphery of video interviews; they often arise between tape changes or after the official testimony has concluded and informal discussion continues in the mistaken belief that the camera is turned off. In typed transcripts these moments often appear to be absent or are otherwise isolated at the margins. In examining these suppressed and often jarring moments in testimony—which underscore what an archive attempts to leave out—one can gain a stronger sense of an institution's investments in mediating acts of remembering. It is often in those margins that witnesses assert agency in their testimony and at times even confront the interviewer on issues of the authoring of their interview.

Finally, I examine the ways in which interviewers and witnesses attempt to assert their respective conceptions of individual and collective memory, official history and personal experience, and the obligation to give voice to absent victims. This includes moments when witnesses imbue testimonies with a sense of immediacy and moral urgency in anticipation of an impending moment when their living presence will no longer be able to inform and authenticate what has been recorded on tape.

My examination of those issues begins with chapter 1 through the case study of the Fortunoff Video Archive for Holocaust Testimonies at Yale University. That archive has deep roots in the survivor community and is invested in fulfilling its obligations to preserve the sanctity of its memories. It currently holds approximately 4,400 video testimonies and continues to conduct recordings with witnesses across the globe. The archive is understandably very protective of its holdings, as demonstrated by its withholding of the last names of witnesses in its catalogue and by maintaining a single, on-site access point at Yale University's library. The library catalogue that includes the Fortunoff Archive holdings is available to those outside of the university community, allowing users to locate interviews from remote locations. However, access to the collections is currently only available in person at the Department of Manuscripts and Archives at Yale's Sterling Library. While ensuring that only the most dedicated and rigorous students, educators, and scholars will travel to Yale in order to access the collections, this restriction has limited the broader circulation of its holdings.

Using testimonies, internal documents, and interviews with staff, my research examines how the Fortunoff Archive both acknowledges and downplays the practices and preferences that guide how it collects and distributes interviews. The archive's approach to issues of media specificity reflects its efforts to expand the availability of testimonies working within an archival model that has until recently privileged on-site library visitation rather than remote and more interactive access. The archive further distinguishes itself from other sites of Holocaust testimony by its open engagement with the self-reflexive aspects of the interview process. For example, in recording sessions, the archive privileges the agency of witnesses over that of interviewers in guiding the narrative. Yet it openly acknowledges that testimony is an act of mutual labor between those who give and receive memory, and that the content and form of that exchange are necessarily intertwined.

When circulating segments of testimony beyond its walls (in edited films and educational materials), however, the archive often leaves out traces of its institutional intervention and focuses almost exclusively on the expressions of witnesses. In addressing a wider audience, it sets out to stabilize the interpretative possibilities of its testimonies by positioning them as raw resources absent any institutional mediation. This reflects its ethical and proprietary preferences, which not only privilege witnesses as the primary authors and agents of their testimonies but also aim to prevent the misappropriation of material. However, by regulating the dissemination of its holdings, whether by editing out the presence of interviewers or by keeping most of its testimonies offline, the archive not only limits its wider access but also prioritizes a mode of reception that can obscure the shared labor and mediations of video testimony.[52]

The second case study, examined in chapter 2, explores the United States Holocaust Memorial Museum (or USHMM) in Washington, D.C. While it possesses neither the oldest nor the largest collection of testimonies among the three sites, it is the most centralized and institutionally expansive, bearing the imprimatur of the U.S. federal government. Furthermore, its capacity not only as an archive, but also as a memorial site, exhibition space, and educational center positions it as an illuminating case for examining testimony across phases of collection and transmission. Rather than presenting a comprehensive history of the development of the Holocaust Museum, this chapter provides a focused examination of how the authority and authenticity of its testimonies are channeled by and through that institution.[53]

A unanimous Act of Congress in 1980 gave the museum its official mandate to serve as an interventionist "living memorial" of the Holocaust that could attend not only to that past genocide but also to the emergence of contemporary atrocities.[54] At the core of the museum's charter is a tripartite mission to commemorate, document, and activate the memory of the Holocaust in the face of current events, with its federal authorization solidifying its political and symbolic currency in pursuit of those aims. Its location on the National Mall adjacent to the museums of the Smithsonian Institution and in close proximity to the Jefferson Memorial and Washington Monument places it squarely in the heart of an official American commemorative landscape.[55]

At the same time, museum planners had to explore ways to import the historical and evidentiary authority from the European topography of the Holocaust. A central strategy for accomplishing that aim was a push to collect audiovisual testimonies that would provide embodied resonance to the museum's exhibitions and programming. Originally intended to house the central national archive of Holocaust testimonies, the museum's oral history department has to date collected more than 9,000 interviews, mostly in English, in both audio and video formats.[56] However, one of the museum's central priorities, and in turn a driving impetus for creating a department of oral history, was a mandate from the main planners that the "soul" of the USHMM would be its Permanent Exhibition and that all other activities, including the collection of testimony, would be secondary to developing that core space.[57] While the representation of victims and survivors is central to that effort, the "soul" of the Permanent Exhibition, like the museum's oral history collection, is heavily curated.

The third and final archival case study, featured in chapter 3, is the USC Shoah Foundation—the Institute for Visual History and Education (or Shoah Foundation). It should be noted that the Shoah Foundation is still in a relative period of transition from its establishment in 1994 as an independent operation to its incorporation as a part of the University of Southern California in 2006. Having completed both its campaign to interview Holocaust witnesses and its goal to digitize its holdings of almost 52,000 testimonies, the Shoah Foundation is shifting its attention toward making its archives accessible to students, researchers, and the general public and to addressing genocides other than the Holocaust. This transition from testimony production to dissemination requires not only a major redirection of its energies and staff to new tasks, but also involves the foundation's integration into the academic environment of the University of Southern California, including its library collections. In particular, the Shoah Foundation must now confront the challenges of activating its testimonies beyond the archive, making them useful across a diverse range of venues and in response to past and contemporary genocides and human rights abuses.

The structure and interface of the Shoah Foundation's collection of digitized, online testimonies, which is made available through its Visual History Archive (or VHA) on an Internet2 subscriber-based network, presents limitations as well as possibilities. How does the interface of the VHA potentially encourage the process of searching within testimonies, rather than the careful viewing and listening that is often not only an analytical but also an ethical demand of working with such interviews? Does the segmentation and instrumentalization of VHA witness interviews potentially position them as sources of historical illustration rather than as complex and textured sources in their own right? These questions are integral not only to the case of the Shoah Foundation but also to our understanding of other Holocaust testimony archives and the inheritance of traumatic memory.

Although in each of the following chapters I delve into the categories of "exemplary" and "circulating" witnesses, chapter 4 focuses on those witnesses who delivered accounts to each of the three archives at the center of this book. Cross-referencing catalogues of interviewees in each of the three institutions, I was able to generate a pool of at least fourteen subjects who belonged in this category. They are crucial to highlighting the particular qualities of testimony construction by isolating across each of the three sites the interactions between witnesses and a diverse range of archival practices.

The framing of Holocaust testimonies in turn impacts the ways in which other genocides are documented. The conclusion addresses that issue by examining how the Shoah Foundation consulted with and provided training to the Documentation Center of Cambodia (DC-Cam), an independent Cambodian research institute compiling written records, photographs, and video testimonies of the Cambodian genocide perpetrated between 1975 and 1979. DC-Cam staff members have now created their own pilot interviews at the Shoah Foundation's Los Angeles offices, as well as developed a pre-interview questionnaire for their witnesses directly based on the foundation's framework for Holocaust testimonies.

That archival cooperation raises some larger, pressing questions regarding the challenges posed by mobilizing the Holocaust as a paradigm for framing transnational testimony archives. Do the particular cultures and approaches of Holocaust institutions translate to other, non-Holocaust contexts? Can they obscure the historical and individual textures of other suffering? In order to engage those and other issues concerning the future of documenting genocide, it is first crucial to examine the diverse origins and approaches to framing Holocaust testimony.

ONE

Testimonies from the Grassroots

The Fortunoff Video Archive for Holocaust Testimonies

The founders of what would become the Fortunoff Video Archive for Holocaust Testimonies envisioned a "provisional community bound by memory and the recognition of trauma"—one that nurtures a responsibility for witnesses by giving priority to their voices.[1] Its identity as an "affective community" for interviewees was a central focus at an academic conference held in 2002 to mark the archive's twentieth anniversary at Yale University. Conference organizers and participants acknowledged that Holocaust testimony projects were on the cusp of a paradigmatic transition in which the living authority of survivors would be transferred to the archives documenting their memories.

The participants in that event expressed their eagerness to move away from the view of testimony collection as direct, unmediated practice, recognizing instead that "these projects insist that Holocaust history cannot be pursued without a simultaneous inquiry into the conditions of memory and representations within which this history is produced and received."[2] Nonetheless, a published account of that meeting at Yale reveals the participants' primary focus on the dynamic relationships between subject, interviewer, and audience—on the notion that testimonies are products of the context in which they are created and produced, if only in terms of the moments captured on camera. Only by acknowledging the workings of testimony would the Fortunoff holdings become a "living archive" accessed by future generations. That future user of testimony will inherit not only the mutual labor between interviewer and interviewee—that is to say, the acts of testimonial production as captured on camera alone—but also the institutional histories and testimonial exchanges that take place prior and subsequent to the interviews.

The Local Origins of the Fortunoff Archive

The production of testimonies in the Fortunoff Archive can be traced to efforts within the New Haven, Connecticut, Jewish community in the mid- to late 1970s to create a monument to the Holocaust. This campaign ultimately led to efforts to record the testimonies of Holocaust witnesses living in the area.[3] A parallel of sorts led to the development of the United States Holocaust Memorial Museum in Washington, D.C., as will be discussed in more detail in chapter 2. The key point here is that the visions and frameworks for the Fortunoff Archive and the Holocaust Museum were both forged in the late 1970s, a pivotal moment in Holocaust commemoration. In both cases, the initial campaign to create a Holocaust monument became linked to the recording of survivor testimony, sparked by the realization that firsthand witnesses would soon be passing from the scene.

At various points in its institutional history the Fortunoff Archive has entered into collaborative agreements with the Holocaust Museum on collecting video history. Furthermore, Steven Spielberg's Shoah Foundation consulted with the archive as it finalized its own plans for developing a repository of Holocaust testimonies.[4] In other words, the three institutions covered in this book did not develop in isolation from one another; rather, their staffs were often in conversation and even collaborated at various junctures. Yet, despite the similarities in their origins, the histories of the Fortunoff Archive and the United States Holocaust Memorial Museum have diverged in critical ways. While a federal mandate established the Holocaust Museum, the Fortunoff Archive owed its creation to more grassroots efforts. Thus, in February 1979, representatives of the New Haven Jewish Federation and the television station WNH-TV met to discuss the making of a documentary about the creation of a local memorial, which in turn led television producer and personality Laurel Vlock to contact New Haven psychiatrist and child survivor Dori Laub. That meeting led to a video testimony with Laub later that year, and from there four more survivors were recorded.[5] In 1981 the original tapes of what had become the Holocaust Survivors Film Project were deposited at Yale University, and in 1982 the Video Archive was officially established as part of the Manuscripts and Archives Division of Yale's Sterling Memorial Library.[6] The Video Archive later produced an eighteen-minute-long program to be presented at the American Gathering of Jewish Holocaust Survivors in Washington, D.C., in 1983.[7] The intent was to encourage other survivors to come forward and record their stories on videotape. While the planners of the USHMM played a crucial role at that gathering, that museum had yet to develop an oral history department. The Fortunoff Archive was the first American institution to dedicate itself to the collection of Holocaust video testimony. The subsequent campaign to reach out to survivors beyond New Haven and record their testimony on a national scale also grew out of a grassroots effort to organize a survivor community eager to solidify its legacy.

Financial support from the Charles H. Revson Foundation, for the purpose of increasing the number of interviews for the Video Archive, made possible a series of six-week training sessions for potential interviewers in 1984. That same year, Joanne Rudof came to the archive, initially as its manager, later to become its archivist.[8] In 1987, through a major endowment from Alan A. Fortunoff, the Video Archive was renamed the Fortunoff Video Archive for Holocaust Testimonies.

The Fortunoff Archive currently has a collection of approximately 4,400 interviews, constituting more than 10,000 hours of footage in twenty languages, accessible through thirty-seven affiliates across the world.[9] Its subjects include not only Jewish survivors of the Holocaust, but also Roma and Sinti, homosexuals, political prisoners, bystanders, members of Hitler Youth, and other categories of experience. Since the first Fortunoff testimonies date from 1979, compared to the Holocaust Museum's in 1989, and the Shoah Foundation's in 1994, its interviewees were considerably younger during their recordings and closer to the events remembered. Thus, the archive was better positioned to interview survivors whose Holocaust experiences occurred in the adult stages of their lives, and, in this respect, the other two archives encompass a narrower demographic sampling of witnesses.

Conceptual Framework

From its inception, the Fortunoff Archive emphasized the human dimensions of suffering at the heart of the Holocaust, rather than the broader historical picture. Speaking for the archive, the project director and literary theorist Geoffrey Hartman explained:

> It is our wish to document the tragedy and to show it in its full human detail. But we do not try to make historians of the survivors. We listen to them, try to free their memories, and see each person as more than a victim: as someone who faces those traumas again, an eyewitness who testifies in public.[10]

While Hartman values the historical insights that can be gleaned from testimony, he contends that scholars too often neglect the emotional and personal textures of memory. Testimony, he argues, can supplement historians' work, in particular by being directed to what he characterizes as the "audiovisually oriented" younger generations. In his view, the archive aims to give willing witnesses the opportunity to record their testimonies, rather than designating an "elite" cadre of interviewees.[11] The agency of those witnesses, not the agenda of the institution or the interviewer, is critical: "They [the interviewer] should never take the initiative away from the person interviewed."[12]

The Fortunoff Archive's openness to all witnesses has not, however, always implied a mission to reach the broadest possible audience for its holdings. Unlike the Shoah Foundation, the Fortunoff Archive has made its testimonies primarily available through physical, on-site access at Yale's Sterling Library, and it has been careful to regulate the broader online circulation of its collections.[13] On the one hand, it has been actively involved with developing educational programming for such initiatives as *Facing History and Ourselves,* and it co-produced the PBS documentary *Witness: Voices from the Holocaust,* which featured excerpts from the archive's survivor testimonies. But throughout its history, the archive has resisted use of its materials in commercial or otherwise more mainstream venues. To quote Hartman once again, "It is essential that these moving, personal narratives be properly and effectively utilized by public television, museum exhibits, and school programs."[14] Conspicuously absent from this list of platforms are commercial film and television. In the case of the Fortunoff Archive, there has been a long-held and often justified concern with buffering archived testimonies from what are seen as the blurred boundaries between fiction and nonfiction, sanctity and kitsch, often associated with more popular representations of the Holocaust.

To take one example, the Fortunoff archivist Joanne Rudof remarked to me how the release of Steven Spielberg's *Schindler's List* (1993) had the effect of shaping and often distorting testimonies related to the subject of Oskar Schindler that the archive recorded after the film's release.[15] Related, in the report chronicling the Yale conference, participants draw clear distinctions between the Fortunoff Archive and other testimony repositories—arguing that the former facilitates the agency of witnesses, while the latter privilege their own agendas, with the effect of distorting or idealizing redemptive Holocaust experiences. In the report, this perspective is explicitly anchored in the historical origins of the Fortunoff Archive, particularly in its development as a reaction against the representations of the Holocaust in the popular American miniseries *Holocaust* produced by NBC in 1978.[16] As an antidote to what many viewed as this series' commercialization and homogenization of the events, the Fortunoff Archive aimed to restore sanctity and rigor to Holocaust memory.

For certain scholars who participated in the 2002 academic conference at the Fortunoff Archive, the homogenization of the Holocaust promoted by the NBC miniseries was also manifested in Spielberg's film *Schindler's List* (1993) and even in his founding of the Shoah Foundation. Sidney Bolkosky, the head of the Fortunoff Archive's affiliate program at the University of Michigan in Dearborn, contended that the Shoah Foundation adopted an overly interventionist approach to engaging with witnesses, or in other cases edited interviews to omit familiar, canned stories. Both approaches, he suggested, leave out the "shared sense of collaborative labor" that marks testimony.[17] Bolkosky also expressed concern regarding what he regarded as the densely standardized format used by the Shoah Foundation, in particular its long pre-interview questionnaire, its reliance on a list of interview questions, and its encouragement of witnesses to end their recordings with redemptive messages, followed by on-camera scenes with family members. In the eyes of some scholars, this was seen to represent the redemptive dramatization or "Schindlerization" of Holocaust Memory.[18]

Lawrence Langer and Anti-Redemptive Testimony

The involvement in 1984 of literary scholar Lawrence Langer in the Fortunoff Archive, both as a long-time interviewer and as a researcher working with its collections, marks an important period in its development. The archive positions his book *Holocaust Testimonies: The Ruins of Memory* (1991)—based on Langer's close examination of testimonies in the Video Archive—as a foundational work on the subject and a representation of many of the archive's core methodologies.[19] Indeed, the archive soon adopted Langer's work as a text for developing its approach to testimony, and incorporated it into training sessions for volunteer interviewers.[20] Langer's approach to testimony was reflected in many of the interviews analyzed for my book. At its center, his work emphasizes the anti-redemptive experiences and "choiceless choices" of those who survived the Holocaust, rather than privileging catharsis.[21] He underscores how testimony can begin to reveal what life was like for witnesses under circumstances that systematically undermined moral and ethical values. Rather than imposing heroic or healing narrative frameworks on testimonies, this conception of testimony is intended to allow witnesses to express the anti-redemptive aspects of their experiences. While it is impossible for anyone other than a witness to understand what he or she went through, according to Langer, the interviewer and the audience are nonetheless obliged to try to understand, even while knowing the impossibility of doing so. In this sense, Langer advocates a mode of conducting and receiving testimonies that is engaged with witnesses without being appropriative of their experiences; while deeply invested, it nonetheless recognizes the experiential rift that separates witnesses from those who bear witness to their acts of testimonies.

By way of engaging Charlotte Delbo, Langer distinguishes intellectual or "common memory" from the "memory of the senses," otherwise referred to as "deep memory."[22] While survivors express common memory in a chronological and coherent structure—recalling in the present moment how events unfolded in the compartmentalized past—deep memory takes witnesses back to the events, reintroducing them to the range of senses experienced at that time and complicating any efforts to keep that past coherent and compartmentalized. Throughout testimonies, these two threads of memory are often intertwined, so that witnesses find themselves immersed in the past, indeed at a moment that they had initially narrated from a point of distance and separation. It is equally possible for accounts to assume narrative coherence and chronology after an emotionally wrenching return to the past sparks a vivid recollection of a particular name, date, or other historical detail. Langer stresses the evasiveness of deep memory, however, characterized as it is by fragmentation and extremity, making witnesses less forthcoming in laying bare such experiences. And in many cases, Langer reminds us, interviewers reliant upon a standardized interview narrative and protocol are inclined to keep testimonies ordered along the lines of common memory, closed off to the more nuanced layers and turns of deep memory.

This conceptualization of the layers of memory is not simply theoretical to Langer but also clearly informs his approach to conducting interviews for the Fortunoff Archive. His methodology was central to his prior work as an outside consultant helping the United States Holocaust Memorial Museum refine its own oral history practices. In written correspondence in 1991 between Langer and Michael Berenbaum, then project director for the United States Holocaust Museum, Langer discusses the interviews from the Yale archive that he viewed as the "*most* dramatic and eloquent," and thus potentially valuable to the Holocaust Museum as it cultivated its own oral history protocol.[23]

One such testimony was that of Irene W., recorded by the Holocaust Survivors Film Project (the predecessor of the Fortunoff Archive) in 1982. Langer places particular importance on witnesses' transition between chronological or common memory and less structured deep memory, thus underscoring what he describes as the "fluid structure of these narratives."[24] For example, in the midst of Irene's description of hiding her jewelry before being deported, her story jumps ahead to the time immediately after the war when she returns to her house to reclaim those precious items. What happened to Irene, Langer asks, between her deportation and her return home? There is a substantial gap between those two events, he notes, and the listener is left wondering if and how she will return to that middle portion of her story.

The presence of such lacunae, Langer argues, is a recurring aspect of Holocaust testimonies and should not be sutured to provide a sense of continuity and closure.[25] He notes the tendency among interviewers at other archives to rush subjects through their stories or to mold a linear narrative progression, rather than allowing witnesses to wander down the circuitous paths of their memories.

Langer urges interviewers to take responsibility for being sensitive to the individual textures of memory, for example by allowing subjects to return to their respective traumas on their own terms. And that means accepting testimony for how it is performed by witnesses, regardless of whether or not it conforms to a linear narrative or empiricist historical standards.

Langer also stresses the importance of reading the subtext of recurring tropes such as inmates' memories of arrival at Auschwitz, particularly their recollections of asking Kapos about the fate of their loved ones. When giving testimony it is not uncommon for survivors to recall that the Kapos responded by pointing to the smoke billowing from the camp chimneys, proclaiming, "There's your parents."[26] Langer notes in his critique, "This story has been repeated so many times that one wonders if it's become part of survivor folklore or mythology, or in fact happened exactly that way. On the other hand, the Kapos may have developed this gesture among themselves, and repeated it almost mechanically."[27] While Langer cautions Berenbaum that survivors' memories are often informed by family, friends, and the prevalence of particular tropes from collective memory, he nonetheless makes a strong case for conducting a close and deep reading of testimonies in order to grasp how survivors understand and frame their own stories. The documented events are only one aspect of the process and are necessarily refracted through the psychological and narrative complexity of their telling. With that in mind, Langer stresses that both interviewers and audiences must position themselves to receive a very personal history without the pretense of complete comprehension. His comments on the testimony of Leo G., recorded at Yale in 1980, are particularly incisive on this matter:

> He [Leo G.] distinguishes between the impossibility of communicating what he's talking about to 'us,' and the intuitive shared intimacy with actual survivors, who know what he's talking about without asking. The importance of these testimonies is that if we watch enough of them, we become part of his intuitively understanding audience, not perhaps in the same way as authentic former victims, but close enough to move into the subtext of his and their narratives.[28]

This suggests that through close engagement with Holocaust testimonies we can responsibly forge an interpersonally charged connection with witnesses, all the while preserving recognition of the experiential divide between interviewer and interviewee.

Invoking the testimony of Dori K., recorded by the Holocaust Survivors Film Project in 1979, Langer again reflects on the nature of the interviewer–interviewee dynamic. At one point in her interview, Dori attempts to come to terms with the fate of her father after he was taken away, never to be seen again. Langer describes the moment: "She now can imagine his real fate, and sobbing she repeats 'They put him on a train.' She doesn't have to say the rest, we and she can imagine it, and this truth, instead of liberating her, merely imprisons her in a vision of his fate that overwhelms her."[29] In this instance, the absence of a detailed account of what happened to her father compels not only the witness but also the audience to speculate on the precise fate of her father. Thus, Langer concludes: "Holocaust truth thus makes one *vulnerable* as well as knowledgeable."[30] In his assessment, the value of this particular testimony lies not in any semblance of a complete or redemptive account, but in the endless and fractured struggle to reconstruct an event without having experienced it. It also underscores how a survivor's proximity to a trauma—the extreme experiences of deportation or the concentration camps, for instance—does not necessarily determine the level of anguish that he or she experiences.

The Demands of Testimony

A central tension in the work of the Fortunoff Archive stems from its attempts to negotiate both the analytical and the emotional demands of recording Holocaust video testimonies—the need to tend to the affective community of witnesses but also to its university setting. As described by Rudof, the Yale University Library considers the archive to be "one of its premier collections . . . based not on any emotional factors but on the archive's obvious value as demonstrated by its many visitors and the papers, books, journal articles, music compositions, and other works resulting from viewing the testimonies."[31] It has been a delicate balance: archivists acknowledge the historical value of their testimonies, all the while steering clear of prompting subjects to fixate on filling in the historical gaps of their stories, rather allowing them the agency to follow the paths of their own traumatic memories. While interviewers for the archive must have a foundation of historical knowledge, their purpose is not to close themselves off from the more spontaneous and unanticipated paths of testimony. The internal Fortunoff Archive training documents reveal the delicate nature of that dynamic.

Media Specificity

An early Fortunoff Archive training document, "Toward an Understanding of Media-Based Testimony," exemplifies the concern, however rudimentary, for the media specificities of the video testimony format.[32] While this memorandum's observations exhibit a limited perspective on the critical discourses and practices of the video camera as a recording device, they nonetheless reveal the archive's preferences for how testimony is to be mediated. The document attempts to direct interviewers' attention to the spectrum of choices and mediations presented by the production process, while at the same time stressing the possibility of extracting raw encounters with traumatic memory. In this latter regard, the video camera is to function as a "passive recording device," able to document an empirical record of an event: "The purest form of this is exhibited in instrumentation or data recording of an event such as a scientific experiment."[33] This seems consistent with the archive's conception of testimony and its emphasis that while emotions are a necessary dimension of the interpersonal bond between interviewer and interviewee, they should be grounded in sober, restrained, and more objective interview and framing techniques.

The training document describes the conditions under which testimony is produced, including consideration of how the foreign space of the studio, the camera's presence, and the disembodied voices of those working on set all potentially contribute to a witness's unease. It argues that interlocutors should provide as much comfort to the witness as possible in order to bridge the potential "psychic distance" between interviewee and interviewer and between interviewee and the "camera as viewer."[34] There is thus a stated ideal of a noninterventionist and more objective approach to camera placement. Yet the perspectives represented in the document are quite limited, since it suggests that the camera's ability to express a point of view is restricted to "the single technique of zooming in and out."[35] In this regard, the memo contends that the zoom, which it refers to as the "mobile documentary style of camera," is frequently overused at the expense of the "purity and objectivity of the recording."[36] Therefore, the training document suggests a mode of representation that captures a sense of continuous time and space by eliminating editing and camera alternation. This "unvarnished minimalist" approach to production indicates the "veracity" and "integrity" of a testimony.[37] Such a perspective assumes that raw footage can somehow be culled from an interview. In so doing, the Fortunoff Archive memo neglects to address how the camera's framing of the witness and the spatial positioning of interviewers and interviewees, among other technical aspects, are crucial to shaping the interpretative possibilities of testimony.

For one, the archive's approach to camera coverage of a witness's physical form can reveal or conceal how she or he performs the gestures of memory. While the memo acknowledges that use of the zoom can be distracting, notably by signaling a rupture in its preferred mode of realism, it says nothing about how the framing of the face and body conveys knowledge. Although focusing tightly on a witness's face can often seem abrupt, it can also permit a measure of intimacy, depending on the context of the interview. Furthermore, while a medium shot capturing subjects from the waist up might compromise facial detail, it can provide a wider spectrum of gestures, giving the viewer a sense of the discomfort or intensity experienced by the interviewee. Yet the memo is chiefly concerned with achieving an objective representation, rather than accepting that the process is necessarily mediated—a preference that is reinforced through the archive's standard use of unedited long-takes in recording testimonies.

Although the Fortunoff Archive's training and interview protocols were not formalized until 1984, there are nonetheless some fundamental consistencies among the interviews recorded at Yale and its affiliate projects since the establishment of the archive in the 1970s. With some exceptions, video interviews were shot with a single camera positioned in the zero-degree style—with the camera placed in front, though slightly to the left or right, of the subject, with the interviewers sitting just off to the side of the lens. There are occasionally moments when the camera zooms in for a tight close-up of the witness's face in an attempt to capture a particular facial expression or to provide dramatic punctuation to a specific moment, with the effect of accentuating the intervention of the recording process. Yet for the most part, the camera is locked down into a medium close-up, exposing subjects from the chest to the head in an attempt to foster a seemingly more neutral, objective, and static composition. While early archive testimonies, as well as those from the initial affiliate programs, would often position interviewees against more prominent backdrops including brick walls or bookshelves, most testimonies were conducted against a black backdrop with a standard three-point lighting scheme, and recorded onto videotape. These approaches were intended to emphasize the primacy of the witness and to privilege her or his performance, conveying a sense of a direct and more austere encounter by minimizing the distractions caused by elaborate settings or camera angles. Ultimately, while the Fortunoff training protocol acknowledges the participation of multiple participants in the production of testimony (the interviewer, interviewee, and various crew members), it still suggests some notion of attaining unvarnished testimonial truth.

Interview Methodology

In keeping with Geoffrey Hartman's inclusive description of the Fortunoff Archive as a supportive, emotional community, the archive invites all survivors and witnesses of the Holocaust to give their testimony. At the same time, it does not actively promote its testimonial project with the same level of publicity associated with the Shoah Foundation and Holocaust Museum. It relies instead on word of mouth and its well-established reputation to draw interest. The archive currently has a small full-time staff in addition to volunteer interviewers who conduct testimonies, primarily on-site at Yale or through affiliate projects at other locations, including but not limited to the United States, Israel, the United Kingdom, Ukraine, Canada, and Poland. The agreements between Yale and these affiliated projects stipulate that although the Fortunoff Archive conducts training and integrates the affiliate tapes into its collections, the participating members assume financial responsibility for their interviews.

The archive did not develop a formal pilot system for affiliate members until the late 1980s and into the early '90s, when it began to require the submission of fifteen video testimonies to Yale for analysis, in order to ensure that affiliates met the archive's methodological and technical requirements.[38] Trainers from the Fortunoff Archive would then observe and supervise a small number of these affiliate interviews. It is important to reiterate that the archive lacked a formal training policy until 1984, when Joanne Rudof joined the staff. The earlier testimonies recorded both at Yale and by affiliates are consequently less standardized than those composed after 1984. The affiliate programs' interview activity within the United States was halted, in large part due to funding shortages and the emergence of the Shoah Foundation as a major force in conducting large quantities of video testimonies starting in 1994.[39]

The Fortunoff Archive usually assigns two interviewers to each testimony, first training them to be historically informed and yet open to the tangential, less anticipated paths of memory. As Dori Laub, one of the co-founders of and interviewers for the Fortunoff Archive has written: "The listener must be quite well informed if he is to be able to hear—to be able to pick up the cues. . . . Yet knowledge should not hinder or obstruct the listening with foregone conclusions and preconceived dismissals should not be an obstacle or a foreclosure to new, diverging, unexpected information."[40] To advance that principle, interviewers conduct bare-bones pre-interviews with witnesses three to five days prior to the taping, taking notes on the major historical and biographical information that will be relevant to researching and conducting the testimonies.[41] This approach is intended to prevent witnesses from having to repeat on tape aspects of their story that they have already given in the pre-interview process, thus encouraging a fresher, more spontaneous expression of memory. One of the archive's fundamental rules mandates that interviewers neither bring their research with them to the interview nor take notes in the course of the taping. This is intended to forge a more engaged bond between the parties and to ensure that interviewers listen more carefully to witnesses, rather than looking ahead to questions or giving the appearance of making judgment on portions of testimony. It corresponds with what Rudof has described as a teacher–student dynamic, whereby interviewers create conditions for learning from witnesses, being careful not to interrupt them but rather practicing "active listening" to the various paths of memory.[42]

These instructions attempt to prevent interviewers from imposing their own prior agendas on the interview process, thus giving witnesses primary agency and authorship over the testimony, and creating what Laub has described as an "open, or nondirective, interview that encourages a testimonial alliance between interviewer and survivor."[43] This philosophy underscores that the foundation of the Fortunoff Archive's testimonial approach is a combination of emotive and intellectual engagement—an arrangement that asks interviewers to be both historically informed and emotionally available. When training interviewers, emphasis is placed on detecting the right moments to speak and how best to allow long silences to emerge and tangential routes to be explored. The hope is that by "letting them [the witnesses] just be," they will recover memories that are buried beneath the surface.[44] To facilitate those kinds of silences and avoid imposing limits on the interviewee, the Fortunoff Archive does not set time limits for its interviews, allowing them to continue as long as necessary.

Interview Assessment

The review of completed testimonies is an important part of the Fortunoff Archive's interview training, with emphasis on identifying the limitations, strengths, and potential "entry points" for interviewers, as well as instances of both "inappropriate" and "successful intervention."[45] In conducting training sessions for affiliate projects, Joanne Rudof and the Fortunoff Archive interviewer Dana Kline placed emphasis on examining the "dynamics of an interview" in all facets, ranging from administrative matters like release forms to strategies for listening silently as witnesses tell their stories.[46] Rather than compartmentalizing the administrative and interview processes, Rudof and Kline treated each aspect as a crucial element of the testimony, helping to create a comfortable space where witnesses are able to tell their stories. With that in mind, they encouraged interviewers to explain the process to the witnesses, ensuring that they were briefed before and after each interview. Rudof and Kline suggested that interviewers reflect on their own past recordings, in order to both improve their approach and relate their experiences to academic discourses on the subject of Holocaust testimony, notably Langer's *Holocaust Testimonies*, which became part of the training curriculum in 1993. In addition to reading the book, volunteer interviewers were encouraged to relate it to their own experiences.[47] The training placed a particular emphasis on maintaining a "heightened" awareness of when and how volunteers were to use their own voice and trainees were instructed to withhold statements that might draw conclusions for, or cast judgment on, the witness.[48] Expressions of excessive pathos by interviewers during testimonies were also discouraged. Although interviewers were asked to engage the witnesses on a personal level, that should not be explicitly communicated or made visible on the videotape.[49]

An internal Fortunoff Archive document assessing the interview techniques for the testimony of Fred O., recorded at Yale in 1987, forcefully articulates these principles. For example, one of his interviewers for that testimony is criticized for having asked, "Why didn't you and your family leave?" on the grounds that such a question expresses a judgment of the witness's actions and projects an external agenda onto the testimony.[50] The same interviewer had also pressed Fred about why it had taken him so long to record his story. The witness responds that it had been too painful and emotionally draining; he had lived his life trying to move forward rather than dwelling on the past. The interviewer persisted in pursuing her own agenda and asked Fred about the transition to life under Nazi occupation: "When did you first realize that there was a dramatic change?" Fred responds: "I wouldn't use dramatic change. The changes didn't come in a dramatic way. The changes came insidiously, degree after degree."[51] While the interviewer expected there to be a dramatic framework for Fred's experience, the interviewee contradicted that notion, and the notes given on this testimony critique the interviewer for failing to listen, understand, and remain sensitive to the witness's initiative. The evaluator makes a similar assessment regarding the testimony's conclusion, noting that the interviewer imposes a redemptive vision of the Holocaust in an attempt to disavow the "legitimate cynicism" of the witness. As Fred O. concludes his testimony, he remarks:

> I have emotionally exhausted my emotional strength for the day. But so what? I am cynical about it. It's told, it's written. It's video taped [*sic*]. People can see my beautiful face on the tape. But so what? So someone will write a thesis someday? Comparing this Holocaust to the Armenian holocaust or to the Cambodian holocaust?[52]

At this point the interviewer interjects: "No, not if there is a breath left in any of us, like Elie Wiesel who gets so angered." Fred O. interrupts her, "Are we on tape now?" The interviewer responds by trying to end the testimony, stating, "I think we better cut," but not before Fred remarks on camera: "Because you mention Elie Wiesel and I don't want to go public on what I feel. . . ."[53] Then the screen cuts to black.

That dialogue on Wiesel, while seemingly peripheral to the testimony, is exposed (though ultimately truncated) once the interviewer takes the conversation down a path that is less diplomatic than she intended to have recorded on tape. It is a profoundly revealing moment in which the preferences of the interviewer and the voice of the interviewee come into tension, ultimately bringing the testimony to a halt. The interviewer's approach to the testimony with Fred O. clearly contradicts the prescribed methodology of the Fortunoff Archive. Critical notations cover the written analysis of this testimony, signaling the various points at which the interviewer should have withheld vocal responses and personal agendas and avoided attempts to cast the testimony in a cathartic light. The few positive notes commend the witness for his sober description of hunger—"excellent description, clinical, not emotional"—suggesting that the Fortunoff Archive stresses that interviewers help facilitate testimonies that, while informed by emotional experience, are nonetheless effective at making a story understandable in more intellectual terms.[54]

The archive's training materials carefully delineate boundaries for how interviewers are either to withhold or contribute their voices. Archive protocols instruct interviewers to avoid twelve categories of questions that, broadly speaking, cover inquiries driven by assumptions, prior agendas, embedded answers, or statements of judgment.[55] The category of "inappropriate questions" includes those deliberately intended as being emotionally charged, such as "How did you feel?" or "What was the worst thing that ever happened to you?" Such questions would project and exploit the affective dimensions of testimony, rather than allowing the witness to initiate the emotional contours of stories on her or his own terms.[56] Interviewers are also asked to consider the number of questions presented, and are cautioned about posing "small questions" that can often lead to small answers.[57] While the Fortunoff Archive remains concerned with reconstructing the details of the historical record, it also attempts to keep testimonial agency in the hands of witnesses.

In pursuit of that aim, although the Fortunoff Archive encourages interviewers to address historically inaccurate information or myths, it works to create a space where survivors and other witnesses could at least reflect upon those myths without incessant intervention. To take one example, in regard to the often repeated fiction concerning the processing of Jewish victims into soap, interviewers are instructed to ask witnesses questions such as, "Did you know that then?" or "How do you know that?" in order to differentiate between firsthand and secondhand witnessing or individual and popular memory.[58] Though interviewers are trained not to directly contradict the witness, they are also instructed not to give him or her too much historical authority. In one notation on the testimony of Peter C., recorded at Yale in 1987, the interviewer is encouraged to refine her approach in a line of questioning about the formation of Jewish ghettos.[59] As the witness starts to drift from a discussion of his firsthand memory of events into a more sweeping, secondary description, a note suggests that the interviewer might ask, "What did you see?" or "What did it mean to you?" in an attempt to maintain firmer boundaries between actual experience and memory without adopting an interrogative stance.

These recommendations represent an approach to testimony that is less encyclopedic and more reflective about the workings of memory and the interview process. It is a method that seeks to acquire details through the agency of witnesses, rather than through the agenda of the archive. Unlike other archives that often provide exhaustive (and exhausting) lists of questions for interviewers, the Fortunoff Archive prohibits such lists from the studio during an interview. It is a system that acknowledges witnesses as agents of their own stories, rather than regarding them as informants of a predetermined history.

The Circulation of Testimonies

The holdings of the Fortunoff Archive have been catalogued and made accessible in keeping with conventional library practice. Its holdings are searchable through Yale's Orbis catalogue employing the MARC standardized library catalogue format; as such, it is searchable for geographic place names such as *Warsaw* or experience categories such as *Forced Labor*. Importance is placed on cataloguing testimonies in accordance with standardized library protocols to ensure that they can be cross-referenced with other sources and library catalogues, "conforming to established archival practices and employing authoritative and standard vocabulary."[60] The Fortunoff Archive is inter-operable, allowing users to search between different bibliographic sources and to more easily include testimonies in their research agenda. While the archive is protective of its interviewees—to ensure privacy, it identifies witnesses only by first names and last initials—it has nonetheless made the holdings searchable (but not accessible) through Orbis. To further that aim, each of the interview findings on the catalogue contains brief content descriptions with linkable search terms.

The Fortunoff Archive is developing plans for facilitating remote access to its digitized testimonies to universities and Holocaust museums across the world. However, from its establishment in the late 1970s until as recently as the spring of 2014, requests for access to testimonies have been handled directly through archive staff, with requested tapes (usually no more than three or four at a time) left at the desk of the reading room within the library's Department of Manuscripts and Archives. This space has dedicated video viewing stations for Fortunoff Archive testimonies. Consistent with its rigorous rules regarding decorum and protocol, the reading room creates a suitably distraction-free environment for engaging the testimonies. Rather than being accessed through a digital interface, viewing copies of interviews have been transferred onto VHS tape; typed finding aids for each testimony list brief summaries of the contents, corresponding to a time-code that is visible on the screen for each recording. While this procedure falls short of providing a transcript (as is often available at the Holocaust Museum), it is a reliable research tool for helping to navigate through portions of the interviews. The archive plans eventually to digitize its finding aids, making them available within the library to researchers and staff who want to refine their search beyond the Orbis terms. This search tool would be accessible through direct consultation with the archive staff, but not placed online. As with the withholding of witnesses' last names, this represents another effort to protect the identities of witnesses and the proprietary standards of the archive.

The library protocol speaks to one of the strengths and limitations of the Fortunoff Archive. Its protectiveness of its holdings is understandable, given concerns of the archive and certain witnesses regarding the intensely private and intimate nature of these resources. The archive has deep roots in the survivor community, and it is justifiably invested in fulfilling its obligations to preserve the sanctity of its memories. At the same time, the protracted and yet-to-be completed process of making its testimonies available through online or other remote venues has thus far made broader access much more challenging.

Those Who Were There

While not nearly as extensive in its outreach as the Shoah Foundation or the Holocaust Museum, the Fortunoff Archive has—as noted—made some attempts to raise awareness of its work. The archive's first major attempt to do so came in 1983 with the production of a promotional video entitled *Those Who Were There*, which was screened that year to the American Gathering of Jewish Holocaust Survivors, an event bringing over 20,000 survivors and their families to Washington, D.C. Produced four years after the archive began recording interviews in 1979, the video was released at a time when the American survivor community was becoming more fully mobilized, through the campaign to construct the United States Holocaust Memorial Museum, the formation of the American Gathering of Jewish Holocaust Survivors, and growing efforts to establish oral history archives of the Holocaust. The video functioned both as a call to give testimony, particularly in light of the aging of survivors, and as a primer for witnesses apprehensive about telling their stories in front of the camera. *Those Who Were There* features interviews with survivors who were initially reluctant to give testimony but who realized that their stories would be lost if their accounts were not documented. The video includes interviews with both witnesses and scholars such as Erich Goldhagen, who appear on screen to lend historical credibility to the archive, as well as to stress the importance of oral histories by the victims to counter sources left behind by the perpetrators.

Those Who Were There encourages survivors to come forward and lend their voices through the technology of video, which had yet to achieve ubiquitous domestic use at the time. The work discusses in detail the process of conducting interviews, with footage of the studio, control room, and other aspects of the testimony process. The video portrays the Fortunoff Archive as a supportive environment for survivors—one that creates a space and fosters a dynamic that grants them agency in giving their histories. Interviewer Dori Laub appears in the tape to testify to the nature of that interaction: "A listener to a survivor needs to be a full participant in every aspect of the shared experience. There is no place for fleeing from it. The survivor is contacted ahead of time, the project is explained, and from that period onwards there is a companion with them on the way to this opening of the painful secret of his life."[61] Rather than characterizing survivors as historical informants, Laub emphasizes the mutual process and responsibility that mark a testimony. Acknowledging the immense psychic toll that can accompany the endeavor, he assures potential witnesses of the archive's commitment to making survivors the primary authors of their testimony; there are no tape limits on testimonies and the technological interaction will be as nonthreatening and as comfortable as possible.

Elie Wiesel, then the chairman of the United States Holocaust Memorial Council, also has a key role in the video, due to his identity as an iconic survivor and the political and moral authority bestowed upon him by the federal government through his involvement in the Holocaust Museum. His address to the video's audience is framed as a mandate for their participation in giving testimony:

> And to you, to you who are there. I know how difficult it is to speak. You have children, you have friends and you don't want to open wounds—why should you? But you must. When you choose not to speak, your story will not be told, not even in silence. You are more than a witness, you are a hundred witnesses. You belong to a very special minority. A minority that will very soon be gone. And with you or with me, that part of the story will be gone too. You must share. You must.[62]

Wiesel describes the act of giving testimony as psychologically traumatic, yet morally necessary. He underscores the stakes of the endeavor, citing the impending absence of survivors and the fading of their living memory. Consistent with the ethos of the Fortunoff Archive, he nonetheless acknowledges the impossibility of fully conveying the extreme nature of the events experienced by survivors. Later in the video, Wiesel speaks to the potential nonsurvivor audience: if they can never know what it was like to experience the Holocaust, by carefully listening and attending to survivors, they may "come close to the gates" of that history.[63] Thus, while Wiesel presents the possibility of generating an ethical bond between audiences and recorded witnesses, the divide between those two parties is ultimately unbridgeable.

Witness: Voices from the Holocaust

After the release of *Those Who Were There*, the Fortunoff Archive continued to expand as one of the preeminent sites of Holocaust testimony in the United States. In 1999, it co-produced another video, *Witness: Voices from the Holocaust*, a documentary directed and produced by the independent filmmakers Joshua Greene and Shiva Kumar, who had earlier worked with the archive on thirty-minute programs for cable television. Completed in 1999, the 90-minute *Witness* aired on PBS in 2000 on Holocaust Remembrance Day and was consistent with the archive's intention of circulating a small sampling of completed testimonies beyond Yale's Sterling Memorial Library. The video illuminates the Fortunoff Archive's attempts to make its archival holdings more accessible, while struggling to maintain its particular archival and institutional standards and principles.

The opening titles for *Witness* are surprisingly sentimental given the more sober leanings of the Fortunoff Archive. They feature a mosaic of stock Holocaust images—flames, barbed-wire fences, faces of anonymous victims—with a caption stating that the video's interview footage comes from the Fortunoff Archive, particularly its earlier testimonies, and was not generated specifically for the video. To produce the full-length documentary, Greene and Kumar screened more than six hundred hours of "raw, relentless testimony" spanning one hundred interviews, from which they excerpted more than twenty for the final work.[64] The documentary has no "voice-of-God narration" and features no experts or other figures who did not give witness testimony to the archive. The filmmakers emphasize not only the rawness of the edited footage, but also the visceral and labored nature of the endeavor of testimony. The editor's introduction to the book adaptation of the documentary describes the process of reviewing and selecting testimony for the film as "exhausting," but the filmmakers pressed ahead because of the fragments of insight they uncovered in searching through the myriad testimonies.[65]

Greene and Kumar overstate the extent to which their source material and the video represent the varied and textured dimensions of archived testimony. They characterize *Witness* as a "multivoice narrative" in which the complexity and contradictions of experiences can be viewed *across* and *between* the different witnesses featured in the documentary. Yet they do not engage with the multiple voices that exist *within* individual testimonies, since they mostly edit out the participation (that is to say, the voices) of interviewers and focus, with only a few exceptions, on the words of witnesses. This appears to be an extension of one of the Fortunoff Archive's driving principles—its emphasis on allowing witnesses to be the authors of their own testimony. And while the archive acknowledges, through both its training methodology and supported scholarship, the critical role of interviewers in facilitating testimonies, that role is downplayed in *Witness*. What remains in that work is an underlying notion that the archive can uncover a purer, unadulterated form of memory.

The filmmakers assert that they attempted to use testimonies for their documentary "without romanticizing, without fanfare, in a manner that reflects meticulous research and inquiry, and with profound respect for the words of the witnesses."[66] Elaborating on that aim, they note that they strive "not to comment on the testimonies but to carefully sequence them into a narrative that roughly traces life, before, during, and after the Nazi era—to edit without editorializing."[67] This perspective fails to acknowledge adequately how the acts of excerpting and editing interviews themselves constitute forms of commentary and editorializing. Furthermore, while the directors describe witnesses as "experts" in their own stories, they do not discuss how those subjects express their memories in dialogue with either an institution or individual interviewers.

Witness: Voices from the Holocaust employs specific framing devices. By virtue of its three-part structure the documentary attempts to excerpt testimony in a more accessible, sequential format. That approach may be difficult to avoid in light of the sheer magnitude of testimonies housed within the Fortunoff Archive, but it nonetheless belies the filmmakers' claim that an editing process can exist without editorializing. The archive's guiding ethos and interview methodology often creates circumstances that allow the often nonsequential paths of memory to be pursued. At the same time, however, the process of adapting testimonies into films or pedagogical programming can complicate efforts to preserve the traces of that approach. Constructing such a work requires not only excerpting portions of testimony that advance the narrative in the order of events from before, during, and after the war. It also involves choosing which witnesses and testimony segments best represent certain thematic and chronological divisions. While those choices are arguably unavoidable, the decision to structure the video along sequential lines complicates the Fortunoff Archive's investment in conveying the openness and frequent lack of closure in its testimonies. By adopting a sequential rather than a mosaic form, the documentary imbues the footage with a coherent trajectory. The video is broken down into chronologically advancing categories that include such topics as Hitler's rise to power in Germany, the process of ghettoization, and the events of liberation.

While the documentary's interview segments are initially captioned with first names and last initials of witnesses, as well as their places and dates of birth (e.g., "Helen K., born Warsaw, Poland, 1924"), the date and location of each interview is omitted. Leaving out that information reinforces the notion that the accounts of witnesses, and not the context for their dialogues with interviewers, should be the exclusive focus for the analysis of testimonies. The documentary's incorporation of documents, photographs, and other artifacts, including stock moving images, also raises significant issues. Witnesses are often shown on screen holding photographs of their loved ones or pictures of themselves before or after the onset of the war, but their voices are also superimposed over archival images that—while they may reference general events being discussed at that point of the interview—do not always directly correspond to the personal experiences of the witness. For example, Robert S., a contrite former member of Hitler Youth, recalls being seduced by the allure of Nazi torchlight parades in his German hometown. As he describes the scene, his testimony can be heard over familiar footage of Nazi torchlight parades, but there is no mention or captioning of the context or origin of that footage. Similarly, as the Jewish survivor Joseph W. remarks on the emerging threat of the Nazis—"the clouds were getting dark"—his testimony is intercut with archival images of Nazi propaganda and of antisemitic warnings being placed on the windows of Jewish storefronts.[68] These moments complicate the attempts of the documentary and the archive to allow the testimonies to stand on their own terms rather than rendering them as more general exemplars of Holocaust experience.

Equally important, the recurring use of generic film footage works against the rigorous epistemology of the Fortunoff Archive that privileges firsthand accounts of what was seen and heard, as against more sweeping historical generalizations or unverified secondhand speculations. At one point during an interview with John S., a Czech Catholic priest, the witness recalls having seen the deportation of a group of Jews, though he ultimately remained a bystander, too afraid to intervene on the victims' behalf. It is an emotionally charged moment in which John S. reflects on his failure to take action and his inability to ever forgive himself. Rather than allowing segments of that testimony to appear on their own, the filmmakers intercut footage of Jews loaded onto a train for deportation. This footage appears to be the same material that is rather prominently displayed by the museum of the Anne Frank House in Amsterdam in an exhibit on the deportation process at the Dutch Westerbork transit camp.[69] While the footage in question represents an invaluable trace of the deportation process and serves as material testimony to the Nazis' genocidal machinery, it appears here without its very particular historical context, instead employed as a stock image of Jewish deportation in general.[70] To suggest a correlation between the horrors that John S. witnessed that day and the stock images presented on screen is to render his encounter in universalizing terms. Just as audiovisual testimonies are shaped by the institutions and parties that take part in an interview, found film footage from the Holocaust also carries a history of production and reception that goes beyond what is simply captured on celluloid. Although the included film footage can be traced back to actual historical contexts, *Witness* does not attempt such a contextualization, instead relying on the images to provide emotive resonance and generic historical illustration for particular moments of testimonies.

The co-director Joshua Greene seems to hedge in his published comments on the use of both testimony and nontestimony footage in his work. He contends that his documentary is compelling despite its heavy dependence on shots of witnesses sitting in front of the camera; such scenes violate a primary lesson often taught in film school: "Talking heads won't hold viewers' attention."[71] However, Greene's use of stock moving and still images not only takes their illustrative value for granted, but also serves to prop up the testimonies by interweaving them with recycled visual tropes, rather than allowing the "talking heads" to speak for themselves or to be placed in constructive conversation with the found footage.

The profound limits of that approach to "talking heads" are evident in one of the video's more emotionally wrenching moments: a segment in which Abraham P., a Romanian Jewish survivor, describes his arrival at Auschwitz-Birkenau and the process of selection that continues to haunt him. Abraham recalls with great anguish having encouraged his youngest brother to join his parents in the selection line, unaware that they would be chosen for execution: "I can't get it out of my head. It hurts me, it bothers me, I don't know what to do."[72] At this point, the image of Abraham speaking on camera immediately cuts to a montage of iconic moving images of Auschwitz-Birkenau, including the infamous gate to Auschwitz and the barbed-wire fence surrounding that camp—punctuated by a pensive piano score that intensifies the pathos of this already intensely emotional moment. Just as it is essential to contextualize Abraham P.'s background and experience beyond the segments shown in the film, it is equally crucial to rigorously use found footage that can generate new knowledge, rather than to recycle well-worn symbols. In their current form in *Witness*, found moving images appear as icons of a general sentiment or moment rather than as sources to be examined in their own specific contexts.

Finally, the interview segments with Abraham P. underscore one of the larger issues relating to the documentary *Witness*, namely the editing out—with one or two exceptions—of interviewers' voices from the original testimonies. Abraham's original archival interview took place in 1984 at the Fortunoff-affiliate project at the University of Michigan at Dearborn, with Sidney Bolkosky, the project's founder, serving as the interviewer. Bolkosky asks Abraham a series of penetrating questions, such as: "What are your dreams like?"; "Are you regularly affected by your experiences during the war?"[73] These questions spark the witness's reflections on how the past continues to mark his present life, including how he handles his ongoing confrontation with the memory of his younger brother during the camp selection. By omitting such interactions, *Witness* emphasizes the voice of the subject in isolation, at the expense of airing it in dialogue with the interviewer.[74] Excluding the voice of the latter can obscure the audience member's position as a witness to the act of witnessing that unfolds on camera. While the talking heads of survivors, liberators, and bystanders predominate in *Witness*, the crucial role of interviewers and the operative influence of the Fortunoff Archive methodology are mostly obscured.

Exemplary Witnesses

The Fortunoff Archive's exclusion of testimonial dialogue between interviewers and interviewees in a work to be screened outside the archive's walls is especially striking because of the archive's dedication to developing a deeply interpersonal and at times self-reflexive approach in its interviews. That dedication was evidenced in the late 1980s, when financial concerns led the archive's planners to look back on their past work and assess future directions. Each of its chief interviewers, including Dana Kline, Lawrence Langer, Dori Laub, Geoffrey Hartman, and Joanne Rudof, submitted the names of five witnesses whom they thought should be re-interviewed in the hopes of addressing particular elements of the testimonial encounter.[75] Langer was a strong advocate for these re-interviews. In a letter to Michael Berenbaum of the Holocaust Museum, he explained the great value of revisiting certain witnesses when there is a sense that some order of experience was yet to be raised by the survivor.[76] Langer ended up playing an active role in the re-interviews, both as a member in each of the new interview teams and as a participant in developing new sets of questions and lines of investigation. In contrast to the first interviews, the second round was intended to be more structured, less open-ended.[77] Rather than focus on reconstructing the personal history of the subject, interviewers were to directly raise larger questions of language, the workings of memory, and the challenges of cognition; in addition, they were to ask witnesses to reflect back on their earlier experiences of giving testimonies.

A sampling of these repeat testimonies reveals much about how the passage of time affects a witness's recollection of events. But they also speak to the Fortunoff Archive's changing preferences and approaches. Due to their deliberate reexamination by the archive's core interviewers, the testimonies in question are revealing in their exploration of interview methodologies and dynamics. They ultimately provide invaluable insights into the investment by the Fortunoff Archive—as against the two other featured archives—in reflecting, outside of closed doors and in open conversation with witnesses, on the framing of its testimonies. That degree of transparency is illuminated in an interview with one particular repeat witness, Eva B., who had her testimony recorded by the Fortunoff Archive on three different occasions.

The First Testimony of Eva B.

Eva B., a Czech Jewish survivor born in 1924, was interviewed by the main Fortunoff Archive at Yale (as opposed to an affiliate project) in 1979, 1983, and as part of the re-interview project in 1988. Her first testimony—like others conducted by Fortunoff before the mid-1980s—is notable for its less polished quality, reflecting the fact that it was one of the earliest interviews, conducted before the archive established a firm institutional identity or methodology. Unlike later testimonies, there is no mention of either the interviewer or of the location, though the citation and finding aids identify archive co-founders Dori Laub and Laurel Vlock as the interviewers. Eva is not asked to provide fundamental biographical information such as her name or date of birth. Rather than being framed against a black backdrop, she sits in an orange reclining lounge chair placed in front of a bookshelf, in what appears to be an office.[78] In contrast to later, more standardized interviews, Eva tilts to her right, facing the off-screen interviewers, rather than looking toward the camera with the interviewers placed just adjacent to the lens, thus providing a less direct mode of address. She is initially framed in a medium close-up but with a static lens, though the camera eventually racks back and forth into tight close-ups of Eva's face, punctuating particular moments in her story, including her description of the rising threat of Nazism.

That latter technique seems to reflect Laurel Vlock's interest—perhaps related to her background as a television producer—in having the camera intensify the dramatic effect of a particular testimony. In addition, Vlock's use of a series of often prying questions seems to reveal an investment in capturing an emotional reaction from witnesses. In contrast, Laub, as consistent with his more psychoanalytically informed approach, allows more room for silences and moments of reflection to make their way into Eva's testimony. The distinctions between their respective styles are evident in the kinds of questions they posed. Vlock adopts a much more aggressive tack, often posing one question after another: "Were people in contact with the outside world?"; "Do you remember the old city [of Prague]?"; "Was there much discrimination before the war?" In pursuing these lines of inquiry, Vlock is asking Eva to compile a detailed chronicle of her experiences, pinning down the facts of what happened, but in the process framing Eva's testimony in Vlock's terms, rather than allowing her memories to emerge through more indirect, carefully placed inquiries. Whereas Laub's questions—such as "What stayed with you [after the war]?"—ask for Eva's perspectives on the workings of memory and the legacy of the Holocaust, Vlock shows more of an interest in reconstructing historical details from the past, including extensive questions about life in Theresienstadt.

Despite Vlock's attempts to mold this first testimony, some moments emerge without having to be overly prompted. Eva comments that not until five years earlier had she been able to openly discuss her experiences with her children, who had previously been unaware of the full details of her wartime history.[79] She later remarks in the testimony, "I just pushed it away, I couldn't think about it, I couldn't cope with it. I was so busy adjusting, repressing, living." Eva's coming to terms with the legacy of the Holocaust seems to mirror a broader discourse among survivors living in the United States. The more open confrontation of their experiences included mobilizing the memory of the Shoah through such endeavors as the formation of the United States Holocaust Memorial Museum, resistance to the planned neo-Nazi march in Skokie, Illinois in 1977, and many critical responses to popular representations of the events such as in the television miniseries *Holocaust*.

In spite of the litany of questions posed to her, Eva—often in tension with Vlock—finds spaces for drifting through recollections of the past, rather than strictly chronicling events from a more distant present. When asked early in the interview to provide a sense of her family life before the war, Eva assumes a sullen mien and mournfully reflects on the loss of her high school sweetheart: "A very talented individual, he never came back." The moment falls outside of the topic and sequence of the question—the realm of common memory—and leads down the more unanticipated path of deep memory. Eva seems to personify Lawrence Langer's description of the anti-redemptive nature of Holocaust remembrance. Even in describing her liberation from Mauthausen, she speaks not of freedom but of irredeemable horror. She recalls seeing the emaciated bodies of fellow inmates: "You see these pile[s] of corpses, these pictures of corpses, that everyone I think has seen by now and I think the much more horrible thing is to see these corpses walk. Walking into this typhoid-ridden place was liberation for me." As the testimony heads toward a conclusion, Vlock departs from her list of questions and openly expresses her sympathies for Eva, "I just want to hold you and tell you I want to be your family. I don't want you to feel alone. That's just how I feel." At that moment, the camera suddenly zooms back and the camera goes to black. The audio remains on, and we hear Eva remark: "Thank you, I appreciate it, I think I'm through. I don't think any more details would be interesting." While Vlock attempts to comfort Eva by openly expressing and potentially imposing her concern and desire to care for her, the intensity of the witness's despair seems to evade that kind of nurturing. As the testimony concludes, Eva seems to still be grappling with many of the stories she has presented on camera.

The Second Testimony of Eva B.

The second interview with Eva at Yale, conducted four years later in 1983, reveals not only the witness's firmer grasp of her story, but also how the Fortunoff Archive had begun to move toward a more formalized process of conducting its testimonies. This time, when we encounter Eva, she no longer sits in an office space, but is rather against a more neutral black backdrop, sitting in a chair and more directly facing the camera, with the unidentified interviewer just off the side of the lens. Though only four years have passed since the last interview, Eva appears to have aged considerably; her hair is now completely gray. She is, however, much more assertive in initiating her account. Rather than having to face a litany of questions concerning her life before the war, Eva raises those issues on her own, with self-confidence and clarity that perhaps reflect her opportunity to confront memories that had been largely unaddressed until the prior interview. To some extent it appears that Eva has internalized or at least anticipated that the interviewer would inquire about the historical dimensions of her story. In contrast to her earlier interview, Eva keeps her story moving forward with a fluency that appears to be firmly grounded in her familiarity with a common memory of the events. Having delivered her testimony on videotape before, she now appears to have developed some mastery of her story and of the generic conventions and performance modes of testimony.

Despite Eva's apparent composure and sense of historical grounding, there are moments when she seems to lose her footing, and her memory departs from the chronology and drifts forward to the experience of losing her beloved high school sweetheart. It is a moment that speaks to both the repetitious yet also seemingly spontaneous and authentic nature of Eva's testimony. While she repeats many of the same details from her prior interview, the breakdown in her recollection seems to constitute evidence of the persistence of trauma and the impossibility of fully containing the excesses of her memory. At one point in this second testimony, Eva openly addresses the difficult and incomplete nature of giving testimony. Her son would urge her to tell him the whole story, but he would run away in discomfort before she could finish. As a result, she felt compelled to put her thoughts down on paper and at one point even attempted to record her recollections on audiotape—but the project was left incomplete. It was not until her first taping at the Fortunoff Archive that she realized just how alive her experiences were, and she began to feel obligated to tell her story, all the while acknowledging that these experiences would continue to cast a shadow over her.

In this second interview, Eva frames her testimony as an obligation to herself and to her family to confront her past. Rather than seeming to facilitate closure, the more she tells her story the more she expresses the fragmented, singular nature of her experience. It is a "worm's-eye view" of the Holocaust, she remarks, but "as a worm's-eye view, [it] has its own value."[80] The interviewer, rather than focusing on that singular story, presses her to extrapolate some universal lessons, asking: "Do you have any thoughts on those who listen. Learning lessons . . . teaching?"[81] Eva is mostly resistant to the idea as the interviewer continues to press her for thoughts on the pedagogical utility of her experience. At one point, Eva responds: "I have no desire to tell anybody who doesn't want to know. I'm not sure that any lessons can be learned." Just as the testimony appears to come to a close, with the screen cutting to black, Eva reappears on tape and begins to sing a song that she learned in Auschwitz, passed from one inmate to another as a means of boosting morale. As she performs this song, she looks directly into the camera, with the lens zooming in for a close-up to punctuate the moment. Eva translates the song: "Be of good mood and strength, keep your belief alive." It was, as Eva recalls, one of the few things that lifted her spirit in the camp: "It would give you a cohesion. A sense of belonging."

This moment is one of the most striking in this testimony, in part because it emerges in a seemingly peripheral juncture after the interview appears to cut permanently to black, only to resume with the performance of the song. But it is also compelling as a trace of the voices that sang this song, of those who ultimately perished. Eva serves as a surrogate of sorts, reenacting a song transmitted between and across the inmates of Auschwitz. This moment in her singular testimony gives voice to a larger collective experience. Though Eva cannot attribute the song to any writer, the interviewer presses her for its provenance. Eva can only reply: "It wasn't told. I was just taught it by people who were earlier than I." In reciting the song on camera, she too has transmitted the story to future generations, and in that sense takes responsibility for a survival that is larger than her own. However, Eva actively resists assigning a redemptive meaning to her survival. On hearing the song, the interviewer asks Eva if she ever has felt the inclination to see any of her fellow survivors from Auschwitz. Eva unequivocally rejects the idea: "No, listen. Auschwitz was so horrendous that the faces kind of merge, they were shadows." The interviewer continues to inquire about Eva's possible desire to communicate with other survivors, but she seems less invested than the interviewer in constructing such an affective community with other living witnesses.

Posing what is phrased as one final question, the interviewer asks Eva: "People have said that they think it is impossible to cry about things that happened forty years ago, people who were lost forty years ago, one doesn't cry about losing a parent or a child when that much time has elapsed and yet almost uniformly people's eyes get filled when they talk about the concentration camp experience. Why?" With this line of inquiry, the interviewer places Eva in the position of having to generalize about the mindset of other survivors. She briefly indulges the questioner: "Because the way they lost people was so traumatic. But of course I didn't lose anybody that close." Then her thoughts travel yet again to her high school love—someone, she remarks, whom she would have married had they both survived the war. Eva attempts to downplay her own turmoil during the Shoah, suggesting that because she survived, her proximity to real loss is not as profound. This is the moment of recollection, similar to her performance of the song, when Eva seems to be immersed in her memory, seemingly off the track of the testimony. Her voice grows increasingly hushed as she looks toward her lap and squints her eyes: "He was a pianist and an artist and an engineer. He was a lovely person. It hurt. His death hurt me more than my family, although I was very young. He was part of my life for many years." At this point the interviewer interjects, seemingly off-point, "You married a Czech man? You needed that?" But Eva is still pondering her prior utterance, and she signals an interest in finishing the testimony: "I didn't think we would talk that much more." At this point the testimony abruptly comes to an end, as the camera cuts without any formal conclusion.

The Third Testimony of Eva B.

Whereas the first two interviews with Eva B. had been directed toward reconstructing a narrative of her experiences during the Shoah, the third and final testimony, recorded in 1988 as part of the re-interviewing program, is almost completely dedicated to the meta-discursive elements of the testimonial process. Eva sits against a black backdrop, centered in the frame, with the two interviewers seated to the left of the camera. Unlike in the other two testimonies, the interviewers here (Dori Laub and Lawrence Langer) introduce themselves at the beginning of the tape before deferring to Eva to begin talking. Although at the time of this taping Eva is sixty-four and thus almost ten years older than in her first interview, she appears stronger and more upright, and she speaks with an even greater sense of purpose and confidence. She reveals that she is now working as a psychotherapist. And while she does not elaborate upon that fact, it is a revealing admission in that it suggests a continued, dedicated, and formalized engagement with trauma and memory, which seems to inform her demeanor and performance throughout the third interview.

The motivations for the re-interviewing project and the fact that Eva is now delivering her testimony for a third time give this process a critically self-aware dimension. Eva remarks that in her first testimony in 1979 she "treated it in a clinical way, conveying the facts but none of the emotions."[82] She reflects how at that time she played down her own emotional struggles, noting that since her father had died before the war and her mother had survived with her, she somehow believed that she had not suffered as much as others, leading her to feel guilty. But she realizes now that "it [the Holocaust] has very much affected my relationship with people. I really keep my distance." Her remarks are followed by a very long silence until Langer assures her that her accounts will have educational value and that it will be useful for future audiences to hear her thoughts on the process. As against Langer's more direct approach, Dori Laub conveys a gentler disposition, attempting to take Eva back to particular memories about her hometown of Prague. Laub asks: "There is a memory of Prague that is life. How do you remember it, not the facts?" He is interested not in uncovering a place that has yet to be described, but rather in finding an entry-point into *how* she remembers: "How do you remember? Not what but how?" When Eva drifts into discussions of particular details of her life before the war, rather than on reflections on the process of memory, Laub keeps her on track: "We're going to try to keep you away from facts."

At more than a few points throughout the recording, the particular agenda of this re-interview—the focus on "emotions" rather than "facts"—has the effect of shaping Eva's remembering in very precise, deliberate ways. She expresses having felt a sense of guilt over the fact that her mother survived on account of not having worn glasses, while the bespectacled mother of a close friend was selected for extermination. As she attempts to come to terms with that ever so small yet critical twist of fate, Laub interjects, asking her to describe what is going on inside her head: "When you mention these incidents, are there pictures, like the glasses the woman wore? Are the memories images of moments?" And while Eva describes certain events in terms of their visual resonance, they appear to be embedded in a particular narrative account that initiates the process of taking her back to that moment in time. As in her two prior interviews, she recalls her high school sweetheart in a manner so intense that it underscores the persistence of her feelings of love and loss: "I have memories of the things we did together. Playing tennis with him. I remember he came, we had a sandwich together, I remember where we were sitting."

The self-reflexive approach to this interview draws out perspectives that never arose in the prior interviews by shedding light on both the form and content of Eva's memories. At the same time, however, it constitutes a representational framework that ultimately looks past the more subtle and unanticipated moments in testimony. Rather than fostering more spontaneous moments when the witness and the prospective audience can look for meanings in the silences of testimony and in tensions generated between interviewer and interviewee, the very subtexts of witness narratives that Langer powerfully describes are made explicit in Eva's testimony without sparking closer analysis.

In one particular exchange in the testimony, Eva reflects on the guilt she feels for having survived while others perished during the Shoah. Langer, who in his scholarship on testimony eloquently writes of the "choiceless choice" facing the victims, projects his concern with that subject onto Eva by asking a leading question: "How did the absence of choice affect your thinking about it [her survival]?" While Eva affirms Langer's assessment here, it is difficult to ascertain if this is the result of her own initiation or on account of the interviewer's prodding. There is a sense that both Laub and Langer are turning to the re-interview process as a way of reexploring certain of their own preferred lines of inquiry, often at the expense of the archive's aim of granting primary agency to witnesses. In one exchange, Laub asks Eva why she viewed her first testimony as primarily factual rather than as emotional:

> DORI LAUB: Do you really think it was factual only?
> EVA B.: That's what I thought at the time. Am I deceiving
>   myself, you think?

Laub and Langer attempt to give Eva an opportunity to reflect on the first interview and the evolution of her perspective on the testimony. Yet Laub's attempt to move her toward the emotional core of her story is to some extent at odds with the mechanisms she has adopted for confronting her past. As the testimony comes to a conclusion she dryly comments: "There were a few traumas in my life. So I'm more comfortable with facts than with emotions." At this point Langer concludes the testimony: "Well, thank you for the facts and for the emotions." The camera holds still on Eva looking away from the camera, and she appears and sounds exhausted and emotionally depleted. The screen then cuts to black.

Langer and Laub had attempted to penetrate the emotional core of Eva's testimony by capturing both its raw and constructed qualities. This is one of the limitations of the Fortunoff methodology, as it often operates on the presumption that unvarnished testimony can somehow be captured on tape, rather than being mediated by institutional frameworks. Nonetheless, this closing moment ultimately sheds light on how the emotional and analytic aspects of Eva's testimony are entangled rather than discrete, displaying how Eva can negotiate the affective burden of her memory through the mastery of facts.

The Exemplary Testimony of Baruch G.

The Fortunoff Archive has identified a number of compelling survivors in addition to those invited to give more than one testimony. They notably include those whom the archive highlights on its website and at least one who was rec-

ommended to me on my first visit to the archive. The latter is Rabbi Baruch G.
—a witness whom Joanne Rudof suggested to me during my initial research trip
to the Fortunoff Archive in 2006 when I asked to see an illustrative sampling of
the collection. One of a group of witnesses included in the book adaptation of the
archive's video *Witness: Voices from the Holocaust,* Baruch is also featured in a section of its website that contains excerpts of witness testimony intended to provide insight into the general nature of the archive's testimonial project.[83] Moreover, as will be explored in the next chapter, he appears as an exemplary figure
in internal discussions within the U.S. Holocaust Memorial Museum.

The testimony of Rabbi Baruch G. (born 1923) was recorded at Yale on 6 September 1984. Despite falling short of the consistent production standards eventually adopted by the archive, Baruch's interview does illuminate the interpersonal
dynamic that the archive attempted to foster between interviewer and interviewee. The interviewer, identified on the finding aids as Dana Kline, is not introduced at the beginning of the tape. Baruch sits on a brown couch in front of a
beige curtain, directly facing Kline, who sits just off the right of the camera. Her
first question reveals the archive's preferred interview approach: "Why don't we
begin by thinking about the past almost as if you are looking at an album with
pictures in it from your family, from your early years—and can you tell me your
name and where you were born?"[84] This question privileges the visual compo-
nent of memory and glosses over some crucial biographical information—we
never learn his birth date, for instance. However, it rather quickly compels Baruch to ponder his deeply embedded remembrances of the Holocaust. By turning the pages of this internalized picture album, Baruch associatively calls up
his younger sister, a figure who will often return throughout the testimony. He
tenses up at the thought of her, putting his hands to his pursed lips and with a sullen, unsteady delivery comments: "I missed my sister for a long time. For some
reason I felt, I thought that for some reason she had survived and for many, many
years I dreamt that someday I would hear that she was still alive. So when you
talk about my brother and sister, this comes to mind always." Thus the interviewer has Baruch frame his memory of his family in a way that enables him to
arrive at a moment of intimate memory, rather than relegating his biography to
a litany of census-like questions. She facilitates a space for a more multilayered
recollection of memory, one that cannot be viewed from a distance but rather is
experienced as the interpenetration of past and present.

Another such moment emerges when Kline asks Baruch about his family:
"You said you were from a religious family. I bet you can describe a Seder." Baruch proceeds lovingly to recall the details of the Passover feasts from his youth,
remembering how his father sat at the head of the table like a king. His fond
memories of those prewar experiences, rather than following along the sequen-

tial trajectory of common memory, quickly jump ahead to his more anguished moments from many years after the war. In tenderly recalling the plenitude of past Seders, he cannot help but reflect upon the glaring absence of his extinguished family. He recalls with great anguish that, at his son's bar mitzvah, no one from his side of the family was present to celebrate the joyous event as they would have been in those years before the Shoah. In many ways, Baruch's sense of loneliness is more pronounced in recollecting those postwar moments of expected joy and celebration than in his memories of the war. At this juncture, he reveals that events during the Shoah may present fewer difficulties than do the challenges of grappling with its aftereffects. Perhaps most compelling is the fact that these revelations surface in the first fifteen minutes of an almost two-hour-long testimony.

While Kline allows Baruch the room to follow the unanticipated paths of memory, she carefully brings him back on track with comments like: "Let's leave 1948 for a minute and go back to 1933, '34, Hitler comes to power in Germany, and does this have any impact on your life?" When Baruch responds by commenting that he did not think it would be that bad, that God would eventually intervene, Kline asks for clarification: "Do you remember thinking that now or thinking that then?" So while the interview foregrounds the interpenetration of past and present, Kline also attempts to parse out the various levels of knowledge, including considerations of retrospective insight. Ultimately, however, she enables Baruch to linger on the painful moments and to create a space where his performance of testimony can serve to reenact and reembody the presence and gestures of those whom he lost.

It is not only the memory of Baruch's sister, but also that of his father that continues to resonate with him, and in his recollections of this figure one senses Baruch's role as a surrogate witness. He remembers how his father was assigned to a forced labor camp and was never the same man after his return. He never told Baruch what had happened to him during his absence, but the impact was evident on his body—the shaven beard of a pious Orthodox Jew and the meek disposition of a once strong and charismatic man demonstrated these changes. As Baruch speaks of the physical denigration of his father, his own body begins to wilt, his lips quiver, and his voice begins to tremble. A period of silence is followed by tears.

As Baruch proceeds to tell of his arrival at Auschwitz, Kline asks him: "What did the name [Auschwitz] mean to you?" Here, too, Baruch uses bodily expression to invoke his own and others' experiences. Unexpectedly, he responds to the question by pulling back the left sleeve of his dress shirt to reveal the large tattooed numbers "76300." He deciphers the numbers as designating both his individual identity in the camp and the series of inmates taken from his hometown.

In that sense, revealing the tattoo chronicles not only his dehumanization but also the larger suffering of fellow Jews from his community. Baruch explicitly comments on how his testimony functions as both a form of individual preservation and collective commemoration. One of his main motivations for coming forward is his recognition that he is the last surviving member of his family. Without his testimony, "There will be no one to tell of the existence of the Goldstein family in the city of Mlawa. It sounds silly, doesn't it?" Baruch is torn between the obligation to remember and the pain of revisiting the past. He recognizes that time is running out for survivors and that he has no right to "bury" his story; still, he is plagued by the questions of his own survival and his reasons for giving witness: "I sometimes feel guilt. Why have I survived? Have I fulfilled a basic obligation that one should carry with him to tell the world about it?" Baruch had tried to tell his story soon after the war but, like many witnesses, he had found it difficult to be heard. He also reveals that after the war, he became terribly afraid of doing harm to others, of making anyone displeased with him. He thinks that he should have seen a psychiatrist, and that perhaps now he is making up for that by telling his story on camera. At the same time, he seems to recognize that the process of giving testimony, while constructive, is not completely cathartic. He states: "But I can tell you that I wasn't well mentally. By not well, I don't mean that I was crazy, but my inside was definitely, is still definitely scarred." Baruch briefly slips into articulating his suffering in the past tense, but quickly reaffirms that his pain remains palpable in the present.

Baruch's testimony also illuminates both the entanglements of past and present trauma and the mediated, contested, and cross-generational dynamic of transmitting Holocaust memory. He appears to be someone who has struggled with the revelation of his story. Baruch remarks that his son was upset with him for not having opened up earlier about his experiences, causing a rift between the two: "He [his son] has gone to therapy and I have not. He urges me to go." Baruch is reluctant, but eventually reconsiders his position after viewing a documentary film dealing with the generational inheritances of the Holocaust. In particular, he recalls a scene in the film about a female survivor who is afraid to love her daughter because the loss of her family during the war makes her resistant to getting too attached. Baruch considers whether this might apply to him—that he buried himself in his work in order to avoid becoming too attached to his son for fear of losing him: "Is it fear to come close to him? Or is it wanting to become normal so much so that I immerse myself in my work, or what? But I suppose these are the scars I mentioned before and that are with us and I suppose will be buried with them." The encounter with a mediated representation of another survivor's experience triggers Baruch's resolve to record his own testimony and grapple with the strained relationship with his son. Baruch may not have talked openly about his experiences with his child, but the resonances were nonetheless transmitted to the next generation. In his remarks, Baruch echoes a not uncommon tendency to pluralize his experience, commenting on the scars that will be buried with *"us"* [survivors], suggesting the collective legacy of the survivor community.

In keeping with its exemplary status, Baruch's interview resurfaces in 1990 in the Fortunoff Archive's training documents as a model case study for volunteer interviewers for affiliate projects, including endeavors in New York and Houston.[85] Even more revealing are the examinations of Baruch G.'s testimony by Lawrence Langer in 1991. In that year alone, Langer offered a deeply compelling analysis of that interview in his foundational work *Holocaust Testimonies: The Ruins of Memory* and in his written correspondence while working as a consultant to the Holocaust Museum's oral history department. He submitted evaluations to the museum of what he considered to be the Fortunoff Archive's most compelling and instructive testimonies.[86] His memorandum to the project director Michael Berenbaum discusses Baruch G.'s enduring postwar pain:

> He describes it as "life around you seems to be normal, but you are abnormal," and he speaks at length about the difficulty he had adjusting after he was "liberated." The overwhelming loss casts a permanent shadow over his present joys, not undermining them, but causing them to exist within the framework of irretrievable loss. This passage begins about 11 minutes into the tape, and is a locus classicus on the subject.[87]

Consistent with his discussions of the anti-redemptive, noncathartic, and temporally interwoven dimensions of testimony, Langer characterizes Baruch's perspectives as the personification of that idea. He also emphasizes Baruch's experience of what he calls "humiliated imagination," as the witness continues to feel guilt and a sense of unworthiness, and by an irreconcilable tension between a traumatic past and a "normal present."[88]

In 2000, Joshua Greene and Shiva Kumar adapted the Fortunoff Archive's documentary *Witness: Voices from the Holocaust* as a book, with the same title. While the book includes excerpted transcripts of testimony for all of the witnesses included in the video, it also features testimonies from other interviewees, including Baruch G. The volume retains the video's thematic structure, covering subsets of experiences before, during, and after the war, as well as its sober ethos. Lawrence Langer's foreword stresses that survivors avoid speaking in terms that can be rendered as redemptive lessons. The book's final segment, "It Started with Dreams: Aftermath," incorporates the conclusion of Baruch's interview, including his remarks:

Do we have the right to bury this [story] with us? We have no right to do it. It's got to be told. It's got to be, it's got to be recorded. For one reason and one reason only: not so much to know what happened, but rather what assurance do we have that it's not happening again? Actually, it is happening in one way or another. And this must not be permitted to go on if we, if we are humans. And I hope we are human.[89]

Although the ambivalence of Baruch's testimony is difficult to deny, this passage is introduced as the closing encapsulation of his experience, suggesting an even starker representation of his interview. While the following segment of Baruch's original, archived testimony for the Fortunoff Archive (not included in the book or on the website) does not appear to be fully hopeful, it nonetheless conveys the sense that the witness has held out some prospect for hope, as reflected in the following exchange:

> DANA KLINE: Is there anything else you would like to add?
> BARUCH G.: One thing that I'll be thinking a lot is the work you're doing so quietly. It is good to point out that there is still humanity. And while my experience has been so much the brutality of the human condition, human beings, I've learned also goodness . . . if we keep increasing in number the people who do care, the world will be a better place.[90]

While Baruch acknowledges that he continues to endure much suffering, he reaches out to the future both on behalf of others and for the sake of his own psychological well-being. The act of giving testimony is for him a way of rebuilding the world, even though he will never recover those lost to him in the Holocaust. That note of even partial redemption is mostly absent from either the book or video version of *Witness*.

Expanding the "Frame Conditions" of Fortunoff Archive Testimony

Examinations of the Fortunoff Archive and the other two archives featured in this book underscore the multivocal aspects of testimony—the impossibility of representing these collections as monolithic, despite efforts to impose certain frameworks and standards on the interview process. The self-recognition of that impossibility is one of the strongest underpinnings of the Fortunoff Archive. Notably, it invests in deferring to witnesses to tell their singular stories rather than strictly adhering to a predetermined interview agenda. As Geoffrey

Reframing Holocaust Testimony

Hartman has written, the archive considers each of the witnesses it documents to be an agent rather than a patient or legal witness of his or her testimony; examining individual details across their interviews allows both the uniqueness and commonalities of those testimonies to surface.[91] However, the emphasis on facilitating testimonial authorship carries with it a set of operative, representational preferences.

For example, the Fortunoff Archive's aversion to redemptive closure in testimonies can miss those moments when a witness actually expresses some semblance of redemption. In his forward to the book adaptation of *Witness: Voices from the Holocaust*, Lawrence Langer reiterates one of his recurring arguments about Holocaust testimony: witnesses are not shown to be heroes or martyrs—"labels they firmly reject"—but rather adopt the role as "chroniclers of a melancholy and dreadful tale."[92] Langer wants to counter the romanticizing of Holocaust testimony and the tendency to equate survival with victory over oppression—"an act of will worthy of celebration."[93] Joshua Greene echoes those sentiments in his introduction to the same book, contending that in screening the testimonies, not one of the subjects "ever celebrated the act of survival."[94]

However, those firm, continued claims to the anti-redemptive strains of survivor testimony can limit understanding of how archived traumatic memory often works. Based on the interviews analyzed here, it is clear that certain witnesses can and do express at least partial redemption or catharsis through the delivery of testimony. For example, particular portions of the testimony of "exemplary" witness Baruch G. that were not selected for the book do speak to his belief in the constructive social and familial value of acts of remembrance. I mention this example to underscore the ambivalences of memory and the tensions that emerge between witnesses and the institutions that record and disseminate their stories. While Langer takes an ethically charged position to safeguard testimonies from shallow romanticizing and kitsch, his (and the archive's) preference for stressing anti-redemptive modes of testimony constitutes a framing paradigm. Even an interview agenda that intends to foster agency by witnesses is an agenda nonetheless and should be analyzed as to how it shapes the generation and transmission of Holocaust memory.

Rather than characterize testimonies as anti-romantic or anti-redemptive, they should be viewed and listened to in ways that emphasize the interplay between often competing yet entangled impulses of remembering. To return to the case of Baruch G., I would neither discount Langer's description of its tragic, dehumanizing aspects, nor would I ignore the traces of moral redemption in the conclusion of his testimony, which are elicited when the interviewer asks: "Is there anything else you would like to add?"[95] The conflicted nature of his survival comes to light precisely when the voice of the interviewer comes into dialogue with the witness. Such vital dialogue is exactly what is absent from the documentary *Witness* and its book adaptation.

This absence speaks to a larger issue related to how Langer, Hartman, and other advocates of the Fortunoff Archive discuss the process of mediating testimony. In his letter to Michael Berenbaum in 1991, Langer elaborates on some of the distinctions between literary and oral forms of testimony. In his written analysis of another Fortunoff witness, Barbara T., who was recorded on November 8, 1986, Langer points out how at one point in the interview Barbara, who happens to be an author, cites her autobiographical historical novel to recall certain experiences.[96] Langer is skeptical about such a mingling of video testimony with novelistic genres, arguing that people do not talk in the same manner in which they write—that the latter form is less spontaneous and more stylized than the oral expression. While Langer's scholarship has been groundbreaking in its attention to the complexities of Holocaust testimonies, he seems averse to drawing attention to the mediated, stylized aspects of video interviews. In the memo to Berenbaum, Langer describes the "artlessness" of testimonial recollection by witnesses and their ability to verbally express pure, raw expressions of memory absent from the "enhancement of narrative style and tone and form" associated with written forms.[97]

However, audiovisual testimony is never free of those stylized elements and is always generated in concert, and at times in conflict, with institutional histories and practices. To some extent, the Fortunoff Archive and certain scholars working for or in dialogue with the institution acknowledge the need to look beyond the impact of testimony on the witness and toward issues related to the prospects of its future use. Again, to invoke the Yale conference *The Contribution of Oral Testimony to Holocaust and Genocide Studies*, participants in that event regarded it as a turning point in addressing how testimonial resources would be utilized in light of the passing away of survivors and other witnesses.[98] According to the published report on that conference, "formerly dominant discussions of the practical and ethical dimensions of recording testimonies" must give way to "questions concerning the future of the archive."[99]

Yet rather than separating those two lines of inquiry concerning testimonial production and transmission, it is imperative to examine the ways in which they are intertwined. That is to say, the practical and conceptual aspects of recording testimonies profoundly affect the ways in which future generations will use those materials and in turn create new archives. Many of the scholars who have developed and written about the Fortunoff Archive have also discussed how Holocaust memory can be instrumentalized by the "politics of memory—that is, with the interests, institutions, and conceptual frameworks that mediate what we know of the past."[100] Nonetheless, the report from the Yale conference offers little actual discussion of the institutional frameworks that affect the construction of testimonies at the Fortunoff Archive. What Geoffrey Hartman calls the "frame conditions" of that archive are not determinative of testimonial meaning—they work in conversation as well as in conflict with the personal textures of memory. And they underscore the need to preserve not only testimonies as they appear at the center of the screen, but also the debates, methods, and voices that are often found behind the scenes.

TWO

Centralizing Holocaust Testimony
The United States Holocaust Memorial Museum

The United States Holocaust Memorial Museum (USHMM) possesses neither the oldest nor the largest collection of testimonies of this book's three case studies. Alone bearing the imprimatur of the United States federal government, it is, however, the most centralized and institutionally established among them. Not just an archive, the museum is also a memorial site, exhibition space, and educational center, making it an illuminating case for examining testimonies across phases of collection and transmission. What follows is not a comprehensive history of the development of the U.S. Holocaust Memorial Museum, but rather a focused examination of how testimonial authority and authenticity are channeled by and through that institution's particular memorial, pedagogical, and social mandates.

Two principles have guided the USHMM from the outset: an emphasis on the uniqueness of the Holocaust and on the moral obligations of American remembrance. The museum's interview guidelines make clear that its "primary mission is to advance and disseminate knowledge about this unprecedented tragedy, to preserve the memory of those who suffered, and to encourage its visitors to reflect upon moral and spiritual questions raised by the events of the Holocaust as well as by their own responsibilities as citizens of democracy."[1] The USHMM's charter—authorized through a unanimous act of Congress in 1980—declares its mission to serve as an interventionist, "living memorial" to the Holocaust that could attend not only to that past genocide but also to the emergence of contemporary atrocities.[2] This mandate informs its aims to commemorate, document, and activate the memory of the Holocaust in the face of current events, and its federal authorization solidifies its political and symbolic currency in pursuit of that aim.

The museum's location adjacent to the National Mall places it squarely in the heart of an official American commemorative landscape.[3] At the same time, the museum's planners had to explore ways of importing its historical, evidentiary authority from the European topography of events. As expressed by Michael Berenbaum, the first project director for the Holocaust Memorial Museum and a principle figure in its development, this task demanded no less than Americanizing the Holocaust by bridging the historical, cultural, and spatial distance of the events for the visitors: "To move them back fifty years in time, transport them a continent away . . . in 90 to 120 minutes, we must discharge them into the streets of Washington with a changed understanding of human potential and commitment."[4]

To establish the foundations for that experiential encounter, the museum's planners, staff, and chief donors made a series of official visits to the European sites of destruction, beginning in 1979 with a trip to Poland by the Presidential Commission on the Holocaust, the predecessor to the United States Holocaust Memorial Council (or USHMC), the museum's governing body.[5] Its intent was to provide museum dignitaries with an opportunity to stand close to the physical evidence of the crimes and to absorb the moral implications and visceral charge of the Shoah. In the assessment of then-presidential commission chairman Elie Wiesel, by visiting the places of destruction and then returning to the United States, the museum backers and planners would be better able to "touch" and sense the "feel" of the events, and in turn place that experience in the American context.[6]

Subsequent trips abroad by museum staff and dignitaries aimed to secure access to original artifacts and forge institutional arrangements with European Holocaust museums, memorials, and historical sites. During one such trip members of the U.S. Holocaust Memorial Council formulated an arrangement with the museum at the former Majdanek death camp in Poland. The agreement called for the USHMM to provide the camp museum with video equipment for conducting testimonies with survivors and other witnesses in exchange for securing shoes and personal effects that could be placed on display in Washington.[7] In this contract, the better-endowed American museum provided its institutional capital and technological infrastructure in return for the much needed evidentiary and moral weight bestowed by original artifacts from Majdanek.

The United States already had access to an equally essential source of historical authority and authenticity in the form of a culturally and politically active Holocaust survivor community. Indeed, a central aim of the Holocaust Memorial Museum was to anchor its institutional birth on the still living authority of those survivors. Just as the survivors relied on the museum's institutional authority and legitimacy to give official expression to their experiences, so too the museum required their stories as a means of transmitting its moral and civic pedagogy in person-to-person terms.

The museum's moral capital was further bolstered through its official merger with the National Registry of Holocaust Survivors, which had been established by Benjamin and Vladka Meed to collect the names, locations, and other details of Jewish survivors living in North America.[8] For Benjamin Meed, who later assumed a pivotal role in the museum as chairman of its Content Committee, the alliance enabled the National Registry and the survivor community at large to link their ephemeral legacies to a concrete national institution.[9] In addition to the institutional legitimacy that the museum bestowed on survivors, it also served as an affective community for fostering networks between the survivor population and the general public. It created a space where survivors could make their stories known, including in the form of audiovisual histories collected by the museum's oral history department. Ben Meed viewed survivor accounts and artifacts from the Shoah as necessary for the institution's legitimacy and authenticity; to this end, he stated that "the Museum needs *our* [survivors'] participation to insure that the Permanent Exhibition . . . tells *our* story accurately, authentically, powerfully."[10] Meed's successful efforts to merge the Registry with the USHMM further illustrated the proprietary aspects of Holocaust memory. In achieving a centralization of Holocaust memory, this merger joined the definitive national memorial with a registry of survivor names that numbered more than 70,000 in 1990.[11] Not simply a fusion of administrative and networking resources, it meant a convergence of affective and preservation discourses, one that stressed the importance of nurturing survivor outreach and documenting as many stories as possible before witnesses passed from the scene.

The joint efforts of the USHMM and the National Registry thus marked an intersection between institutional and more vernacular strains of Holocaust memory. Just as the community of survivors represented by the Registry required the museum's political and institutional currency, the USHMM in turn relied on the support and participation of survivors and their embodied, ethically charged presence. In 1989, the national leadership board of the American Gathering of Jewish Holocaust Survivors issued a resolution declaring that "Without our testimony no one would have known of the magnitude of the uprising in Warsaw, the revolt in Treblinka, the escape from Sobibor."[12] In this sense, the American Gathering and later the Registry reflected unease that traditional history alone would be insufficient to foster a postmemory legacy. In the language of the American Gathering's resolution: "We have all seen the skeletal remains of once vital people, but we must give flesh to the bones and see the people as they once lived."[13] By collecting and centralizing survivor memory in the United States, the USHMM in conjunction with the Registry aimed to renew and preserve three different bodies of memory: the body of recorded testimonial work representing the individual and collective experience of survivors; the bodies of absent victims left behind through traces in photographs, human remains, and personal artifacts; and the museum's institutional body, a memorial structure serving as a foundation of commemoration and advocacy for the legacy of the Holocaust.

Elie Wiesel, as the first chairman of the United States Holocaust Memorial Council, wanted to incorporate survivors into the museum in ways that preserved the sanctity and incomprehensibility of their memories, while at the same time integrating them into projects of moral pedagogy. As Wiesel stated in guidelines to the USHMM's Content Committee in 1985:

> At times one must attempt to do the impossible. Perhaps this is such a time. Fully aware that there exists a human suffering that cannot be communicated, we must try to transmit it. We realize that due to its magnitude and character the subject lies outside time and space, yet we are called upon to use temporal and concrete means of communication to share our knowledge of it. The Holocaust defies language and art and yet we must do both to tell the tale.[14]

Wiesel wished to stress the impossibility of representing the interior of Holocaust experiences. At the same time, he asserted that the voices of survivors must be heard, that they must be registered in the public consciousness as witnesses of a uniquely Jewish event with universal humanitarian implications. Yet this brought the dilemma of potential commercialization of the Holocaust. Wiesel had himself been a strong critic of the 1978 NBC television miniseries *Holocaust*, accusing its producers of trivializing the events with melodramatic storylines and crass consumer exploitation.[15]

Consequently, Wiesel pressed the Content Committee to envision a site that would inspire among visitors a sense of transcendence and solitude, allowing them the space to identify with the suffering of the victims. He hoped that confrontation with the "people, objects, words, images that have survived the dead" would perhaps "bring back an echo, at least an echo, of the screams, of the shouts, of the silences, the faces."[16] But Wiesel thought that these people, objects, words, and images could speak for themselves, without extensive historical contextualization or commentary. To preserve the sanctity of the museum, he envisioned that survivors would circulate through the exhibition as docents, guides, and storytellers, anchoring the photographs and documents on display to the authority and authenticity of their experience, effectively allowing them to assert: "Look, that is the place; I was there, and if you look closely, that is me."[17] For Wiesel, survivors were the crucial connection between the European Holocaust and the landscape of American remembrance: "So that the educational process links the survivor to the story and the story to the visitor. No one can move people better than survivors, and therefore we must organize them and that will be the educational arm of the Museum, providing the explanation, the background, and the emotion."[18] Better to tell the story of the Holocaust with a "whisper" and to keep its visual representation to the smallest possible scale.[19] Ultimately, and despite his formative role in the USHMM, Wiesel's preference for limiting the visual representation of events proved difficult to accommodate.

The Visceral and Intellectual Demands of Exhibiting the Holocaust

In the end, the members of the Content Committee—not Wiesel—had primary responsibility for vetting the details of the exhibition spaces, in line with the USHMM's pedagogical and socially transformative mandates. The museum was to be not only a place of quiet contemplation; it would also foster a more interactive and dynamic transformation of the consciousness of its visitors. For the committee, this entailed a more integrated approach to exhibition space, one that allowed sacred, educational, and often politically charged activities to coexist under one roof. Thus the planners who guided development of the museum's content confronted the challenge of both popularizing and dignifying the Holocaust—of attending to both the intellectual and affective aspects of memory.

Although the Content Committee struggled to devise ways of making Holocaust history felt by those with no direct link to the events, they recognized the limits of recreating trauma. While interactive and immersive displays would generate a sense of authentic historical experience, planners were concerned about compromising either the authority of historical scholarship or the sanctity and singularity of individual suffering. Nevertheless, the terms of historical rigor and representational excess were often highly contested among planners. Eli Pfefferkorn, a member of the Museum Concept Planning Committee, summarized the debate in stark terms: "It's a controversy between . . . those who advocate the visceral experience and an intellectual [experience]."[20] As the committee attempted to address that challenge, there was a recurring concern that the farther the museum ventured into the emotive and experiential realms of remembrance, the more it would diverge from the historical specificity of the events.

One of the central priorities of the museum, and in turn a driving impetus for establishing its oral history department, was a mandate from the main planners that the "soul" of the United States Holocaust Memorial Museum would be its Permanent Exhibition and that all other developments, including that regarding testimony, would be in service of formulating that core space.[21] As an extension of the museum's deliberate conceptualization as a storytelling site, the Permanent Exhibition (known internally as the PE) provided the axis point through which oral histories, written narratives, authentic objects, and still and moving images would guide the visitor through an emotionally driven narrative staged in three acts: "Nazi Assault/1933–1939"; "The Final Solution/1940–1945"; and the "Last Chapter—The Immediate Postwar Years."[22]

With these recommendations in hand, Wiesel convened a meeting of the Museum, Process, Education, and Archives committees in June 1983. Its agenda was to develop programmatic requirements to achieve the commemorative, educational, and preservation mandates of the Holocaust Museum, which would be presented to the U.S. Secretary of the Interior for his approval by the middle of 1985.[23] The committees summarized their work in a report called "To Bear Witness, to Remember, and to Learn: A Confidential Report on Museum Planning," referred to internally as the "Red Book." With its three-pronged emphasis on remembrance, teaching, and documentation, the Red Book dealt with every aspect of planning for the USHMM, from its exterior and interior design to thematic structure for exhibitions and education programming.

The Red Book urged planners to imbue every detail of the museum with a sense of witnessing the events of the Holocaust, in order to "evoke in visitors empathy and reverence for the nearly six-million of others who suffered and perished, and to provoke in people of all ages and backgrounds questions that engender yet more questions," thus making clear the multivocal dimensions of the Shoah. At the same time, planners should ensure that the "obligation to remember [is] . . . fulfilled with absolute authenticity and expressiveness. Visitors must experience a sense of immediacy in direct relationship to the persons, artifacts, and documents that bear witness to the Holocaust."[24]

Within this schema, survivor stories were to have a fundamental mediating presence between the often-competing impulses to consider the Holocaust as something distant and scholarly or as a subject for more popular and interactive representation. Stories would foster interactive education but also contribute to a mood of solemn contemplation. As initially proposed in the early 1980s, the visitor's first experience in the Permanent Exhibition space would be an encounter with audiovisual testimonies of witnesses and survivors, each narrating a brief but personally compelling account of life stories related to the themes and artifacts of the exhibition.[25] By the time the museum opened in 1993, however, the plan to embed the visitor's journey in testimonial encounters had been reversed; indeed, testimonies appeared now in the final segment of the Permanent Exhibition.

One reason the USHMM moved away from relying heavily on testimony was the anticipated passing of survivors and the emergence of a postmemory landscape. In response to that impending development, the foundation for the journey into the museum became an encounter with official documents, artifacts, and academically vetted historical accounts. In other words, the official history as it exists "on the record" became the source for authenticating and authorizing the integration of corporeal referents, including witness testimonies. While these sources work in concert with one another—the testimonies do, after all, lend a unique moral and evidentiary voice to the exhibition—the presence of human witnesses is ultimately subordinate to the museum's "official" account of Holocaust history. The core challenge was to reach an audience with little or no direct experience with or knowledge of the events.[26] If survivors were to serve as exemplars of those three concerns, their stories would first have to be grounded in an established historical record.

The museum's first director, Jeshajahu "Shaike" Weinberg, found that his investment in moving patrons on an affective and visceral level was what favorably distinguished the Holocaust Memorial Museum from its counterparts: "Whereas the traditional, cold museum conveys impressions and a measure of information, it does not raise the blood pressure of its visitors. . . . The USHMM on the other hand, definitely intends to make not only an intellectual, but also an emotional, impact. It will be a hot museum, emotionally loaded, upsetting, disturbing."[27] Within this conception, the museum positioned original and replicated artifacts to provide both moral authority and historical authenticity to the central exhibition, lending a "perceptual advantage" to visitors by bestowing both an evidentiary and moral charge to the storyline.[28] In the assessment of the Content Committee's chairman Meed, the Permanent Exhibition had to provide both information and moral understanding. Rather than offering a "textbook on the walls," it was to present "authentic, accurate history to create a compelling narrative, a visual epic of the Holocaust."[29] The exhibition's display of artifacts including shoes, eyeglasses, prayer shawls, brushes, and other personal effects were to serve as material anchorage for the museum as it confronted both the opening of its doors and the fading of the Holocaust survivor community. Because of survivors' instrumental role in granting moral authority and authenticity to the museum, anxiety mounted within the institution that the impending absence of living witnesses required urgent efforts to secure not only their recorded testimonies, but also their personal effects and documents. This collection process went hand in hand with the museum's oral history department's development of a protocol for soliciting donated items—often designated as "object survivors"—from witnesses to be used during the pre-interview process of testimony gathering.[30]

In this sense, the Holocaust Museum developed as a site not only of historical preservation but also of communal and individual surrogacy. It archived the stories and physical artifacts of victims and survivors, all the while positioning itself as a proxy, living body in its own right.[31] Shaike Weinberg articulated these imperatives just before the museum's opening:

Reframing Holocaust Testimony

The soul of the United States Holocaust Memorial Museum will be its permanent exhibition. . . . Through oral recollections, written narratives, authentic objects and still and moving images, the story of the Holocaust will unfold for the visitor. . . . Serving as guides will be the people who lived the story—victims, bystanders, public officials, liberators, rescuers, and perhaps even perpetrators—creating an intimate dialogue between the visitor and the dramatic historical events of the Holocaust through personal narrative and memorabilia.[32]

Despite this conceptual discourse of intimacy and embodiment, notions of what constituted the body and soul of the Holocaust Memorial Museum remained contested. On the one hand, the museum relied upon authenticating objects and firsthand accounts—documents, photographs, torture implements, testimonies—to advance its storyline by fostering identification with its victims. At the same time, it placed limits on the types of artifacts and bodies put on display. Evoking authenticity was carefully calibrated to balance the cognitive and visceral aspects of commemoration with the sensitivities of the survivor community. Central to the debate was this question: For whom was the Holocaust Memorial Museum being constructed? For the survivors or for future generations with limited exposure to the histories and the material artifacts? In an effort to address the needs of both interests, the museum provided access to images of death and destruction, but it placed the most gruesome representations behind privacy walls or used castings or photomurals for highly charged objects.

Weinberg, the former director of the Museum of the Diaspora in Israel, was initially hired as a consultant in 1985, when the museum was still soliciting plans for exhibition development. His ideas were crucial to shaping the contours of the institution. For example, he thought it essential not to emphasize analytical engagement with the Holocaust at the expense of minimizing its emotional dimensions, although he also supported framing affective encounters in a chronological, three-act sequence of events before, during, and after the Shoah. This format enabled visitors to be immersed in their own visceral experience while still being guided by a historical narrative trajectory. For Weinberg, the planning process presented the challenge of negotiating the institution's monumental and informational imperatives. As he articulated in a proposed outline for the museum in May 1985: "The more monumental its exhibits, the less information the Museum can present."[33] As museum planners developed conceptual models, they drafted a series of guidelines on the use of print and visual materials in an effort to ensure the objects' authenticity, while also adapting them to the exhibition's storytelling needs. The objects should be sufficiently "evocative" or "expressive" to bestow universal meanings beyond their historical particularities.[34]

As the scholar Edward Linenthal has documented, Elie Wiesel had resisted any attempt to make the Holocaust accessible in visual terms. In 1981 Wiesel commented to fellow members of the United States Holocaust Memorial Council: "I believe that we are dealing here with something so sensitive, something . . . so sober, so austere as an ancient prayer. Now how do you translate ancient prayers into something visual? I think everything must be pure."[35] Although Wiesel's position did not prevail, and the museum adopted a less austere visual historiography for the exhibition, planners remained concerned with the prospect of de-sanctifying the Holocaust through visual, particularly cinematic renderings. This issue flared up in 1988, when the Content Committee was considering applications for the position of director of the Permanent Exhibition, and its members expressed concern that the leading candidate, Martin Smith, would rely too heavily on his background as a documentary film director and producer in Great Britain. Although then project director Michael Berenbaum regarded Smith as an accomplished storyteller, he was uneasy that the filmmaker's experience consisted largely in weaving a two-dimensional narrative and presenting it to a seated rather than a kinetic audience.

In light of these concerns, the committee designated Smith as executive producer of the design process, but also chose Ralph Appelbaum as Exhibition Designer, taking advantage of his museum experience, which involved juxtaposing three-dimensional fixed objects with "stable images and a moving audience."[36] The Content Committee was "assured that Mr. Smith will not be making a movie but rather will be leading a design team that will shape a Museum and that will tell the story outlined in the approved narrative storyline."[37] This decision to split responsibilities between Smith and Appelbaum reflected institutional anxiety over the prospect of converting the Holocaust Museum into a "movie house" that would privilege technological distraction and redemptive narrative closure. Raul Hilberg, the renowned Holocaust scholar and a member of the Content Committee, warned that the museum must be on guard against "transforming the Holocaust life experience into a technological experience."[38] He also questioned Berenbaum's belief that the sensitive integration of Holocaust survivor testimonies could offset the technological imperatives of exhibition design. Because survivors' recollections cannot always be historically confirmed, Hilberg advised against integrating information, whether as testimony or material for interactive computer terminals, which had not been completely authenticated.[39] Reflecting skepticism toward both recorded survivor testimony and computer technology, he argued that such less "official" and more interactive sources lacked the rigor of more "traditional" sources, such as recovered documents and physical artifacts. For Hilberg, recorded testimony and interactive displays ran the danger of mediating the events of the Holocaust in ways that might redeem a sense of triumph and resolution from the "abyss" of the Holocaust.[40]

Members of the Content Committee determined that the mystery of the abyss had to be converted into tangible moral pedagogy. Despite Hilberg's objections to oral history, the Content Committee, which included as a member the Holocaust survivor Sam Bloch, saw a role for survivors' living and recorded testimonies as intermediary points between the impenetrability and accessibility of the Shoah. Moreover, they thought that the historians on the committee had a responsibility to consult with survivors as they proceeded to develop content for the Permanent Exhibition.[41] For Bloch and his fellow survivors on the committee, such voices would provide a strong interpersonal anchorage for the museum.

The details of this debate directly affected the contours of the USHMM's educational mission. Contrary to Hilberg's rigorous and sober approach to research and education, Berenbaum and most of the other planners realized that this museum's mandate went beyond the traditional curatorial mission of presenting historical information; rather, its mission extended to the task of moving the "hearts and minds" of its audiences in morally grounded terms.[42] The Holocaust Museum's brand of pedagogy aimed to activate both the cognitive and visceral registers of experience in its visitors, lending an affective and analytical charge through the "direct effect of its imagery."[43]

The U.S. Holocaust Memorial Museum as a Storytelling Site

Shaike Weinberg further intensified the emphasis on the museum as a storytelling site. His earlier association with interactive media at the Museum of the Diaspora in Israel had initially provoked internal resistance when he was hired as a consultant in 1985, raising concerns that he might turn the Holocaust Museum into a site of attractions, rather than a space for serious, solemn contemplation. Although assuring the Content Committee that as chief consultant he would not attempt to push through his earlier recommendations, Weinberg also emphasized the importance of adopting innovative storytelling approaches through the use of audiovisual technology, while maintaining historical standards. For example, while he recognized the importance of collecting authentic historical materials such as currency from the Warsaw Ghetto or posters announcing race laws, he recommended that curators enlarge photographs of those artifacts, thus dramatically accenting the storyline. He also underscored the importance of using video testimonies of survivors and witnesses and contemporary film footage as "strong storytelling instruments."[44]

While the museum tried to secure original materials from foreign institutions, Weinberg emphasized that in the absence of certain authentic objects, a sense of authenticity could be achieved with castings of original objects or through the use of items—such as the proposed Polish boxcar that was "of the kind" used for deportations.[45] The boxcar became a particular point of contention. When it arrived from Poland in 1989, Content Committee member and survivor Sam Bloch expressed his concern that the boxcar looked too "fresh" after its painting by Polish authorities. As a result, it was restored to its "authentic" condition, in order to correspond more closely with the iconography of the Holocaust.[46] Rather than stressing the provenance of the boxcar and other holdings, objects on display were meant to advance the experiential and narrative aims of the institution. To quote Michael Berenbaum: "Artifacts, architecture, and design are subservient to the tale that is to be told. They are the midwife of the story."[47] In that sense, collected artifacts were valued for their rhetorical flexibility—conveying symbolic and thematic meaning while at the same time providing material traces of a traumatic history.

The earlier visits to Poland by the Presidential Commission on the Holocaust in the late 1970s, as well as tours of Europe by the Content Committee in 1989, reflected this approach. The requested items from abroad are highly personal in nature. For example, a letter of agreement between the USHMM and the State Museum at Majdanek in Poland refers to the acquisition of 2,000 shoes of former inmates; 50 inmate uniforms; 100 hand mirrors; 100 brushes; 4 prostheses; and batches of human hair.[48] This small segment of the personal artifacts collected by the museum speaks to the drive to fill the Permanent Exhibition with objects tied directly to victims of the Holocaust, which the museum then interweaves with more iconographic pieces such as castings of a gas chamber door and a duplicate of the entry gate at Auschwitz.

The museum's effort to define and preserve the embodying functions of personal artifacts was particularly evident in its approaches to handling the ultimately 4,000 inmate shoes on loan from Majdanek. A report by USHMM conservator Katherine Singley observed as follows:

> More than any other article of clothing, a shoe makes a personal statement for its owner. Generally, there is only one wearer. This collection would reflect the socioeconomic diversity among the Jewish population of Poland, and the personal tastes, values, and even personalities of individuals within the group. Information on individual heights, weights, and physical problems possibly could be extrapolated from the collection using forensic techniques.[49]

Thus the shoes embody their absent wearers, even allowing curators to extrapolate gender, class, and physical attributes. A condition of the loan was that the

USHMM agree not to restore them to their form at the time of their initial confiscation during the war. Rather, the museum was to clean and stabilize the shoes against further deterioration, maintaining their faded appearance at the time of donation.

The museum's particular approach to preserving authenticity thus meant that it would neither restore objects to the "ideal" form at the original time of their confiscation, nor allow them to decay. In a sense it would attempt to maintain its holdings in a state of suspended animation. Unlike the shoes' deteriorating *in situ* presentation at Majdanek, where they were housed within originally placed barracks, in the USHMM the shoes would be subjected to preservation in order to maintain their living essence in a space far removed from the site of destruction. Indeed, the greater the distance between the shoes or other artifacts and the original site of annihilation, the more intensely the Holocaust Museum labored to preserve their condition and frame their historical value. In an internal memorandum, Martin Smith offered his suggestions for displaying the shoes: "My instinctive attitude is pile 'em high, do it cheap. Majdanek has done so and the impact of the message behind the shoes is very strong."[50] If the USHMM was unable to benefit from Majdanek's location within the topography of the Holocaust, then it would attempt to replicate that site's large-scale display of artifacts.

The collection of shoes and other personal effects, including glasses, prayer shawls, and brushes, would provide a material foundation as the museum anticipated both the opening of its doors and the diminution of the survivor community on which the living memory of the Holocaust depended. The collection of testimony and artifacts proceeded hand-in-hand as the museum distributed donation forms to survivors during the pre-interview process. One survivor among my sample of testimonies, Max "Amichai H.," agreed to donate his childhood drawings and other effects to the museum, which in turn designated them as "object survivors."[51] The USHMM's access to institutional resources and political capital enabled it to secure artifacts and testimonies that could bridge the spatial, temporal, and experiential divide between the museum and the Holocaust. Its planners endeavored not only to create the largest clearinghouse of Holocaust-related testimonies and artifacts in the world, but also to serve as the primary center for authenticating and legitimating other works, including films, that represented the Holocaust.

Such was the case with the Holocaust Museum's attempts to legitimate and regulate the historical perspective of Steven Spielberg's critically acclaimed film *Schindler's List,* released in 1993, not long after the Holocaust Museum had opened in April of the same year. Prior to the film's general release, on 30 November, the USHMM hosted an event at which Oskar Schindler was posthumously awarded a U.S. Medal of Remembrance. The audience included the film's director, Steven

Spielberg, the central cast, and the recently appointed Supreme Court Justice Ruth Bader Ginsberg.[52] Spielberg's film had not only been embraced by film critics, but had been lauded by Holocaust survivors and educators eager to use the work as a gateway text for teaching the lessons of the Holocaust. While the work of a definitively populist auteur, the film was praised for its sensitive and historically grounded treatment of the subject and for its ability to penetrate the conscious of the mainstream public. Spielberg could benefit from the institutional and historical legitimacy of the USHMM, and the museum could in turn capitalize on the popular appeal of the filmmaker and the cultural phenomenon of *Schindler's List*.

The museum's internal discussions of the film are illuminating, in particular the efforts of staff and administrators to vet Spielberg's project in an effort to ensure its commitment to historical fidelity and thus grant the film institutional recognition. In the process, tensions emerged between the museum's institutional culture and Spielberg's commemoration of the Holocaust. In November 1993, the USHMM offered an advance screening for staff members, who submitted their responses in internal memos. The staff's overall reception to the work was enthusiastic. They accepted it as essentially accurate, though only insofar as it reflected a movement away from mass culture and toward established history. One staff historian, Severin Hochberg, praised Spielberg's commitment to history but suggested that expositional captioning would have given the narrative a more authoritative voice, placing events in their appropriate context and chronology. He concluded: "Spielberg, up to now a successful director of entertainment and fantasy, now takes his place among the best directors of serious film in our time in my judgment."[53] In this sense, it was Spielberg's progression away from popular moviemaking toward "serious film" that won him support from museum staff. It represented less of an acceptance of his work on its own artistic terms than a guarded embrace of Spielberg's turn toward the historical "real."

The museum's senior staff was more critical. Raye Farr, then director of the Permanent Exhibition and later head of the Steven Spielberg Film and Video Archive at the USHMM, reported that her "primary concerns" were that the film was "playing loose with historical facts and fundamental processes of Holocaust events, in order to achieve powerful drama."[54] Museum Director Shaike Weinberg summarized staff reactions in a letter to Marvin Levy, the head of Universal Studios. He began diplomatically with praise for the film as a powerful work that remained sensitive to both historical issues and the subject's emotional intensity. His concerns revolved primarily around representational accuracy, particularly the film's misleading sequencing of events related to deportations: contrary to the film's representation of events, deportees surrendered their personal belongings *after*, not *before* arrival at the camps, a strategy crucial to maintaining the deception of resettlement in the East. Had deportees followed the film's scenario, they would have been aware of the fate that would befall them. The most frequent criticism concerned the scene in which a group of Jewish women were forced into what they thought were gas chambers, only to be relieved when the showerheads released water—not gas pellets. Weinberg pointed out that upon arrival most prisoners did not know of the gas chambers and would have expected showers.

Weinberg expressed particular regret about the shower scene because of its potential to fuel the cause of Holocaust denial—a threat that Raye Farr raised in explaining the narrower "margin for error" in representing the events of the Holocaust. In light of this concern, Weinberg urged Levy to have the shower scene removed before the film's release: "We hope you will not mar the accomplishment through inattention to the real, and not always present, world in which the history of the Holocaust is debated."[55] Ultimately, Universal Studios rejected the editing suggestions from Weinberg and the faculty and staff of the USHMM. Yet the administrators' efforts revealed a profound tension within their institution concerning the attempt to strike a balance between integrating popular forms of representation with attention to historical authenticity. Many of the internal debates concerning representations of the Holocaust in *Schindler's List,* particularly on matters of dramatization and the limits of graphic representation, played out throughout the conceptual development of the Holocaust Museum and its oral history department.

"A Conceptual Museum"

In 1991, two years before the museum's opening, Weinberg circulated a manifesto entitled "The USHMM: A Conceptual Museum." It emphasized that although the museum would possess one of the largest collections of Holocaust-related objects in the world, the Permanent Exhibition's chief purpose was not to showcase this collection, but rather to weave a pedagogic narrative.[56] As I indicated earlier, Weinberg's multifaceted approach to visual historiography integrated historical information into a carefully constructed storyline told through a precise placement of artifacts, photographs, and audiovisual displays. That approach played a central role in shaping not only the narrative flow of the Permanent Exhibition, but also its display of testimonies as embodied history. The chosen strategies aimed to regulate the cognitive and visceral demands of Holocaust memory, ensuring that depictions of extremity and the creation of surrogate suffering on the part of museum visitors would not overwhelm moral pedagogy or hinder the ethical obligations to respect victims and survivors.

The Content Committee addressed some of these issues by commissioning an internal report, "A Working Response to the Question of Explicit Imagery Including 'The Pornography of Murder,' Nudity and Violence," prepared by Michael Berenbaum and consultants Alice Greenwald and Shomer Zwelling. The report stressed that the debate did not concern *whether* "difficult material" would be presented, but rather *how* it was to be handled. Documentary images of brutality, emaciation, and systematic dehumanization were unavoidable; nonetheless, the museum must make a determined effort to avoid exploitation that would further humiliate victims and their families, or engender in visitors a sense of historical voyeurism. Although the report argued that the museum must include even the most graphic representations, it must also mitigate any sensationalist appeal by providing careful historical citation and contextualization about the lives being presented.

Central questions remained: What constitutes a "shocking" or "powerful" image, and how are those categories distinguished from one another? Which images are clichés and which are penetrating? And what representations should visitors encounter when they enter the exhibition? In designing the initial segment of the Permanent Exhibition, planners ultimately decided to include an opening image of American liberators encountering the charred remains of concentration camp inmates. In this way, they deliberately created a space where visitors could identify with the liberators discovering the reality of the Holocaust, rather than positioning them as voyeurs to the suffering of the victims. It is also important to note that the planners, in reviewing documentary footage, particularly that of human corpses and liberated, emaciated inmates, demonstrated sensitivity to the clinical presentation of the human body and recognized the need to restore some sense of dignity, physical embodiment, and soul to the victims captured in the images.

In an effort to negotiate those concerns, the planners salvaged and reconstructed the living traces, voices, and bodies of history, thereby generating a sense of lived intimacy and restoring victims to the "fullness of their lives." However, a process of careful segmentation and instrumentalization determined the placement of specific bodies. As Farr explained, the space—except for a dedicated Anne Frank section—was designed to evoke a sense of "individuality," rather than an encounter with specific "individual persons."[57] Edward Linenthal argues that the presence of survivors, whether through testimonies or in-person accounts, further reflected an increasing fascination with and sacralization of survivors, witnesses, and victims of the Holocaust.[58] He suggests that the museum, while striving to personalize those subjects, particularly survivors, tended to homogenize their experiences by assigning them a universal moral currency and bestowing a redemptive value on their stories. Although I agree with Linenthal that the museum attempted to instrumentalize survivor experiences by mining them for their precious knowledge and moral authority, I would argue that it was

Reframing Holocaust Testimony

a far more complicated process. While the museum strived to deploy documents, material objects, and testimonies in service of its institutional preferences, the collection, display, and interpretation of those holdings revealed the specificity and excesses of those individual traumas that were rendered.

The deliberations of the Content Committee regarding the collection of original artifacts—specifically the boxcar and a casting of the crematorium model on display in the Auschwitz Museum—illustrate that conflict. Earlier, I discussed objections to the railcar on grounds of historical authenticity. Those passionately raised by Content Committee member and Holocaust survivor Hadassah Rosensaft invoked her own experiences of deportation and the loss of a young son during the Holocaust. In urging her fellow members to "draw a line" that excluded objects that could cause emotional distress to survivors and visitors, Rosensaft invoked the moral authority not only of her own experience but also her collective authority as a representative of Holocaust survivors more generally: "I often hear the words that our Museum in Washington is not being built for the survivors; I agree, but it is being built because of the Holocaust and because of the survivors; it will tell *our* story, *my* story."[59] She also asserted a personal and communal imperative to monitor the museum's representations in order to ensure that the Holocaust would be endowed with a respectful and sacred quality befitting the once- and still-living traces of that experience. Her concern was not whether the railcar in question had been authenticated as having transported Jews, rather:

> I looked carefully at the showing of artifacts that we consider to expose, and I saw myself. Well, *it is* me (saying me, I mean all the survivors . . . who was brought . . . in the cattle car). *It is* me that was standing at the selection . . . before entering the camp. *It was* me, whose entire family including my first son—age six—was consumed by the flames. . . . *It was* me whose head was shaved.[60]

Rosensaft shifts between singular and collective expressions of authority, speaking for the larger experiences of the Holocaust and its survivors while also drawing from her own firsthand encounters. For her, the material objects of destruction are not so much artifacts of a contained past as they are emotionally charged embodiments of a suffering that will never be fully alleviated.

While the display of the boxcar or the model of the crematorium might foster experiential engagement in the museum's visitors, Rosensaft's comments remind us of the ethical and emotional challenges of reconstructing the Holocaust. Though the USHMM was designed to generate what Alison Landsberg terms "prosthetic memory," whereby the memory of the Holocaust is transferred to those with no firsthand experience of those events, the notions of what constitutes prosthetic or "experiential" learning are variable and highly charged.[61] Rosensaft's opposition was not to the idea of displaying the railcar or the crematorium model in theory, rather to showing those objects removed from their original sites. In her assessment, the farther those objects are situated from their European context, the greater the risk of appropriating and exploiting the memory of the Shoah: "I know how important it is to expose the artifacts, but we must draw a line. Tools of torture, tools used by the Germans to kill . . . must remain in the places of the crime. We should never sanctify the Museum or enshrine their tools of torture!"[62] Ultimately, Rosensaft and her allies lost the debate, and the railcar and crematorium model gained places in the Permanent Exhibition. However, they were displayed in such a way as to mitigate the traumatic impact. An alternate route for the boxcar installation allowed visitors to bypass the space.

These kinds of tensions were particularly evident during debates within the Content Committee related to displaying human hair shorn from concentration camp inmates. The museum had secured a sizable collection of that hair from Poland and had initially planned to exhibit it in a large bin on the third floor of the Permanent Exhibition.[63] Advocates for its inclusion stressed the strong visual and analytical impact—its ability to encapsulate wordlessly what Raul Hilberg had called the "ultimate rationality of the destruction process."[64] Hilberg, who had previously expressed his concerns that the museum would be an "empty" space devoid of sufficient material evidence, viewed the acquisition of hair as a major step in constructing a "full museum."[65] The majority of the Content Committee initially determined that the hair would serve a compelling visceral and didactic function by instilling a sense of fear in the visitor while simultaneously encapsulating the genocidal teleology of the Nazi regime.

However, the display did arouse intense resistance among certain committee members, particularly survivors who feared that the sanctity of the victims' bodies would be compromised. One such member, Helen Fagin, expressed the concern that the display might include the hair of her deceased relatives.[66] Although project director Michael Berenbaum assured her and the rest of the committee that human hair does not in fact hold sacred, bodily value in Jewish religious practice, many members remained firm in their opposition.[67] In the end, only a photomural of the hair was put on display, with the original material placed in storage in a warehouse outside of Baltimore, Maryland.[68]

Establishing the Department of Oral History

The development of the Holocaust Museum's collection of survivor testimonies was itself enmeshed in the process of collecting and curating the artifacts that would embody the living memory of the Holocaust within the Permanent Exhibition. Originally intended by its planners to house the central national archive of Holocaust testimonies, the museum's Department of Oral History has of this date collected more than 9,000 interviews, mostly in English, in both audio and video formats.[69] A contemporaneous memorandum on the role of the oral history department invokes the urgency of its founding mission: "Because of the schedule for opening the museum and the aging of survivors, it is imperative that the interviewing process begin as soon as possible."[70] The planners of the oral history department began their work aware of the growth of efforts to record survivor testimonies on videotape since the late 1970s, particularly the Fortunoff Video Archive. Framing the collection of testimony as a public duty to scholars and educators, they sought to position their institution as the definitive, central repository of Holocaust testimonies.[71] They also recognized the value of recorded interviews to a museum still in need of content.[72]

In order to identify potential interviewees, the new department turned first to the immense database of the National Registry of Jewish Holocaust Survivors, whose founder—Council member Ben Meed—was a strong advocate for oral history: "The survivors are dying at a rapid pace and we must assume that within the next 5–10 years, the majority of them will be gone or incapable of giving testimony."[73] Although he acknowledged that many of the registry's survivors had already given testimony elsewhere, Meed was adamant that the USHMM record as many witnesses as possible: "It is true that there are bound to be repetitions, but in each personal testimony, there may be something which may shed a different light and contribute to better comprehension."[74]

The American Gathering of Jewish Holocaust Survivors was another source of survivor names. In 1991, museum representatives attended the organization's meeting in Los Angeles, where they distributed promotional material and survey cards calling on survivors to "become part of our history" by recording their personal stories for the USHMM.[75] The cards had spaces for general biographical details as well as information on Holocaust-related experiences. Museum administrators, including Weinberg and Berenbaum, also realized the necessity of evaluating the testimonies held by other U.S. institutions in order to formulate a list of interview priorities for the museum's nascent collection. By cultivating relationships with both local and national survivor and archiving institutions, the museum hoped to find local survivors and their interviews and then transfer their testimonies to its centralized site. If the Holocaust Museum could not be the first U.S. archive to extensively document audiovisual testimonies of the Holocaust—the Fortunoff Archive already had that distinction—then it would be the "first *national* archive of Holocaust video and audio testimony"[76]

The fact that the Fortunoff Archive had been acting as a repository of Holocaust testimony for a decade complicated the USHMM's assertion of priority. Despite its federal mandate, substantial funding, and vast educational network, the museum lacked the Fortunoff Archive's academic credibility and proven track record. Moreover, a 1981 agreement between the United States Holocaust Memorial Council and the video archive at Yale University—renamed the Fortunoff Archive in 1987—granted official status to the latter as an official archive for audiovisual materials for the future Holocaust Museum.[77] In analyzing Yale's holdings with an eye toward potential exhibition use, USHMM planners also looked to this archive as a model for conducting and cataloguing Holocaust testimony. The museum would retain some elements of the Yale approach, particularly an early emphasis on trying to grant as much agency as possible to the interviewee, but tensions marked the attempt to blend the two sites' methodologies and institutional cultures.

The opening of a USHMM oral history department was formalized in 1988 with the hiring of Dr. Linda Kuzmack as its first director. Tensions soon arose between the fledgling department and the more established Yale project. The frictions grew as planners increasingly sought to consolidate the museum's position as a leading center for Holocaust-related holdings in the United States. Although the Fortunoff Archive provided assistance in securing audiovisual materials for the museum's future use, it did not relinquish its institutional independence or the pursuit of its own projects. Concerned that Yale's ongoing archival work would compromise the museum's emerging status, in April 1990 Kuzmack sent an internal memorandum to Weinberg, arguing that the USHMM must "combat Yale's image as the only archive where organizations may deposit their tapes. Right now, Yale is trading on their image as the only Holocaust archive."[78] This concern prompted Kuzmack to begin cultivating relationships with grassroots testimony projects, including those that had preexisting affiliations with the Fortunoff Archive, in an attempt either to appropriate their holdings or standardize their interviewing techniques along the lines of the museum's guidelines.

This growing competition between the two institutions hindered their agreement. In 1990, the museum sought to extend the cooperative arrangement so that they could use Fortunoff testimonies for exhibition and public education. The Yale archive agreed to loan the museum 150 video testimonies on a renewable basis, with the museum bearing all costs, in addition to publicly acknowledging Yale's "pioneering role" in the area of video testimony.[79] The Fortunoff Archive seemed to be motivated in part by a need to benefit from the museum's promotional prestige, while the museum hoped to gain from the archive's intellectual credibility and resources. More specifically, the museum wanted to request testimonies that would serve its particular criteria for dramatic impact, historical value, and range of personal experiences. Rather than a considered strategy for expanding the museum's fledgling audiovisual archive, the agreement aimed to fill immediate exhibition needs, with an eye toward generating clips of testimony footage for the Permanent Exhibition. Ultimately, however, the agreement fell apart as the Holocaust Museum severed its ties with the Fortunoff Archive for failing to budge on the issue of allowing scholars (as opposed to museum staff) to access the archive's testimonies without added cost to the museum.

The failure of the two institutions to come to a new agreement also revealed a larger divide between their respective institutional cultures and practices. While the Fortunoff Archive was intent on regulating access to its holdings, the Holocaust Museum saw testimonies as a means of extending its mission to the broadest possible audience. A more detailed description of the museum's approach to audiovisual testimony will demonstrate the profound implications of these institutional differences for the aesthetic, pedagogical, and ethical dimensions of testimony.

The Museum's Oral History Methodology

The Holocaust Museum's investment in collecting interviews was grounded in the imperative to both archive and exhibit testimonies, although the latter took precedence as the museum's opening approached. Thus exhibition director Smith was given supervisory authority over oral history director Kuzmack on the collection of audiovisual interviews. Smith's primary focus was on advancing the museum's interpersonal and narrative approach with an "Exhibition Storyline" that included the experiences of survivors and witnesses.[80] Although he realized the importance of drafting a list of potential interviewees to fill the historical and geographical categories needed for the Permanent Exhibition, Smith's background as a documentary filmmaker informed his view that these testimonies would differ from the historical material traditionally pursued by scholars. Thus, he asked Kuzmack to locate testimonies that would cover such "nodule points" of the exhibition's storyline as conditions in the ghetto, camp life, and liberation. She was also to secure "the little nuggets that are likely to be our most frequent requirement"—that is to say, fragments of drama and pathos with which visitors would identify.[81]

In March 1989 Weinberg, Berenbaum, Smith, and Kuzmack met to develop a set of priorities guiding the collection of testimony, focusing on three main areas: the Permanent Exhibition, the archive, and special programs (this latter category including a learning center, temporary exhibitions, and educational programs). Initially, they would create a database of preexisting interviews, but they also sought to acquire collections of other testimonial holdings in order to pinpoint "dramatic stories" for the Permanent Exhibition. Since the breach between the museum and the Fortunoff Archive had not yet occurred, the Holocaust Museum invoked the "Yale Method" as the paradigm for its pilot oral history program. Indeed, it later commissioned Lawrence Langer, who as a scholar and interviewer had a strong intellectual influence on the Fortunoff Archive, to examine three hundred of the Yale tapes for the purpose of identifying potential interviewees and recommending interview techniques.

Early on, Smith placed an emphasis on forging personal connections between interviewers and witnesses, which would in turn give visitors access to the more intimate textures of the Holocaust. As in the case of the Fortunoff Archive, the museum's interviewers would ask fewer questions during the testimonies. While this seemingly accorded witnesses more agency as to how they narrated their stories, this approach suited Smith's preference for producing usable footage. Echoing his preference for "quiet empathy," Smith remarked: "Interviewers will be neither seen nor heard in edited video."[82]

Smith found the first testimonies recorded by Kuzmack in early 1989 too focused on the historical rather than the personal nature of experience. His review reiterated the dominant criteria: the storytelling needs of the Permanent Exhibition and an investment in "unique testimony to offer to posterity."[83] He also made recommendations on the form, composition, and effectiveness of the interviews in an effort to create a standard methodology for future testimonies. Smith's comments reflected first and foremost his concern for interviews' exhibition rather than archival value. In order to mine recordings for the much-coveted "nuggets," there had to be certain protocols for the generation of footage.[84] This requirement appears to have been the underlying reason for his suggestion that Kuzmack and her staff of volunteers ask fewer questions during the interview and avoid the use of sympathetic noises or utterances, which muddied the sound track when they overlapped with the voice of a witness. He also wanted the interviewers and camera placed closer to the subject, thus creating a sense of "personal contact," despite the approved restraint in broaching questions. Indeed, interviewers' silence was preferred to speech: "Quiet empathy yields better results than repeated questioning."[85]

Kuzmack questioned Smith's insistence that the interview should focus only on personal experiences and events that a subject had witnessed firsthand. Her experience with interviews had taught her that witnesses would inevitably invoke background that they had not directly encountered: "You would be surprised how many insist they must put the [historical] background or it will have no meaning. They do this no matter what I say."[86] Moreover, when she tried to interject a question in order to lead witnesses back to the personal aspects of their stories, they often lost track. Thus Kuzmack urged Smith to allow witnesses to include historical context in order to better ground their narratives.

Underlying the attempt to reach a balance between the personal and the historical currents of testimony was the larger issue of how to address the interrelationship between deep and common memory. Smith's primary concern was mining testimony for segments that represent the viscerally charged impulses of deep memory—those moments that transcend chronology and place the witness back in the emotional center of events. Kuzmack and her interviewees, however, often needed chronological frameworks to ground both their past experiences and contemporary reflections. In that sense, Smith tried to excavate deep memory as the essence of testimonial value for the Permanent Exhibition, but failed to appreciate how it emerged in process and in dialogue with common memory. In the end, Smith's preferences prevailed over those of Kuzmack and heavily influenced the shaping of USHMM oral history policy.

Smith invoked the Fortunoff Archive as a standard bearer in terms of interview methodology, but modified those methods to accommodate the museum's particular exhibition needs. In particular, he was critical of the production value of the Fortunoff recordings: although dense with pathos, they lacked the "exhibit quality" required for the Permanent Exhibition.[87] Thus he requested that Kuzmack develop a model that would train interviewers to conduct sessions that employed Yale's interview techniques, but used a more refined and standardized approach to lighting and shot composition.

The Holocaust Museum also consciously attempted to recreate the kind of affective community for survivors and witnesses achieved by the Yale project. Like the Fortunoff Archive, it used a limited pre-interview protocol in which interviewers engaged witnesses on the broad historical elements of their experience in order to assist their preparation for the interview and make them more comfortable with the process. In each of the three case studies in this book, the pre-interview stage, although varied in scope, amounted to a testimonial rehearsal with implications for how individual witness accounts would be situated. The museum's policy, however, insisted that interviewers not use information gathered from this pre-interview phase to "control" the testimony. As stated in the initial oral history guidelines: "Effective interviewing must include a great deal of spontaneity on the part of both the interviewee and interviewer . . . the retrieval of 'unrehearsed' information best serves the research historian's needs and works very effectively with museum audiences."[88] So while priming interviewers and interviewees for the testimony was a crucial element of the process, a more open approach was intended to foster a dynamic of discovery.

Originally, the length of an interview was to vary according to the witness. By the time of Kuzmack's tenure, a rule of thumb—with certain exceptions—had been instituted: "Generally an interview of less than an hour is superficial, while a session of more than two hours may become aimless, redundant, and list-less."[89] This rule—upon which I will elaborate later—illustrates a source of friction in the museum's oral history collection. Similar to the conflicts over managing the flow of common and deep memory, planners wanted a process that could rehearse and frame testimony while also engendering spontaneity. But as will be demonstrated in analysis of individual testimonies, a two-hour-long time frame can often truncate the labor of remembrance.

The Holocaust Museum differs from the Fortunoff Archive and Shoah Foundation in using a screening process to determine the selection of interviewees, rather than accepting all those willing to participate. Using an initial set of phone interviews, Kuzmack developed a set of criteria, which included the following: the testimony's importance for the Permanent Exhibition or historical record; the witness's ability to present his or her story (e.g., are there lapses in memory or difficulties in articulating the story?); and determining if the witness's health and age would enable him or her to endure the interview process. This latter criterion was particularly relevant to the museum's exhibition-related concerns. Although health and age might affect witnesses' capacity to tell their stories, they could also affect visitors' ability to relate to them and their accounts.

In this regard, the advancing age of survivors complicated the museum's dual mission of preserving the legacy of the Holocaust and making that history accessible to a wide audience. Paradoxically, the planners faced a closing window of opportunity for documenting the stories of older survivors, yet their exhibition standards sought out only the most articulate and reliable witnesses. The older the survivor, the more likely he or she would be to have experienced a wider spectrum of the Holocaust era, particularly compared to child survivors. Yet Weinberg, Smith, and other planners feared that the advancing age of witnesses would weaken their grasp on details from the past, thus diluting their evidentiary value and potential as personal mediators of the Holocaust.

These concerns emerged during development of the Permanent Exhibition's "Voices from Auschwitz" segment, an installation of survivor audio testimonies adjacent to the display of an original Auschwitz-Birkenau barrack. Kuzmack had originally urged the designers to use video accounts from the oral history archive because visitors would be able to connect better with "living human beings, not with abstract voices which often produce a feeling of unreality in the hearer."[90] For Kuzmack, then, the more fully embodied audiovisual testimonies produced a more "real" rather than "theatrical" effect. The resultant interpersonal connection would be especially crucial for enabling visitors to see survivors' faces, thereby showing expressions of human suffering and more fully capturing the immediacy and veracity of their stories.

On this issue, exhibition director Martin Smith prevailed. His vision of the "Voices of Auschwitz" display would draw exclusively from the audio content of the museum's media archives. Reviewing the audiovisual recordings had reinforced Smith's belief that the visual markers of survivor aging would potentially leave visitors "turned off" rather than immersed in the testimonies.[91] Disembodied, oral recordings would allow visitors to imagine survivors on their own terms, as vital and perhaps young historical agents. In this case, as in others explored in this chapter, the process of screening survivors' voices and bodies involved filtering out elements that complicated the museum's institutional preferences.

This issue became further evident in protocols the museum implemented to evaluate the integration of preexisting video interviews with the other exhibition spaces. In the eventually instituted procedure, Kuzmack, Smith, and other oral history department staff rated testimonies according to the following grades: "Excellent" interviews are "technically, emotionally, and historically outstanding"; "Good" ones are "first-rate dramatically, technically, and historically, but not as stunning as the 'Excellent' category"; "Fair" tapes could "be used to fill in details of life during the Holocaust, but may not provide outstanding drama"; and a "Poor" rating excluded interviews from the Permanent Exhibition.[92] Reviewers also made comments on what they categorized as testimonies' "key segments," such as: "Inside a gas chamber when power failed"; "Selection by Mengele"; "Transport to Auschwitz"; "Buried alive for 16 months in an underground pit"; and "Death march—eating undigested bits of grain from dried cow manure."[93] With few exceptions, the most extreme experiences got the highest ratings, thus allowing planners to better organize segments that would provide pathos and dramatic punch to the exhibition narrative.

The USHMM's Oral History Interviewee Release Form codified the editorial control basic to this segmentation of testimony. Specifically, the witness's signature granted the museum the right to "Publish, exhibit, display, copyright, transfer, edit the image, name, voice, or content in whole or in part for any purposes, including fundraising, education in media both currently in existence or developed in the future."[94] This language, which is almost identical to that of releases used by the Fortunoff Archive and Shoah Foundation, raised concerns about how testimonies might be altered or regulated. In particular, certain survivors worried that by signing the release, they might give up rights to their accounts of their own Holocaust experiences and might therefore be prevented from passing on interview tapes to their families. In response, Kuzmack advised Berenbaum that the museum should revise the agreement in consultation with a group of survivor leaders. The museum's revised release contained the following clarification:

Please note that the second provision of the Form only gives the Museum ownership and copyright of the words and/or photographic images contained in this one particular interview. In other words, you are *not* giving the Museum ownership of *this particular recording* of your personal history. *Therefore, signing this Form will not in any way limit your continuing right to tell your personal story in books, articles, or other interviews in this or other media in the future.*[95]

Museum staff assured prospective interviewees that "Each videotape will remain unedited, preserved exactly as told to the interviewer."[96] Certainly the recorded interviews remained unedited within the archive. They were, however, edited and reconfigured for installations and educational programs both within and outside the museum. The evolving language of the agreement thus speaks to the question: How can testimony be both sacred and pliable?

That issue took on increased urgency when Raye Farr replaced Martin Smith as director of the Permanent Exhibition in 1991. Under her tenure, the exhibition's needs continued to drive the collection of oral histories, although the approaches to that mission radically changed as the museum's 1993 opening date neared. The oral history department was tasked with developing a concluding film segment for the exhibition consisting entirely of its own testimonial footage. In her new capacity, Farr decided that in order to attain a deeper level of response by witnesses, interviewers should abandon the earlier "quiet empathy" approach for a more interactive, question-driven methodology. She hoped that this change would both fill in needed historical detail and spark an emotional response from witnesses.[97] As discussed earlier, Kuzmack was already a proponent of such a method. Indeed, she was aware that Smith's approach had caused her staff to hold back on following up with witnesses on certain subjects or probing deeper on their psychological impressions. The resulting digressions and lengthy descriptions made it difficult to extract the concise, emotionally charged segments useful for the exhibition. Kuzmack expected interviewers to pose questions that would elicit particular answers regarding personal experiences and impressions, as well as broader cultural and historical observations. In addition to questions that would clarify facts and chronology—"what did you do then?" or "what happened when?"—she also pressed for queries directed at recovering emotions—"what was it like for you when?" or "how did you feel when?" Kuzmack further refined the protocol in terms of how survivors were to be handled before, during, and after the interview process and added new sets of prepared questions, which she compiled in the "Interviewing Holocaust Witnesses: Question Guide."[98] The new guidelines established that before the interview took place, the oral history department would send the interviewer historical background and other information as a basis for developing an itinerary weeks prior to the testimony, enabling interviewer and interviewee to develop a comfort level with each other and to engage the main elements of the testimony in advance of the taping.[99]

At the testimony itself, the interviewer was encouraged to keep eye contact with the witness; the camera was placed directly behind the interviewer's shoulder so that the witness would appear to be speaking directly into the camera. The guidelines placed a particular focus on subtly conveying empathy to the witness; thus the interviewer should nod his or her head or perform other "appropriate body language" such as leaning forward during certain critical moments, to reinforce a sense of engagement.[100] Through these guidelines, Kuzmack aimed to achieve "attentive listening," keeping the interviewer engaged without showing vocal signs of empathy. Like Smith's earlier guidelines, Kuzmack's approach was deemed "essential to enabling us [the Department of Oral History] to edit a tape for public viewing," since interviewer questions were not to be included in the content produced from the archive.[101]

Although museum interviewers were given the discretion to select certain topics from a prepared list, a set of required "core questions" addressed the oral history department's designated key themes of a survivor's testimony. These questions were broken down into three parts, covering events before, during, and after the war. The first set posed biographical queries including: "When were you born?"; "Where were you born?"; "Tell us about life with your family"; and "Describe your town before the war."[102] These topics would help reconstruct the witness's familial and communal life before the Holocaust. Similar queries addressed events during the Holocaust, for example: "Describe a typical day in the ghetto" or "Describe how you were deported to camps (if that is relevant to the witness's experience)."[103] Interviewers would also pursue lines of discussion that could elicit emotive aspects of the Holocaust experience, including witnesses' reflections on the kind of legacy they would like to impart.

The attempt by the museum's oral history department to move from a relatively silent to a more interactive mode of testimonial engagement was circumscribed not only by the requirement of standardized questions, but also by a two-hour time limit and a narrative framework divided into the three-part sequential division of events, with the majority of time dedicated to events taking place during the Holocaust era. This model made it difficult for survivors to express seemingly digressive yet nonetheless vital paths of exploration that did not correspond with the itinerary of the oral history department. While some variations were allowed, the focus on sequenced segments played an instrumental role in shaping the narrative possibilities of the recorded interviews. The frame conditions extended beyond the range of the camera and affected how witnesses were handled before and after their recorded testimonies. In order to tend to the affective and psychological aspects of the process, interviewers were given such advice as: "Stay and talk with the interviewee as long as necessary, so he/ she may unwind from the interview. Remember, the interviewee may literally have relived the horror of the Holocaust, and may need some time to unwind from the stress."[104]

The oral history department recognized that collecting testimony for the purpose of generating emotionally charged content necessarily involved examining the ruptures of traumatic memory. Yet even while the museum attempted to tap into that well of pathos through attentive listening, it instituted interview protocols and exhibition guidelines that intended to regulate the overflow and excesses of testimony. In other words, the Holocaust Museum oscillated between activating and containing traumatic memory. These institutional preferences did not determine the meaning generated by testimonies; they did, however, represent a central source of contestation that often emerges in the dialogue between a witness and her or his interlocutor.

A Clash of Oral History Cultures

Frictions often resulted from the USHMM's efforts to replicate the testimonies its planners considered to be exemplars of the Fortunoff Archive methodology. Although the two institutions had failed to reach a new agreement on the sharing of interviews, in 1991 the museum, hoping to refine its approach to conducting further testimonies, nonetheless solicited the consultation of Lawrence Langer. He agreed to survey a collection of the Fortunoff interviews. The resulting list of 150 of the most useful samples, complete with brief summaries and commentary, highlighted the *"most* dramatic and eloquent" testimonies that could serve as models.[105] Langer also produced a half-hour videotape comprising selections from those interviews, structured along themes laid out by Berenbaum, including survival, liberation, resistance, and rescue.[106] Langer's commentary on the interviews reveals the tensions that surfaced when the two archives' methodological and ethical preferences diverged, underscoring the central role institutional cultures play in the formation of archived testimonies.

Langer's report on his findings invoked many of the critiques in his previously mentioned book, *Holocaust Testimonies: The Ruins of Memory*, published the same year that he provided consultation to the museum. His book places a particular emphasis on the recurring manifestation of "humiliated memory"—those moments of misery that a subject would prefer to forget, and that are resistant to redemption.[107] That line of examination directly conflicted with the museum's outlook, given its focus on the transformative moral potential of Holocaust testimonies. In Langer's view, Holocaust testimony is fundamentally anti-redemptive, resisting attempts to impose coherent meaning and closure on its events. He thus considered valuable those moments that reveal the struggles and vicissitudes of memory. Those perspectives are manifest in his review of the Fortunoff testimony of Dori K., a Jewish survivor attempting to come to terms with the fate of her father by replaying in her mind the moment of their separation. As Langer commented on this moment:

> She now can imagine his real fate, and sobbing she repeats, "They put him on a train." She doesn't have to say the rest, we and she doesn't have to say the rest, we and she can imagine it, and this truth, instead of liberating her, merely imprisons her in a vision of his fate that overwhelms her. . . . Holocaust truth thus makes one *vulnerable* as well as knowledgeable.[108]

In Langer's view, testimony is not a cathartic act of retrieving memory. Instead, it is marked by anguishing moments of temporal and emotional collapse when the present moment of recollection and the past experiences of pain are interpenetrated. Rather than marking a compartmentalized and clean extraction of personal or historical knowledge, testimony can make vulnerable not only the witness, but also those who bear responsibility for receiving his or her story. Langer emphasized that the value of Dori K.'s testimony derives not from her proximity to death and destruction during the Holocaust—she was never in a concentration camp nor did she witness her father's death—but rather from the anguish with which she responds to questions such as: "What do you think about when you think of your father's last moments?"[109] No linear narrative could salve the pain she experienced through the reenactment of that painful moment of separation. In Langer's words: "Its legacy leads not to reconciliation, but the difficult struggle with memory that we witness here."[110]

Langer interprets memory as a labor to be shared by both the witness and the interviewer. Visual and sense memory allow the witness to be overtaken by a traumatic past, to be put in a position to reenact profound moments of psychic fracture. As I will explore in later sections of this book, this interior labor is screened before the interviewer and the spectator, as the witness evinces the physical and emotional gestures of translating interior images, sounds, smells, and textures into words that are translated into a non-native tongue. When the testimony also requires linguistic translation—converting memories experienced in Polish, Yiddish, German, or another tongue—an additional process, labor, and mediation are enacted. There is a dual level of translation in that sense, whereby witnesses have to rework their memories into verbal expressions and in turn convert them into a language that is not indigenous to their experiences.

Langer stressed that the collection of oral history requires not only extracting historical narratives but also capturing interior personal experience. He pointed out that the process of identifying deep memory often diverges from a linear historical account. In fact, a good number of the testimonies he designated as most dramatically compelling illustrated the interplay between chronological (or common) memory and associative (or deep memory).[111] In the case of the before-mentioned Baruch G., who gave his testimony to the Fortunoff Archive in 1984, Langer noted that during the first eleven minutes of the interview, as Baruch discusses his Jewish life and rituals before the war, he suddenly moves forward to his life after the Holocaust and the loneliness he felt during holidays and bar mitzvah occasions when he realized that no one from his side of the family remained alive to celebrate those events. In Baruch's words: "Life around you seems to be normal, but you are abnormal."[112] That moment illustrated for Langer the structuring presence of the past over survivors' lives after the war, and underscored how testimonies that begin in chronological sequence can suddenly, without warning, veer from that trajectory. As he remarked in the evaluations, survivors "report a *simultaneity* but not a *sequence*."[113] He thus advocated for careful listening and viewing of the subject during taping, not rushing the witness to reach a pre-designated point of interest or to create a desired effect. This meant encouraging agency on the part of the witness to face events and their consequences on his or her own terms.

Langer further advised the museum against adopting a stance of moral judgment over witnesses given the "choiceless choices" faced by Holocaust survivors.[114] He noted that interviewers sometimes conclude testimonies by asking witnesses to reflect on the moral or redemptive lessons of the Holocaust. But in doing so, they can uncover a profound tension between the attempt to impose cathartic closure on the events and the persistence of trauma that continues to resonate, thus rendering any redemptive resolution illusory. Even while discouraging such concluding questions, Langer noted that the gaps between redemption and trauma that ensue from such gambits may be constructive. They can compel the viewer of testimony to process the contradictions, thus complicating efforts to restore meaning out of meaningless events.

Langer's report did not prompt the museum to consider the self-consciously constructed elements of the testimony process, an issue that had motivated the Fortunoff Archive to institute its re-interview project, as discussed in the previous chapter. On the contrary, the museum often attempted to efface the presence of the interviewer as the institution's intermediary, advocating for silent listening or concealing the interviewer's identity during the testimonies, as well as in some transcripts and catalogues. In a number of the testimonies that were conducted during the department's early years under Linda Kuzmack, interviewer names were misattributed or missing on databases and transcripts. Moreover, the museum's single-shot strategy focused exclusively on witnesses; interviewers never appeared in the camera frame, even at the beginning of testimonies.

The museum's guidelines were shaped both by curatorial needs and the urgency of preserving the living memory of survivors before they vanished. As stated in an internal description of the oral history department from 1990,

> the Museum faces a daunting task—to enable visitors to emotionally feel the terror and reality of the Holocaust, as well as to understand it intellectually. . . . The Museum's oral history department plays a major role in solving that dilemma. Every visitor to the U.S. Holocaust Memorial Museum will "meet" Holocaust survivors, liberators, and rescuers through video- and audio-taped testimonies. . . . Standing "face to face" with Holocaust survivors through the miracle of videotape, Museum visitors may encounter a woman who walked out of a gas chamber when the gas failed to release; one of the few survivors of the Treblinka uprising; and a woman who attacked a Nazi guard and was, in turn, shot in the head.[115]

The epistemology of the museum's oral history department itself encompasses the notion of a direct testimonial encounter. Technology—the "miracle of videotape"—is framed less as a mediating presence in a larger institutional and interpersonal dialogue than as a means to preserve living memory and transfer it to future generations. The affective impact of testimony is just as central as its cognitive valence, and it is precisely that perceived emotional rawness that will be a core asset of the museum's oral history department. A museum press release quoted Kuzmack: "No one, after seeing these tapes, can dispute the uniqueness of the Holocaust with credibility."[116]

This insistence on preserving the seemingly unvarnished nature of Holocaust memory helps explain why the museum keeps the institutional mediations of its testimonies at the periphery. The question remains, however, whether the museum was really able to hide its contributions to testimonial authorship. How does the oral history department's claim that testimonies are unique, authentic, and direct expressions of individual experience hold up to an analysis of individual testimonies or to the museum's use of testimonial footage? How do interview methodologies designed to de-emphasize the mediated aspects of the testimonial encounter affect the ways in which traces of witnesses' lives are placed throughout the museum exhibition?

On a fundamental level, the embodied dimensions of testimony depend on how the camera and microphone record the physical forms, gestures, and voices of witnesses. This factor, in turn, has implications for how interviews are later segmented and repackaged for use outside of their archive. As discussed, while he was still with the museum Martin Smith's primary concern was to secure testimonies for integration into the Permanent Exhibition, in particular for the film to be shown in the "Testimonial Amphitheater," a segment that would conclude the PE. While the museum ultimately subcontracted the film to an independent producer and director, the planners had originally conceived the film as an in-house project, although one that would use footage from other repositories, including the Fortunoff Archive. But on reviewing available footage from within the museum's testimony archive, Smith determined that much of it lacked the refined and consistent style suitable for exhibition use.[117] Smith's search for testimonies with standardized production values and "visually interesting interviews" then led him to mandate Kuzmack and her staff to adopt a uniform approach to lighting and to framing the witnesses. Smith wanted interviewers to sit directly in front of the subjects, as close to the camera as possible and out of the frame, so that the witness seems to look almost directly into the camera. The eye-lines of witness, interviewer, and spectator were all to be level. In Smith's words, the camera should position the witness so that "we are not looking up to a giant or down to a child."[118] Moreover, all interviews were to be shot against a black background with three-point lighting, thus achieving a "cohesive" and "rigorous" appearance distinct from the interviews of other archives. In order to emphasize the face as the central site for screening the emotional texture of memory, Smith also advocated for the exclusive use of close-up composition to achieve the tightest possible framing.[119] This suggestion elaborated on an internal memorandum to Kuzmack that criticized her use of wide framing: "There was too much shirt/blouse and not enough face for the impact I would like."[120] Kuzmack responded that she found such extreme close-ups "too tight and too close to the neck, giving me a bit of a choked feeling."[121]

Smith's views did not prevail in regard to the aesthetic framing of interviews—an issue that reflected the larger question of how to harness the visceral impact of Holocaust testimony through the representation of the body on screen. His preference for frames that were so tight that the camera could capture sweat and tears on a witness's face would have concealed the wider range of gestured expression. Or consider the tattoos on the left arms of Auschwitz survivors, which are usually outside the frame of a tight close-up. In most cases they are visible to the camera only when an interviewer asks about wartime experiences, or during a concluding segment of testimony when witnesses are asked to present photographs, documents, and other artifacts, usually shot on display stands with black backgrounds. In either case, the camera breaks from its focus on the survivor's face to move in for a segmenting close-up of the tattoo, which is then—like photographs and other material artifacts—abstracted from its larger context, but nonetheless provides authenticating value.

Testimonial and Curatorial Frameworks

There are striking parallels between the design and curation of the Holocaust Museum's Permanent Exhibition and the frameworks that shape the role of oral history within the museum. The layout of the Permanent Exhibition, like the basic outline for the museum's audiovisual testimonies, is divided into three sections covering events before, during, and after the Holocaust, following in linear order and with clearly marked narrative transition points. In addition, the exhibition and oral history departments share a concern with fine-tuning emotional reactions to and imposing analytical coherence on Holocaust history and memory. As I have already mentioned, part of the approach relates to the museum's mandates to import an event from its European context and adapt it for an American audience. And it additionally reflects its investment in preserving attention to the historical specificity of the Holocaust while also endeavoring to forge universal, interpersonal lessons from the events.

Despite its self-proclaimed adherence to historical accuracy, the Permanent Exhibition provides few if any extensive captions for its still and moving images. This contrasts with the fairly detailed texts that explain the provenance and historical context of written documents and other physical items on display. It would seem that the museum's primary interest resides in the illustrative and visceral impact of moving images, rather than in considerations of their historical provenance. The operative assumption is that still and moving images possess an immediately legible moral value and visceral charge that can be abstracted from the details of their individual histories. Within the established narrative of the museum's story-driven exhibition space, images of suffering are not artifacts in their own right; rather, they exemplify a historical storyline. An alternative approach that would deliberately examine how various image artifacts and other materials challenge, interrogate, and reinforce each other was deemed too experimental. Moreover, it could undermine the museum's mandate to counter Holocaust denial, which required uncontested documentation of a particular historical narrative, in addition to potentially confusing visitors with a casual or nonexistent familiarity with the Holocaust.[122]

One illustration of this dilemma is the original film footage installed in the interactive media bays on the Permanent Exhibition's third floor, intended to illustrate such key events as Nazi rallies at Nuremberg and the 1936 Olympic games. The few citations that accompany their presentation obscure their provenance and fail to stimulate discussion of how images of the Nazi regime were propagandistically constructed. Similarly, a monitor in the third-floor section on life in the ghetto displays Nazi propaganda film footage of Jewish life in the Warsaw Ghetto, amidst a collection of other artifacts, including one of the famous milk canisters in which the collections of the secret Ringelblum archive were hidden. Yet no museum label explains the origins of the footage, thus obscuring the fact that Nazis were responsible for creating it for their own propagandistic purposes.[123]

Questions of citation also informed the development of the exhibition's "Tower of Faces," a central three-story exhibition. Consisting of 1,500 photographs duplicated in their original condition from the personal collection of the Holocaust scholar Yaffa Eliach, the images chronicle the life of inhabitants in the shtetl of Ejszyszki in Lithuania.[124] The fifty-four-foot-high tower space is covered on all four sides with images ranging in size from one- to three-feet high, placed against enamel panels. Because 95 percent of the shtetl's inhabitants featured in the photographs perished during the Holocaust, Eliach considered the exhibit to be a form of familial and communal reclamation, restoring life to those who were lost. These "survivor photos" are some of the few remaining traces of Jewish life in Ejszyszki. As Eliach wrote in a journal essay:

> Intended simply as mementos of happy times and family occasions, the tower of survivor photos now has the weightier task of restoring identity and individuality to the otherwise anonymous victims of the Nazis. Together with the pertinent documents and captions, the photographs "rescue" these victims and their lost civilization posthumously, redeem them from the conflagration that left behind mere ashes, smoke, and pits filled with bodies. The photographs in the tower will become their memorial, a visual record of Jewish life.[125]

These images serve a restorative function by providing an overwhelming collective as well as a personal perspective on the life that both thrived and perished in that shtetl.

Yet the completed Tower of Faces exhibition ultimately lacks the accompanying "pertinent documents and captions" mentioned in Eliach's essay, which was published before completion of the exhibition. In a letter to then Permanent Exhibition director Raye Farr, Eliach pressed for the inclusion of captions to provide context for the photographs, noting: "A photo without a caption loses much of its impact."[126] By persuading Eliach to omit captions, Farr conferred on the images a more universally identifiable value. The opening museum label makes the photographs' overall historical context clear, but the individual images remained uncaptioned in order to encourage a more immersive and universalizing experience. In other words, the historical specificity of the images had to be balanced against the need for an accessible, visceral impact. While the tower's images stand in for their corporeal referents, the identities of those in the photographs remain unknown to most museum visitors. Their emblematic quality makes them more broadly representative of shtetl experience and of Jewish life in Eastern Europe.

The fact that the tower exhibit includes images of those who survived (however few), as well as of the many who perished, leaves room for interpretation by museum visitors. The enormity of the space conveys the feeling of being immersed in and overwhelmed by both the individual details of the photographs and the mosaic quality of the piece. The result is a powerful visceral and emotional experience, but one that is grounded less in historical specificity than in broader tropes of Holocaust experience. The tower itself is segmented into two parts: "A Shtetl," on one floor, and "End of a Shtetl" on another floor. But all of the photographs on each level of the exhibit capture moments of everyday life in Ejszyszki, ranging from families out on bike excursions to workers posing with the tools of their trades. They provide a compelling chronicle of Jewish life as it existed in the looming shadow of the Holocaust—that which was present and then irrevocably lost. However, the absence of captions renders the particular details of individual names and experiences peripheral relative to the display's larger emotional, experiential tapestry.

The design of the Tower of Faces accommodates the exhibition's overall narrative framework: it provides referential, experiential anchorage for a story of Jewish life in Eastern Europe before and after the war, while also enabling visitors to project their individual interpretations onto the images, thus creating their own stories for those who are represented in the panels. The individual images in the mosaic have their own particular, inescapably unique gazes, features, and gestures; however, they are first and foremost framed to stand in for Jewish and human experience in broader terms. So positioned, the subjects captured in the photographs become sources of interpersonal connection spanning the spatial and historical divide of the Holocaust.

If the Permanent Exhibition represents the "soul of the museum," then the Tower of Faces constitutes its emotional core. During a walkthrough of the display, Raye Farr recounted to me how during the PE's construction, workers emotionally drained by its stark images would frequently head to the Tower of Faces as a "restorative spot," where they could regain perspective on their task at hand and attend to the psychic effects of their work.[127] This function continued after the museum's opening. In Farr's words: "This is where the life-force is for the exhibition."[128] It is also one of the few places within the Permanent Exhibition that includes images of Jewish life as captured by Jews and not by perpetrators or liberators. Eliach's grandparents, Yitzhak Uri Katz and Alte Katz, photographed most of the images, and the photos capture a sense of comfort and intimacy that would be difficult to imagine with a photographer from outside the community.

The Tower of Faces, like the screening of Holocaust testimony analyzed later in this chapter, advances the Holocaust Museum's mandate as a "living memorial," one that renders Holocaust commemoration in terms of an official American narrative, while at the same time emphasizing the interpersonal and the experiential dimensions of remembrance. The collection of photographs from Ejszyszki constitutes an archive of shtetl life lost and yet salvaged. Initially recovered as part of Eliach's personal collection, these images—like the museum's Holocaust testimonies—constitute a public, institutional archive housed within the walls of the USHMM. While less numerous than the collected video testimonies, the photographs provide a rich and overpowering illustration of the human dimensions of history. Also like their counterparts in the testimony archive, they have the potential to be instrumentalized for institutional pedagogical and commemorative purposes, as exemplars of a more universal, viscerally inflected experience, at the expense of engaging the particularities of history. Their value for embodying traces of the Holocaust is not inherent, but rather is contingent upon their use. The next sections of this chapter will explore how the museum similarly mediates the holdings of its oral history department in order to activate their memorial potentiality.

Screening and Screening Out Testimonies

The Testimony Amphitheater at the end of the Permanent Exhibition reflects the Holocaust Museum's efforts to calibrate the impact of its testimonial content. While earlier exhibition segments—such as the Voices from Auschwitz installation—had used audio-recorded testimonies, the amphitheater is the only area in the museum that displays archived *audiovisual* testimonies. The evolution of the Testimony Amphitheater concept speaks to the larger challenge of balancing thematic and narrative coherence with the representational complexities of trauma. In Martin Smith's original plan, a computer-programmed multiscreen installation was to randomly display pre-edited segments of testimonies from the holdings of the museum's oral history department. Segments of interviewees from varying backgrounds, religions, and categories (survivors, liberators, and rescuers) would be edited to correspond with a particular theme or event. The installation would cycle through twenty-four hours of footage before resetting, thus replicating a fundamental temporal measure of everyday human experience. Smith intended the display to be a permanent body of individual and collective memory within the exhibition.

Like the Tower of Faces, the Testimony Amphitheater would present a mosaic of human experiences to complement the exhibition's more "traditional" sources. As Smith described his conception: "'Testimony' [the installation] must be more than a film or video. It has to be a timeless presentation about the Holocaust from the victims themselves. . . . It is essential that 'Testimony' breaks the shackles of the usual media time frame—and not even [the film] *Shoah* did that."[129] For Smith, it was vital that the installation break new ground, even if that meant pushing the temporal boundaries of Claude Lanzmann's epic 1985 documentary *Shoah*. Smith wanted both to capture the richness and multivocality of Holocaust experiences and memories and to create a rationale for visitors to return to the museum, eager to explore the "fresh evidence" gleaned from a growing display of survivor testimonies.[130] The amphitheater could capture the rawness and spontaneity of traumatic memory—avoiding the "artificial linkages" of film editing to present stories in their unadorned immediacy.[131] It was precisely the dynamic and unanticipated quality of the installation, Smith argued, that would prevent the false imposition of closure on the traumatic excesses of testimony.

However, with Smith's departure from the museum in 1991 and pressure from its planners to strengthen the exhibition's thematic coherence, the original vision for the Testimony Amphitheater installation was scrapped in favor of a new proposal to develop a single film entitled *Testimony*, comprising three fixed ten- to fifteen-minute long modules featuring twenty-four survivor and liberator interviews, edited around a linear, three-part structure according to themes of resistance, rescue, and defiance.[132] Although the work was inspired by testimonies originally housed in the museum archive, the job was contracted out-of-house. Filmmaker Sandy Bradley rerecorded each selected interview in order to achieve more thematically grounded itineraries and higher production values. Unlike the original video format, the new work was reshot on film, and subjects were placed against colorful domestic, rather than more neutral black institutional backdrops.

In the official proposal seeking federal authorization for *Testimony*, museum planners laid out their vision for how the film would integrate individual eyewitness accounts into an exhibition space that had largely relegated testimonial material to its periphery.[133] Overall, the exhibition placed an emphasis on official documents and histories, coupled with original or replicated personal objects and other material artifacts ranging from concentration camp uniforms and confiscated eyeglasses, to castings of a gas chamber door and reconstructed barracks from Birkenau. *Testimony* was intended to supplement that display strategy by giving "voice to individual witnesses of the Holocaust."[134] Explicit in the proposal was the notion that the film would facilitate the convergence of both the analytical and visceral demands of the museum. Through its screening, "Museum visitors will have the opportunity to come closer to the events of the Holocaust as they see the faces of survivors and listen to accounts of a world full of contradiction, confusion, and choices."[135] Planners hoped that the film could be used to flesh out the subjects of history by concluding the exhibition with a more living, albeit highly mediated, presence of survivors who would lend faces and voices to otherwise less embodied history.

Although the museum's planners conceived of the film as a means of reflecting the diversity and complexity of Holocaust experience, they also designed it to ground its representations in direct and unified moral lessons. The development of *Testimony* thus illustrates a larger set of tensions concerning the epistemological contours of the museum's exhibition space. The new, thematically grounded film would serve as a corrective to the more fragmented elements of Martin Smith's first design. At the same time, planners attempted to preserve some of the less traditional vestiges of that earlier concept, particularly by running the film on a continuous loop, withholding any explicitly clear markers of a beginning, middle, and end, and allowing visitors to enter and leave the space when they wished. Ultimately, however, those attempts to incorporate Smith's suggestions were largely cosmetic. Any efforts to create an open format with the film were illusory considering the thematic and linear trajectory of the work, coupled with its use of voice-over narration to highlight thematic transitions and provide the personal backgrounds of the witnesses.

Sandy Bradley, the film's contracted director, viewed the interview process that generated the footage for the project as an opportunity to forge a direct connection with her subjects and to shed light on what she regarded to be the unadorned truths of their experiences: the film would "have no formal structure or storyline . . . allow[ing] essentially no visual, no sound effects, no music, in short, nothing to aid the raw content of what is said other than the careful weaving of film editing."[136] Despite her investment in uncovering the "deeper reflections" that emerge through testimony, Bradley was constrained by a temporal and thematic format that limited her ability to capture the messier, less overt processes that drive the work of traumatic memory.[137] She deliberately chose to position her subjects in their own domestic settings, hoping that the more familiar, intimate locations would put them at ease. She elected to frame the witnesses in tight close-ups with soft backgrounds to ensure that spectators would focus on the faces of the subjects. In the official proposal for the film, Bradley stated: "I think most people in the audience will only see and hear the survivor him/herself. The film will seem to be purely: people."[138]

Despite this rhetoric of pure, direct access to testimonial truths, creating *Testimony* was a highly edited and contested process. Once the new testimonies were recorded in May 1992, Bradley and the main museum planners, including Raye Farr, Shaike Weinberg, and Michael Berenbaum, collectively reviewed the new footage to select segments for inclusion in the final cut. The reviewing committee expressed particular concern with ensuring the exclusion of footage that challenged the museum's commitment to historical authenticity. One testimony, for example, raised suspicions that the unnamed witness had embellished, if not outright concocted, his story.[139] In arguing against inclusion, Farr referred to the witness as a "fantasist": "It's genuine and sincere but he is imagining." Michael Berenbaum agreed: "If in doubt, leave it out."[140]

The rejection of a "fantasist" as witness underscores the museum's shifting criteria for defining standards of evidence depending on the category of artifact. It was sufficient that the contested Polish boxcar displayed in the Permanent Exhibition was "of the kind" used for deportations, and that the Warsaw Ghetto film footage of Jewish life did not reveal its Nazi provenance, but audiovisual testimony of survivors was held to a higher standard of authenticity. Here the burden of evidence was proportionate to the survivors' contributions to the experiential anchorage and moral authority for the museum, where they served as living delegates.

The selection committee acknowledged that the merits of a particular testimony often relied on the abilities of a witness to perform her or his memory. Notes taken during the process of assessing videos describe an approach often akin to film or television casting. Descriptions of Gerda K. in her white sweater and pearls as "handsome," or of Emanuel T.'s "handsome, intelligent face," demonstrate the considerable attention paid to finding witnesses who could capture the eye and imagination of the viewer.[141] As "primary interviews," Emanuel T. and Gerda K. were given more screen time; "secondary interviews" would provide color, but not serve as main characters: "Some stories are marginal but can be kept in the film for pacing and effect, as long as [the] main focus remains on themes."[142]

Conceived as the culmination of the Permanent Exhibition, *Testimony* is the exception in a presentation otherwise dominated by more official, top-down historical accounts of the Holocaust. While the film's footage of survivors is no less mediated or segmented than the written documents or found footage on display within the exhibition, it nonetheless provides the only moments when witnesses are shown to be telling their stories through both audio and visual representation. After traversing the Permanent Exhibition's three levels, the visitor has seen many personal artifacts, photomurals of human hair, and implements of torture and death, but rarely has encountered the faces and voices of victims. It is startling to finally come across *Testimony* with its embodied human quality.

Testimony reanimates the history represented in the preceding exhibition segments by projecting human voices and figures back onto the historical fragments in the Permanent Exhibition, endowing them with visceral charge and moral authority. I am not trying to contend that the film provides a full counterpoint to the curatorial concept operative in the prior segments of the museum. Edward Linenthal has taken such a position, arguing that the collection of individual voices and experiences captured in *Testimony* complicates the dominant narrative of the USHMM: "In the midst of moving and horrible accounts of resistance, rescue, near rescue, theological certainty, and theological doubt, the presence of the Holocaust as a living thing is overpowering."[143] Visitors may in fact find it overwhelming to confront the burdens of memory in the filmed faces, gestures, and voices of survivors as they bestow the artifacts of that history with a semblance of living memory. But the film as a whole does not necessarily undermine the museum's more universalizing and unifying impulses or preclude certain impositions of redemptive closure.

The concept of *Testimony* as a multiscreen work without a clear beginning, middle, or end is belied by the caption that appears each time the film completes a loop:

> This film exhibit is a living legacy: eyewitness testimony from survivors of the Holocaust. It concludes the Permanent Exhibition of the United States Holocaust Memorial Museum, running continuously without beginning, middle, or end. Visitors to the Museum are free to enter and leave at will.[144]

Whereas Smith's approach would have maintained the less anticipated and structured aspects of testimonies, the film's current version strives to fix spectatorship even when making gestures toward temporal openness. The captivating faces, gestures, and voices provide a compelling counterpoint to the exhibition's less personalized aspects. They are, however, subject to a rigorous thematic structure, which is in turn aided by a female voice-over narration that provides historical exposition and signals the changing of thematic segments. While the film is introduced as a "living legacy," it is one that is highly structured and circumscribed. Comparing the reshot film footage in *Testimony* to its original archived video sources makes clear that the process of reframing survivor accounts works in conjunction with a particular institutional perspective on Holocaust historiography. In their original archived interviews, witnesses are often more interested in telling the stories of others than in recounting their own experiences. Although much of the featured survivor Abraham M.'s original archived testimony focuses on remembrances of his father and the profound loss suffered as a result of his death, his appearance in *Testimony* involves only the harrowing story of his own survival in hiding.[145]

The interviews conducted for *Testimony* also have a more public dimension than the original archived versions, in large part because witnesses were aware that a substantial number of museum visitors would have access to their stories: in effect, the witnesses were sharing extremely intimate, private remembrances with a public audience. Yet the process of editing testimonies for the film involved screening survivors' accounts in ways that withheld traces of the labor and, often, frictions that mark the process of giving and receiving testimony.

From the Archive to the Screen

The omitted traces of interviews are illuminated by comparing segments of testimonies newly created for the film with their original archived versions. Consider the previously mentioned Gerda K., one of *Testimony*'s primary subjects.[146] Her initial interview for the museum's oral history department in 1990 contains several moments when she asks the interviewer to cut the camera because she cannot bear the emotional burden of recalling encounters with her father wearing a yellow star and then seeing him for the last time before his death. At one such point during the archived interview, she turns to the interviewer just off to the side of the camera and remarks: "There's just one more thing I want to mention. Before my father left, he asked me. . . ." Unable to continue, she begs the interviewer: "Cut. Please. Will you cut it out?" The interviewer replies: "This will all be edited. It will not be seen by the public."[147] The screened footage for *Testimony* excludes all such unanticipated exchanges found in the archived recordings. The typed transcript in the museum's oral history database also omits Gerda's full exchange—as it does other "off-camera" comments—which it designates as "technical conversation."

And yet this exchange does appear to those who view the original archived testimony in its entirety. That moment locatable in the archive underscores the conflict between the institutional call for remembrance and the personal challenges for survivors sparked by reenacting traumatic experiences from their past. It reveals the difficult, dialogical nature of testimonies in which survivors cannot always accommodate the preferences of the institution recording their accounts. However defining these moments are, they are largely absent from the film *Testimony* and from most other exhibition versions of interviews. Obviously, the filmed iteration required editing of witnesses' stories. Nonetheless, it is important to underscore that the film's thematic framework, based on resistance, defiance, and rescue, often leaves out moments that do not fall within those headings, yet are crucial to a more nuanced understanding of survivor experiences.

Again citing Gerda K., *Testimony* highlights the story of her liberation from a concentration camp near Volary, Czechoslovakia, by a German Jew, Kurt, who, after fleeing to the United States, had returned to Europe as a G.I. We learn of their encounter through a series of crosscuts between Gerda and Kurt, whom the film later dramatically reveals to be her husband. That revelation plays a culminating role in the melodrama that juxtaposes her profound devastation with a romantic bond amidst the ashes of the Holocaust.[148] The story of Gerda and Kurt marks the restoration of both her feminine identity and some semblance of hope in humanity. And while it is an incredibly powerful moment in the film, it emerges not through a sustained engagement with Gerda's or Kurt's testimony, but rather through the imposition of institutional authorship, as expressed in the selection and crosscutting of what the film's planners and producers considered to be the defining moment of these two witnesses' experiences. Consequently, what is missing from this sequence is the excess of emotions and the breakdown in narration that accompanies the return of memory throughout Gerda's original archived interview. While the film moves these two stories beyond the archive and through editing enables the two subjects to speak to each other, the difficulties of recalling their traumas are largely left on the cutting-room floor.

The essentialization of Gerda K.'s experience actually began before the re-recording of her testimony for the film. During her initial archived recording, the interviewer was already familiar with many details of her story, not only through the oral history department's pre-interview process but also because of Gerda's prominence in the survivor community and her many public addresses about her wartime experiences. With that prior knowledge in hand, the interviewer often attempted to guide Gerda's testimony in the direction of what the oral history department had judged to be the core aspects of her Holocaust experience: her dramatic liberation and romantic union with Kurt. It is as if the interview had been leading up to this point all along, and when it arrives, Gerda's performance of memory suddenly seems more rote and restrained. She appears to have recounted this part of her story many times before, and it largely lacks the uncertainty and unsteadiness that mark her earlier recollections of losing her father. The moment of liberation and romantic renewal appears to serve as a grounding memory that relieves her of the burdensome aspects of telling her story. The familiar and accessible melodramatic conventions steer her, as well as the interviewer and spectator, through these touchstone events.

A comparison of Kurt's footage in *Testimony* with his original archived interview reveals a similar process of extraction.[149] Based on an analysis of the original archived version, he does not appear to be as polished or composed as Gerda. He reveals some discomfort with the process, often turning his eyes away from the interviewer and toward his lap, sighing and struggling as he tries to collect his thoughts. Like Gerda's original archived interview, Kurt's testimony was guided toward the camp liberation and his meeting with her. Yet this effort comes at the expense of engaging a profound element of his wartime experience: his flight from Germany to the United States before 1938. He painfully recalls leaving his parents behind and the letters he received with their accounts of Kristallnacht. He speaks not so much of his own experiences, but of his parents' fate as told through their letters. They are the only surviving traces of his parents' experiences, and the interview provides him with the prospect of giving them a voice as well as enabling him to fulfill his obligation to remember.

Yet the interviewer shows little interest. She hurries him along, pressing him toward his wartime experiences as an American G.I.: "What did you, what did you do now? This is after Kristallnacht. Tell us very briefly [about prewar experiences] so that we can move into the war experience for you." But Kurt is reluctant to move forward in the chronology without first devoting more time to the memory of his parents: "Well, I should however, also mention that you know we kept on trying by every means to get them [his parents] out."[150] Kurt makes repeated mention of his failed attempts. He has kept the letters that his parents sent to him during their time in a concentration camp in France and he notes his own letters to them:

> One of my letters was returned. Address . . . unknown. Left no forwarding address. And as we found out through a tracing bureau after the war they were in fact deported to Auschwitz, along with all the thousands and thousands who were there. This was the time when I was inducted into the Army. So that was . . . all happened together.[151]

Kurt's failure to rescue his parents and his coming to terms with their loss is entangled with the "key" experience of Gerda's liberation. The deep memory of his parents' loss is something he struggles with; his memory of Gerda seems to be more comforting or at least more familiar in that it has been incorporated into common memory, although it nonetheless sparks a return to a far less stabilized recollection of loss.

At no point does the *Testimony* film reveal that Kurt is a German Jewish refugee who lost his parents to the Nazis, nor is there is a glimpse of his documented and archived struggle to confront the enormity of his trauma. The narrative of liberation and romantic courtship overwhelms the entanglements of his deep and common memory. While the story of the liberation is a key part of Kurt's and Gerda's original testimonies, it has a heightened, dramatized charge in the film because of the crosscutting that culminates in the revelation of their union.

The testimonies of Helen W., a German Jewish survivor forced to place her young daughter in the care of a non-Jewish family before her deportation to Auschwitz, similarly exemplify the conflict between the museum's institutional preferences and the agency of individual witnesses. In her initial archived interview, she reflects on her arrival at the camp:

> Probably the most upsetting was this being changed into a different person with losing your hair, losing everything you had, just as you are born. I think that was the greatest shock. You couldn't see yourself, but you saw the others, so you know what you were looking like.[152]

With that, the first half of the interview officially ends, as preparations are made to insert a second tape. Yet the camera is accidentally left running for a time, capturing an off-the-record moment between Helen and the interviewer, which like other encounters of this nature is noted on the transcript only with the designation "technical conversation." In this downtime, the interviewer comments: "You're doing very well. And you look great on the screen. It really looks very good."[153] And at that moment, Helen turns to her right and sees her image on the studio's playback monitor. She appears startled at discovering her recorded self, a response that echoes the recollection of seeing her new identity mirrored in the appearance of other Auschwitz inmates. And at this striking moment, the interviewer interjects to caution Helen not to look off camera: "You're really not supposed to . . . we're back at the camera!"[154]

Helen has thus transgressed a representational boundary set in place by the museum's oral history department, by viewing herself and thus her new identity as an archived witness and by calling attention to the mediated components of the interview. Just as her Holocaust-era encounter with the other victims allowed her to see herself as the prisoner she had become, so her view of the playback monitor potentially opened a window into the framing of her contemporary identity as a documented "survivor." Those two positions converge and surface between the official and peripheral boundaries of Helen's testimony, between the seemingly off-camera and on-camera transitions. Helen's description of her self-recognition as prisoner is not included in Testimony, which instead uses her story of putting her daughter in the care of a non-Jewish family—an event that more clearly fits the film's tripartite thematic structure.[155]

As pointed out, the performative aspects of a witness's interview—specifically, eloquent and forceful accounts—were among the criteria for footage used in Testimony. Every witness included in the film had previously recorded her or his USHMM testimonies, and the museum was careful to select for re-interviews those witnesses whom they felt presented a credible, authentic perspective on the Holocaust. This often involved working with witnesses who were dramatic in their delivery yet expressed their thoughts with consistency and composure.

Consider, for instance, the two versions of testimony given by Agnes A., a Hungarian Jew who survived the war by working closely with Raoul Wallenberg during his time as a diplomat in Budapest. By USHMM criteria, Agnes is a compelling survivor, in terms of both her clear and dramatic delivery and the harrowing and courageous circumstances of her wartime experiences. Extremely sharp and articulate and speaking with a refined Hungarian accent, Agnes is at once foreign and yet accessible to an American audience. She exudes an urbane and cosmopolitan air, delivering her testimony in an upright and confident manner. Throughout most of her original archived interview, Agnes appears to inhabit the realm of common memory, though at key moments she follows the more rupturing and immersive paths of deep memory.

Agnes provides a glimpse into the labored interaction between those two streams of memory only near the end of her archived testimony, at the same time revealing the tensions that often emerge between the voice of the Holocaust Museum and that of an individual witness. This occurs when she reflects on her encounter long after the war with a man whose life she had saved after he and a group of other Jews had been tied together and thrown into the icy Danube by members of the fascist Arrow Cross. During her archived interview she expresses amazement not only that she had survived her dive into the river to rescue victims, but also at such a chance encounter, so many years after that event: "Because you know, after a while, you don't believe it yourself because years going by and I was sick and it [the river] was frozen. But I was the only woman. So, and that is a life. And I thought it was a wonderful life and I am glad I lived through it."[156]

This comment ends Agnes's official testimony. As in the earlier examples, the camera then captures a seemingly off-tape exchange omitted from the typed, catalogued transcript. In that moment, Agnes turns to the interviewer for her response to the testimony:

AGNES: Well, how was it?
INTERVIEWER: Fine. (Delayed pause followed by a sigh). Never before have I, Bonnie (addressing her assistant) I hope we are off tape. I have never felt so much like screaming.
AGNES: Well, why didn't you?[157]

The videotape then abruptly cuts away from this "off-the-record" moment to the "official" photo and document-sharing segment of the testimony. It is a striking exchange on many levels, but most relevant here is how it reveals the Holocaust Museum's approach to representing the workings of testimony. The closing dialogue appears as a breach in the museum's preferred mode of interviewing, laying bare for one brief moment the mediated and calibrated underpinnings of the testimony. It also shows how the museum searches out the deep reflections of Holocaust memory, all the while attempting to keep at the margins the processes of testimonial production and reception that mark their transmission. In this moment, the interviewer withholds and then silences any official traces of her own emotional investment in the process. Analytical sobriety rather than a mutual exchange of pathos take precedence, and consequently one of the most revealing parts of Agnes's testimony is kept at the periphery. That moment, which documents not only *what* Agnes recalls but also *how* she recalls it and the impact that it has on those receiving her account—representing James Young's notion of "received history"—is relegated to the realm of "technical conversation" in the library transcript and later to the cutting room floor for the film.[158] During her interview and in *Testimony,* Agnes's historically exceptional and heroic work for Wallenberg is given precedence, obscuring the traces of the emotional and psychological labor shared between interviewer and interviewee.[159] However, the interviewer's dogged insistence on keeping her visceral reactions off the official record ultimately brings to light the tensions that can emerge between the agency of a witness and the agenda of an institution.

Although *Testimony* rarely speaks to the more rupturing aspects of the interview process, it does reveal other dimensions of testimonies that often remain isolated and unseen within the archive. The film screening of archived witnesses is important in making possible, if in a limited way, the entry of selected accounts into the more public space of the museum, thus in a sense activating their commemorative potential. This extends to something as fundamental as including a recovered photograph or personal artifact into the body of the film. For instance, *Testimony*'s use of a photograph of Abe M.'s father is integral, not only to restoring an image of a loved one, but also to understanding the story of Abe's survival. Namely, in his testimony Abe, a Lithuanian Jew, recalls how he was saved from selection for execution only because he closely resembled his father, who along with the family had been spared due to a personal connection to one of the SS officers. As the officer had no firsthand knowledge of the family, only Abe's appearance could verify that he was in fact his father's son.[160]

Testimony's thematic, narrative, and formal structure attempts to forge pedagogical and dramatic coherence from the testimonies of archived witnesses. The film essentially evokes the presentational form adopted in the archived testimonies, but adds an authoritative voice-over, familiar from "talking head" documentaries. This narration in turn serves an expositional and thematic purpose by introducing larger historical contours and backgrounds, effectively creating a transition to individual witnesses whose stories will exemplify those themes. Thus, a voice-over introduces the theme of resistance: "Many Jews were part of the underground resistance in France. False identity papers were critical to survive."[161] The film then cuts to an interview with Leo B., a Viennese Jew who worked on false identity cards for the French Resistance.

However, a review of Leo's archived testimony seems to provide a counterpoint to its filmed iteration. In both versions, Leo is a strikingly urbane, articulate, and charismatic figure, with dark, handsome features and a youthful yet elegant appearance. However, his original testimony reveals an intense vulnerability and depth of reflection that is not nearly as prevalent in the film. For instance, the film does not recreate the moment from his archived interview when Leo wells up with emotion as he discusses going into therapy after the war. He sighs deeply and in a hushed voice struggles to put his words together as he wipes away tears, recalling his mother's decision to send him away to Belgium:

> My mother was very much bent on sending me away and frankly, it is constantly a source of guilt for me, to know that she had sent me away and they couldn't do it. But then when I consulted a psychiatrist, because I didn't want to have to live with feelings such as these, he confirmed to me that: "Would your mother be able to speak today, she would still say . . . she was glad she did it." I'm breaking down because she never had a chance in life. She and my sisters and fifty-five others of my family never had a chance in life. . . . She was instrumental in saving my life.[162]

Leo's remarks demonstrate how this unbearable memory continues to shape his postwar life. He shares this story in the first third of his testimony, thus in proper sequence, but its shattering legacy of guilt takes him forward to the aftermath of the Holocaust. Rather than extending discussion of the pivotal issue of this trauma, the interviewer intervenes to keep the story on its narrative track:

> LEO: But, I got to get myself together to make this thing.
> INTERVIEWER: Let's pull it back. Pull it back.
> LEO: Pull it back.
> INTERVIEWER: What happened? You are now in Belgium. What did you do?[163]

On one level, this exchange illustrates both personal and institutional attempts to regulate emotion in the museum's testimonies—the attempt by both witnesses and interviewers at the Holocaust Museum to contain the excesses of trauma for the benefit of transmitting a story. The unfolding of common memory—the initiation of a narrative sequence in an effort to recall how things *were*—functions as a gateway to deep memory, marking Leo's journey back to a past trauma and revealing the interpenetration of past and present and the impossibility of keeping those temporalities discrete. Leo's reflections on guilt and the anti-redemptive aspects of traumatic memory are not of primary interest either within the archived testimony or for the testimony produced for the film. Rather, both testimonies emphasize his compelling performance of memory, his charismatic demeanor, and his dramatic and exceptional story, in particular his escape from a boxcar en route to Auschwitz. Yet, this story is one Leo has refined through public talks and in at least three different video testimonies.[164] In telling this "key" story of escape—unlike his discussion of therapy and feelings of guilt—he conveys a sense of mastery over that particular narrative that is missing in the more difficult, fragmentary encounter with the memory of his family separation.

Testimony represents Leo and other subjects as both exemplars of a broader historical experience and as witnesses to their own personal stories. They carry not only the weight of a singular trauma but also the burden of communal remembrance. At the same time, the film carefully employs contrasts and counterpoints among its multiple subjects to underscore the fact that they did not have the same options, that no single approach to survival was effective everywhere and throughout the war, and that each survivor developed his or her own perspective on their pasts. The film does not, however, present the dialogue and friction that often emerge between interviewer and interviewee. As a result, there is little indication of the process of creating a testimony that may have generated the anguished expressions and tears that we do see and hear. *Testimony* obscures the dynamic at the heart of Lawrence Langer's description of the bonds that should be forged between witnesses and interviewers who are able to draw out the subtext of traumatic narratives.[165]

The Conversion of Testimony

Like *Testimony*'s focus on "key segments" or witnesses' core experiences, as against the more labored, contested aspects of testimonial exchange, the museum's Learning Center, outside the Permanent Exhibition and Hall of Remembrance, was designed as a hands-on educational resource venue to provide new media tools to mine the most compelling aspects of testimonial memory, abstracted from the context of the interview process. Rather than encouraging the sustained viewing of testimony and an engagement with how testimony is produced and experienced in its full duration, the Learning Center was designed to stimulate user-driven explorations of digital sources. Users are encouraged to work interactively with testimonies, not watching them as individual stories so much as accessing them as bits of content subordinate to the interactive framework. In one memorandum, the Learning Center advisory committee gave explicit consideration to the interactive potential or convertibility of testimony for educational use.[166] One particular section concerned the criteria for judging a "good" testimony from an educational point of view.[167] More specifically, planners argued for the need to find testimonial segments that were filled with key terms, concepts, and historical markers. Thus, a Learning Center memorandum referred to what it called the "Peanut Butter Theory":

> What are the qualities that constitute good oral history from an interactive point of view? They are the same qualities that make good peanut butter. It should be thick, chunky, and easy to spread. Smooth peanut butter is amorphous stuff . . . what you need are chunks. In video, these are small identifiable segments that have clean beginnings and endings and which can serve some purpose out of context. . . . Is the oral history thick? Is it chunky? Is it easy to spread? Three "yes" responses lend a very powerful endorsement to conversion.[168]

Rather than arguing against all efforts to segment or instrumentalize Holocaust testimony, I contend that institutions must foster new modes of testimonial usability if interviews are to have any role beyond the archive. At the same time, approaches to disseminating footage can extend beyond a search for the useful "chunks" of information it provides, but also for the labor of testimony—at the very least, the dialogue between interviewers and interviewees—that shape the formation of testimony.

Perhaps the Holocaust Museum wished to withhold traces of mediation that might undermine the direct authority of witness testimony, a particular concern given the museum's investment in defending the historical record against Holocaust deniers. Nonetheless, this approach places an unnecessary and unrealistic burden on testimonies. In other words, testimonies cannot be reduced to "raw" history, as no such thing exists. Rather, they are elements in a much wider constellation of historical and cultural sources that include official and nonofficial documents, personal artifacts, topographical remnants, and other traces. Individual testimonies, if evaluated only on their own terms, are rarely, if ever, able to maintain traditional historical standards of consistency: they are inevitably marked by the fissures created by the extremity of events and the passing of time.

A too-close focus on the core or "key" segments of testimonies can cause archives, museums, and their patrons to lose sight of that process, in turn obscuring the ethical and socially engaged bond that must be generated between witnesses and audiences/users. Grappling with testimony in critically engaged, grounded ways, I argue, demands a close examination of form and content beyond the conventional frame of the camera and outside the institutional preferences that can guide the archive. As illustrated by the analysis of the *Testimony* film, some of the most revealing aspects of this process take place outside the boundaries of official testimony, in particular during what are often deemed "technical conversations" or transitions. The Holocaust Museum's oral history department's protocols for establishing silence and easier segmentation or "convertibility," including preferences for emotional reserve and "clean" breaks from an editing perspective, cannot suppress the emotional excesses that often manifest themselves during the course of interviews. Rather than serving as a distraction from our search for knowledge, these interruptions underscore the degree to which testimony is a shared and mediated labor.

An Exemplary Holocaust Survivor

The process of rechanneling Holocaust testimony at the USHMM extends beyond the Permanent Exhibition and the Learning Center. It also shapes how in-person presentations by living Holocaust survivors within the museum, and not only their audiovisual incarnations, reflect that institution's conceptual frameworks. The case of the survivor Nesse Godin is particularly compelling, as she is one of the museum's exemplary witnesses and a living embodiment of its attempts to calibrate the sober and emotive dimensions of testimony. One of the most active Jewish survivor volunteers working within the museum, Godin delivers talks to a diverse range of visitors including student groups, foreign dignitaries, and military personnel. And as I will examine in the concluding section of this chapter, in 2006 the museum featured her as the keynote Holocaust survivor in an official museum ceremony to call attention to the genocide in Darfur.

However, before I analyze the museum's dissemination of Godin's living presence, I want to examine how the oral history department recorded and archived her video testimony in 1989, four years prior to the opening of the museum. Her performance of memory in that original archived interview established her appeal as a witness by representing an approach to testimony favorable to the museum's larger pedagogical and commemorative aims. In that sense, the case of Godin provides a compelling example of how survivors as they are both archived and presented "in the flesh" are subjected to intertwining forces.

A Lithuanian Jew born in 1928, Godin experienced life in a ghetto, the horrors of the concentration camp Stutthof, and the unfathomable hardship of a death march before being liberated. Her archived testimony from 1989 was one of the interviews reviewed by museum staff as it shaped its oral history program, prior to the museum's opening. The reviewers assessed the interview as having "good" exhibition quality, particularly in terms of a "key segment." They annotated her report as follows: "Death March—eating undigested grain from dried cow manure," referring to a way in which Godin was able to survive the march.[169]

Despite the dramatic quality of Godin's story, her testimony for the archive and her subsequent appearances in person at the museum are noteworthy for her poised and measured speech. This is underscored in one particular moment during her video testimony, when she recalls to the interviewer, Linda Kuzmack, the Nazis' execution of a fellow ghetto resident in 1942 who was accused of smuggling bread:

> Well this man was marched in like this. He walked over to the table. He said to the two men, "Thou shalt not kill," you know in Yiddish, "I will do it myself." He hopped on the table, on the chair, they did not even have a chance like you know in some places they tie their hands back or they put cover on their face. Nothing. He hopped, he put a string of his own, the loop you know over his, the noose, whatever it's called, over his neck, and to the assassin, the Gestapo, he said, "You are not going to win a war by killing me." And somebody pushed or he pushed a chair from under his feet and I remember his body dangling like this. I remember it so. Linda, it was terrible times. You know, I always try to control myself, not to be too emotional because otherwise if I get too emotional, I cannot bring the message. You know, you know, this [is] what people have to think about.[170]

The reader of this transcription misses the intensely visual and aural dimensions found on the video. Nesse gestures throughout the description, using her hands to mimic the motions of the condemned man, tying an imaginary noose around her own neck and defiantly repeating the words: "Thou shalt not kill. I will do it myself." And then, as she begins to absorb and reflect on the tragic nature of this memory, she shakes her head from side to side in a struggle to retain her composure. She teeters on the edge of despair, almost succumbing to her emotions but ultimately pressing ahead with her story without breaking down. Godin's voice is plaintive, but she exhibits the fluency of someone who, as she informs us, has told her story several times before and has grown accustomed to negotiating its terrain.

Her remark, "I always try to compose myself, not to be too emotional. This [is] what people have to think about," speaks directly to one of the primary arguments in this chapter—that the Holocaust Memorial Museum weds the emotive, viscerally charged authority of survivor testimonies with a more sober approach to storytelling. The museum's audiovisual pedagogy is developed to evoke and yet contain the excesses of traumatic memory, enhancing the pathos of its holdings, while ultimately preventing its overflow for the sake of narrative coherence and educational transmission. Godin displays a keen awareness of this need to balance affective and analytic impulses, and that is precisely the basis of her utility as a historical interlocutor and exemplary witness for the museum. In contrast to Agnes A., who in her testimony questions the interviewer's stifling of her own emotional response to the testimony, Godin seems to embrace the sequestering of pathos, realizing that doing so serves a particular pedagogical aim.

Godin's testimony also underscores the interpretative consequences of the choice of camera shots to frame an interview. As mentioned, Martin Smith saw the face as the main site for projecting the emotional urgency of survivors, while Linda Kuzmack argued that close-ups were "too tight and too close to the neck, giving me a bit of a choked feeling."[171] In the case of Godin's testimony, however, the wider framing is precisely what captures that "choked feeling" as she reenacts the hanging of the condemned man. In that sense, the use of the medium close-up provides a limited range of representation for her gestured, viscerally charged performance of memory. If Smith's position on the matter had ultimately prevailed, our encounter with Godin's testimony would be quite different, most certainly muting the physically intense nature of her recollection. That is not to suggest that the medium-close-up utilized here and across the other Holocaust testimony archives examined in this book somehow provides adequate coverage of a witness's physical expressions. Rather, it is still a fairly narrow format that often conceals important aspects of the "business" of performing memory—the workings of the arms and feet in expressing the labor of remembrance and the corporeal traces of trauma (often in the case of tattooed arms that are mentioned by survivors but left out of the frame). Yet in Godin's testimony, movements captured on camera—including markers beyond her face—allow glimpses into the emotional and physical labor of her testimonial reenactment. Her gestures lend an intense immediacy to her story and position her as a proxy of sorts, giving voice and an embodied resonance not only to her own experience, but also to that of the hanged victim unable to tell his story.

Projecting Testimonial Authority beyond the Museum

In recent years public campaigns organized by the Holocaust Museum have shown how testimonial mediation operates both within and beyond the boundaries of its exhibition space. The first such effort was sparked by a Holocaust denial conference held in Tehran in December 2006. The seventy participants in the program, titled "Holocaust: A World Prospect," included Holocaust deniers, discredited scholars, white supremacists, and a few members of anti-Zionist ultra-

Orthodox Jewish fringe groups, all convened under the guise of "debating" the Holocaust. One of the more striking dimensions of the ensuing public controversy was the response launched by the North American survivor community. The Simon Wiesenthal Center convened a counter-program called "Witness to the Truth," a videoconference of seventy Holocaust survivors, each giving brief testimony to challenge the premise of the Tehran conference.[172]

The Holocaust Memorial Museum launched its own response by hosting a visit of local Muslim leaders, each of whom toured the Permanent Exhibition and then lit memorial candles in the museum's Hall of Remembrance. With three Holocaust survivors at their side, the Muslim clergy invoked the moral lessons of the Holocaust, calling for tolerance, understanding, and the need for relating to the suffering of others. In her address at the ceremony, Sara Bloomfield, the museum's executive director, invoked three primary forms of evidence that gave her institution the authority to address the pernicious conference in Iran:

> We stand here in this Hall of Remembrance, America's national memorial to the victims of the Holocaust. . . . And right behind us, under this eternal flame, we have the ashes from the camps, the ghettos, and from American military cemeteries for those soldiers who died in the fight against Nazi tyranny. We stand here in this building that houses millions of pieces of evidence of this crime, perhaps the most well-documented crime in human history. . . . We stand here with three survivors of the Holocaust, and with our great Muslim friends, to condemn this outrage in Iran.[173]

This response underscored how the physical remains of the Shoah, the institution's federal mandate, and the living, verifying power of the survivors converged to situate the Holocaust Memorial Museum as a public space for addressing intolerance and Holocaust denial. However, these very discourses also revealed the underlying anxiety that marked the transition to postmemory, when survivors of the Holocaust could no longer attest in person to having "been there." While recorded testimonies will preserve their accounts, their presence will inevitably be transferred to archival and commemorative institutions that are no longer able to mobilize living bodies of survivors in the cause of commemoration. The physical traces of the Shoah—the shorn hair, the human ashes, and the Polish cattle car—are becoming increasingly animated to serve the cause of giving witness in the growing absence of living subjects.

The other emblematic event emerged out of the planning of what was then called the Committee on Conscience (coc), an official department within the Holocaust Memorial Museum charged with activating the institution as a "living memorial" to confront contemporary genocides wherever they occurred.[174] The COC was mandated to employ a wide range of actions, including public programs, temporary exhibitions, and public and private communications with policy makers to address contemporary crises.[175] During Thanksgiving week of 2006, the COC sponsored a photo installation entitled *Our Walls Bear Witness: Darfur: Who Will Survive Today?* Curated by Chicago architect Leslie Thomas, using photographs from her traveling exhibit *Darfur/Darfur*, the event featured rotating images of the African genocide projected onto three panels, forty-square-feet each, on the exterior walls of the museum. Accompanied by mournful Sudanese music, the photographs presented images ranging from malnourished bodies to burning villages and heavily armed child soldiers.[176]

The large-scale projection raised a series of concerns for the COC relating to the delicate balance between representational sanitization and humanization. A handful of the traveling exhibit's more graphic images, particularly a photograph of a murdered three-year-old boy with a crushed face, were not used for fear of offending passersby. This approach was consistent with the museum's display policies, which exclude or conceal excessively graphic images behind privacy walls, particularly those of nondecomposed corpses. It also reflected the mandated guidelines for the museum's architectural design, which stated that the structure should be prominent but nonthreatening, imposing but not too disorienting. It should evoke the Holocaust but not at the expense of compromising the American narrative of the National Mall. Rather than frightening people away by the horrors housed either on or inside its walls, the Holocaust Memorial Museum should inspire a sense of awe and sanctity.[177]

The opening night of the installation was launched with a public program within the museum's Hall of Remembrance, with speeches from Andrew Natsios, who was then the U.S. special envoy to Sudan, as well as from the emblematic Holocaust survivor Nesse Godin, Rwandan genocide survivor Clemantine Wamariya, and Darfurian refugee Omer Ismail, each of whom described their respective experiences with genocide.[178] As with the museum's response to the Iran Conference, Holocaust survivors played a pivotal role in anchoring the *Our Walls Bear Witness* event. Before the opening address began, organizers asked survivors within the seated audience to stand and be recognized, prompting a steady stream of applause. Godin's presence as one of the museum's own exemplary survivors provided the crucial, authorizing link in the chain of other genocide survivors on the dais.

One of the more striking aspects of the *Our Walls Bear Witness* installation was the absence of descriptive captions accompanying the photographs projected on the outside walls of the museum. The members of the COC concurred that the large-scale, viscerally charged projections would speak for themselves.[179] But who are the children carrying guns in the photos? Which village is being destroyed and by whom? These and other questions remained largely unanswered by the installation, which appeared to be more heavily invested in drawing attention to the intensity of the suffering represented in the images than in providing historical or political exposition. This particular approach to visual pedagogy underscores the dilemma of how extreme images can be presented in ways that not only spark an emotional response but can also facilitate potential forms of analysis and action.

Nor did the role assigned to the Holocaust survivors at the event place the specificity of their individual experiences at the foreground. Neither Godin nor certainly the other Holocaust survivors in the audience provided much detail about their stories. Rather, they primarily served as personal markers of historical trauma, attesting to the paradigmatic status of the Holocaust and authorizing engagement with more recent genocides. Their symbolic presence matched the Committee on Conscience's overall approach to evoking the Holocaust.[180] Instead of drawing a direct line from the Shoah to events in Bosnia, Rwanda, or Darfur, it channeled the moral authority of Holocaust experiences through the more general rubric of genocide awareness.[181] In that sense, the COC filtered the ethical imperative of the Holocaust in ways that evaded comparisons of suffering yet still structured the moral imagination for encountering other atrocities. Within this framework, the Holocaust occupies a position as the paradigmatic genocide, one that remains on a separate register of experience, transcending comparisons. As Hyman Bookbinder, a central supporter and ad hoc committee member of the COC, remarked during debates concerning its creation, "When we identify something as genocide, we are not saying it is a Holocaust. Holocaust is still another one . . . it is another kind of destruction."[182]

While survivors' living authority is primary to the U.S. Holocaust Museum's charter as a memorial with a mission, I have emphasized how the institution has carefully and precisely managed the ways in which living and dead bodies are presented both within and outside its walls. Whether by withholding the more graphic photographs from *Our Walls Bear Witness*, shielding certain representations of destruction within the Permanent Exhibition, or isolating the overflow of emotion in its video testimonies to the realm of "technical conversation," the USHMM has carefully negotiated the delicate balance between analytic and visceral forms of address. To repeat the words of Nesse Godin: "You know, I always try to control myself, not to be too emotional because otherwise if I get too emotional, I cannot bring the message. You know, you know, this [is] what people have to think about."[183]

As Janet Walker has reminded us, there is also the frailty of traumatic memory to keep in mind—the unavoidable gaps in recollection that require that we work to reconstruct the past, not simply assume an immediate, unvarnished performance of memory.[184] In the case of the culture of the U.S. Holocaust Memorial Museum, it has expressed profound anxiety toward the vicissitudes of testimony. Ellen Blalock, whom I interviewed while she served as director of the museum's Office of Survivor Affairs, remarked to me that she was increasingly concerned with the failing memories of certain witnesses who had been enlisted to tell their stories to visitors. In response, Blalock contemplated pulling those speakers from circulation, fearing that their faltering delivery would undermine their historical credibility.[185] Therefore, just as the USHMM has struggled to preserve the original condition of its disintegrating collection of shoes and other artifacts, it also faces the daunting task of embalming the living traces of trauma. To compensate for this challenge, the museum has placed an even greater emphasis on its holdings of material artifacts and documents to lend authenticity to survivor recordings and presentations. This marks a major reversal in the flow of testimonial authority. Whereas in its early development period the museum had turned to survivors as the source for authorizing its collections, the material artifacts have now increasingly assumed that role, lending both institutional and evidentiary legitimacy to testimonies.

That is where Lawrence Langer's perspectives on testimony prove to be so instructive. He eloquently describes the painstaking processes and labor of Holocaust testimonies, underscoring that they involve not only retrieving the past but also recording the ways one retrieves that past. Interviewers and future generations who will inherit these resources must acknowledge that testimony is generated as part of a mutual, contingent process, rather than strictly privileging a static or infallible notion of memory. This principle seems to provide a foundation for constructing testimony projects as sites for cultivating that previously mentioned notion of "intuitive shared intimacy" between survivors and those who receive their remembrances.[186] In April 1991, as an outside consultant on issues of oral history at the USHMM, Langer wrote in a letter to Michael Berenbaum: "The importance of these testimonies is that if we watch enough of them, we become part of this intuitively understanding audience, not perhaps in the same way as authentic former victims, but close enough to move into the subtext of their narratives."[187] Although Langer does not delve deeply into the institutional framing of testimony, he does stress that an "intuitively understanding audience" must conduct careful analysis to detect the layered meanings of interviews.[188] As I have argued throughout this chapter, that level of examination must be extended to archival histories and practices in order to understand more fully the agency and specificity of witness accounts and the ways in which they can mesh or clash with institutional guidelines.

A closer look at individual testimonies from the USHMM calls into question the museum's expectation that testimonies necessarily serve redemptive or morally instructive aims. Prior to the museum's opening, Elie Wiesel remarked in a public address to political figures: "The survivors advocated hope, not despair. Their testimony contains neither rancor nor bitterness. They knew too well that hate is self-abasing and vengeance self-defeating. Instead of choosing nihilism and anarchy, they chose to opt for man."[189] Yet actual video testimonies often reveal resistance on the part of survivors to redemptive humanism and an aversion to structuring their story in concert with the museum's preferred agenda and its determination of what constitutes "key segments."

The particularity of individual witness experience often resides not in the foreground, but instead in suppressed or "unofficial" moments of interviews. The richness and complexity of testimony depends less on discrete content than on an integrated evaluation of *how* and *what* a witness conveys about his or her story, as influenced by media- and institution-related aspects of the recorded testimony. While analysis is crucial, it is also necessarily elusive and incomplete as survivors and other witnesses confront the challenge of both reenacting their experiences internally and struggling to translate those interior fragments into comprehensible, externalizable narrative threads. It requires, as Langer contends, a painstaking effort to detect the subtext of their experiences. In that sense, analyzing these interviews requires that very "testimonial literacy" which is at the center of this book.

Edward Linenthal has registered concern that sites like the United States Holocaust Memorial Museum as a whole privilege the increasingly instrumentalized nature of experience, rather than fostering a more direct encounter with the "moral traumas of history."[190] More specifically, he questions vicarious and appropriative encounters—ones that perhaps fulfill a thirst for horrific spectacle—rather than transformative social encounters. While he holds out hope that the Holocaust Museum has the potential to cultivate empathy and civic engagement, he worries that it will fuel voyeurism. I would argue, however, that the fissures and tensions found in survivor testimonies can in part address—if not completely remedy—those concerns. While survivor testimonies can to greater or lesser extent be subject to the narrative and didactic framework of the museum, they can also reveal personal complexities that counter tendencies toward simplistic, redemptive, and monolithic narratives. The USHMM may not promote the messier aspects of testimonies and has often worked to keep them at the periphery. However, these less unified and unifying moments often surface in between the cracks of preferred institutional discourses, and are unable to be contained by the conceptual frameworks of the museum.

THREE

The Cinematic Origins and the Digital Future of the Shoah Foundation

The Survivors of the Shoah Visual History Foundation in Los Angeles was established by Steven Spielberg in 1994, following the 1993 release of his highly acclaimed film *Schindler's List*. As mentioned earlier, this period was a particularly prolific moment for the institutionalization and popularization of Holocaust memory in the United States, especially considering not only the release of *Schindler's List* and the founding of the Shoah Foundation, but also the opening, in 1993, of the U.S. Holocaust Memorial Museum.

While it is not my aim here to offer an extensive discussion of Spielberg's film, it is necessary to recognize its operative narrative elements and how they might inform our understanding of the Shoah Foundation's Visual History Archive (or VHA). *Schindler's List* is a redemptive story cut from the cloth of classical Hollywood cinematic conventions in which a singular protagonist (in this case, Oskar Schindler) serves as the primary agent of historical change. Although certain film and media scholars such as Miriam Hansen have suggested that it constitutes a more modernist film text, its character-centered causality, linear presentation, and firm imposition of closure fit the Classical Hollywood Cinema mode of narration laid out by David Bordwell.[1] Equally pertinent, *Schindler's List* embodies Spielberg's immersive, experiential, "you-have-been-there" approach to representation and reflects his consistent interest in fostering participatory forms of reception. These points are essential, as Spielberg's film serves as a source narrative for the VHA, linking the archival project with its own narrative stakes in fostering hope and tolerance. The VHA not only constitutes an archive of diverse witness narratives, but is itself a narrativized archive embedded within a broader constellation of memorial and representational discourses, among them Spielberg's film.

Illustrating this point, the Shoah Foundation's initial website invoked *Schindler's List* as a cinematic gateway through which to access the VHA. When one arrived at the main portal for the database, a short film narrated by Anthony Hopkins appeared at the center of the screen, showing Steven Spielberg working on location in Kraków, Poland. Hopkins' narration explained how Spielberg's creation of the film and his face-to-face encounters with Holocaust survivors provided him with the central motivation for establishing the Shoah Foundation. Further underscoring the archive's debt to cinema, the foundation's moving image logo was a celluloid filmstrip with flash photographs of Holocaust survivors and victims placed within the frames. That logo, while eventually replaced, underscored the archive's origins as one of several "marketing windows" in a broader network of Steven Spielberg's work on depicting the Holocaust, including *Schindler's List* and the various interactive programs that have grown out of the Shoah Foundation.[2]

Mandate and Scope

Like the mandate that shaped the development of the U.S. Holocaust Museum, the Shoah Foundation's founders intended that it become the central repository of Holocaust testimonies in the world—an aim it has exceeded by developing the largest collection of audiovisual histories of any kind (nearly 52,000 testimonies in 32 languages, conducted across 56 countries).[3] From its inception in 1994, the Shoah Foundation set as a primary goal the collection of at least 50,000 testimonies, with the ultimate aim to digitize the interviews and make them globally available through a secure, subscriber-based interface.[4] While still in formation, the foundation developed a pilot program that, from July to December 1994, created collaborative relationships with, and received consultation from, several Holocaust organizations and testimony repositories, including the Fortunoff Archive and the U.S. Holocaust Museum, the Museum of Jewish Heritage in New York, the Simon Wiesenthal Center in Los Angeles, and Yad Vashem in Jerusalem. Around that same period, the foundation also opened up regional offices in Los Angeles, New York, and Toronto, initiated training sessions, and soon thereafter conducted interviews. In pursuing a global presence, it also developed an initial three-year plan to establish American outposts in Los Angeles, New York, Miami, and Chicago, as well as foreign sites in Canada, Argentina, France, the Netherlands, Poland, Lithuania, Belgium, England, and Australia, to name just a few of its international areas of operation.[5]

In order to create a "historically valuable archive," the VHA's project overview foresaw the need for consultation with Holocaust scholars and oral historians.[6] My analysis of internal institutional documents reveals a clear attempt by the foundation to ensure not only the popular appeal of the enterprise, but also its grounding in legitimate historical scholarship. Yet like the U.S. Holocaust Museum, the Shoah Foundation was motivated by the goal of "collecting as many varied survivor experiences as possible while there is still time."[7] Thus while the foundation invested in efforts to ensure that its institutional culture and methodology met standards of rigorous scholarship, its driving, urgent concern was to embark on the project as quickly as possible in order to reach its goal of 50,000 testimonies. The matter of determining how subsequent generations would use the interviews seemed less urgent. In the end, the push to maximize the number of testimonies came at the expense of developing a more refined methodology for conducting, cataloguing, and disseminating interviews. Subsequently, the dynamic between interviewer and interviewee—and, in turn, between the interface and its users—has had both constructive and limiting consequences.

Domesticating and Standardizing Testimonies

The guiding imperatives of the VHA produced interview and collection policies that were far more streamlined and standardized than those of the Fortunoff Archive or the Holocaust Museum. In particular, the Shoah Foundation's promotional materials stressed the comfort and usability offered by its collection and cataloguing procedures. Most interviews were recorded in witnesses' homes rather than institutional settings, and conducted by one interviewer, working with a camera operator and camera assistant using relatively affordable and easy-to-use Betacam SP video equipment.[8] Recording testimonies in the homes of witnesses rather than in studios or institutional offices reduced both costs and logistical issues; it had the added benefits of putting witnesses at ease in their own surroundings and of helping to create at least the appearance of a more intimate, relaxed conversation. The Shoah Foundation intended that recorded interviews would be easily accessed once the testimonies were catalogued according to an index of identifying keywords, subjects, and phrases, each chosen to ensure ready retrieval of the holdings.[9] Moreover, monitoring of the testimony process by a quality assurance team would ensure the consistency of interview and recording methods.

Once it began collecting testimonies, the Shoah Foundation set a goal of making the VHA available through online secure Internet2 networks through which subscribing institutions would have access to the actual Los Angeles-housed collection, as well as to books, interactive classroom materials, and documentary film and videos containing footage compiled from the archive.[10] The VHA recorded its first testimony in 1994, and the interview process began to wind down in 1998, with most of the remaining interviews to be conducted abroad; it reached its initial goal of recording 50,000 witnesses in 1999.[11] In 2002, the VHA went online via Internet2. After recording its final testimony in 2005, the foundation focused most of its efforts on digitizing its collection and promoting its availability through subscriber contracts with various institutions, which early on included Rice University, Yale, the University of Southern California (USC), and the University of Michigan.[12] There are now more than fifty access points for the VHA located all over the world, covering nations as diverse as Australia, Israel, Poland, Canada, Germany, and Greece.[13]

It is important to note that since 2008, when the VHA was made available in the research library of the U.S. Holocaust Memorial Museum, that institution has become the central repository of Holocaust testimony in the United States since it now houses a combined collection of more than 60,000 audiovisual testimonies from both the VHA and its own oral history department. This merger of testimonial resources also means a convergence of two of the most prominent institutions of Holocaust remembrance in the world. Furthermore, having phased out its own testimony collection operations, the Shoah Foundation currently refers those wishing to give witness testimonies to the Fortunoff Archive, thus underscoring the convergences between each of the three testimonial archives featured in this book.

From the Studio Backlot to the Ivory Tower

The Shoah Foundation's move from the backlot of Universal Studios to the University of Southern California in January 2006 marked a fundamental shift in its institutional mission and culture. Through its formal integration into USC's College of Letters, Arts and Sciences it became restructured as the USC Shoah Foundation Institute for Visual History and Education (subsequently having its name tweaked to the USC Shoah Foundation—the Institute for Visual History and Education). The evolution in its institutional structure and branding is significant. First, it represents a new emphasis on establishing the foundation's place in a legitimate academic environment: by anchoring its endeavors in a highly regarded research university, the foundation seeks to lend scholarly prestige to its work. This connection also presents an opportunity to further develop and refine methods of mobilizing the VHA as a teaching and research resource by providing access to students and faculty within the university. It is also consistent with the foundation's movement away from testimony collection and digitization to expanding access to its holdings. This has in part been attempted through efforts to broaden the scope of its mission. The removal of "Survivors of the Shoah" from the foundation's title is not incidental, but rather reflects an effort to widen its scope by more broadly incorporating visual history. In other words, the Shoah Foundation—having accomplished its ambitious aim of compiling the largest Holocaust collection of its kind in the world—is engaging with the effort to harness the vast potential of its resources.[14]

According to Douglas Greenberg, the foundation's former executive director, the Shoah Foundation remains committed to respecting the wishes of its witnesses by protecting the proprietary integrity of their testimonies and the manner in which they are disseminated.[15] Greenberg indicated, however, that after survivors have passed away, the foundation, and not the children or relatives of survivors, will make decisions concerning the use of their testimonies and related material. To date, while the foundation holds copyrights to its recorded testimonies, it has usually deferred to witnesses, or at least consulted with them on how and where to transmit footage of their interviews. Once witnesses pass on, however, the foundation will be able to broaden its guidelines on collection usage, underscoring the extent to which, as in the cases of the Fortunoff Archive and the U.S. Holocaust Memorial Museum, the Shoah Foundation is assuming a role as an institutional body of memory.

Although the majority of VHA holdings consist of interviews recorded with Jewish survivors, the Shoah Foundation's collection also documents other categories of experiences, including those of Roma and Sinti, homosexuals, and political prisoners, to name a few. The foundation has also consulted on archival projects documenting other genocides and massacres in places like Armenia, Cambodia, Rwanda, and Nanjing, and has begun to make available testimonies from the latter two on the VHA. Nonetheless, and despite its wish to encompass broader concerns such as documenting violence and teaching tolerance in other historical and contemporary contexts, the foundation retains a commitment to maintaining the collection of nearly 52,000 Holocaust-specific testimonies as the archive's core holdings. The challenge, as Douglas Greenberg had noted, is to preserve that foundational commitment while still advancing the VHA's sustainability by making itself relevant beyond the Holocaust, or at least by making the Holocaust relevant to the contemporary moment.[16] Stephen Smith replaced Greenberg as executive director of the Shoah Foundation in 2009, and the introduction of programs such as the Witnesses for Humanity Project represented a new, more aggressive direction for the foundation in addressing transnational and transhistorical acts of genocide. However, there remain fundamental questions concerning the limits of preserving the Holocaust as a historical and methodological paradigm for other documentation efforts undertaken at the Shoah Foundation. In order to better understand those challenges, it is imperative first to consider the epistemological framework and limitations of the foundation's Visual History Archive.

Conceptual Framework

The approach to collecting testimony adopted by the Shoah Foundation adheres to the notion that seeing is believing—that one must view visual artifacts and witnesses of the Holocaust in order to grasp the implications of the events. In this regard, it is aligned with the U.S. Holocaust Museum. This investment in visual pedagogy provides the underpinnings for an immersive and emotionally fueled encounter with Holocaust history. The transformative possibilities of the VHA, however, reside not in the sheer depth of its collection, but rather in the ways in which the archive might be shaped and used as a resource. Rather than negating the archive's historical and evidentiary value, that contention calls for a more rigorous examination of how particular institutional and cultural preferences affect how the VHA represents Holocaust memories.

In order to assess how the foundation might mobilize its resources in the future, it is crucial to consider its underlying mission, epistemology, and infrastructure. As already suggested, the Shoah Foundation has emphasized the far-reaching, monumental, and authoritative scale of its endeavors. In the words of an early promotional mailer inviting witnesses to come forward and deliver testimony to the VHA: "The Foundation will create a permanent record of survivors' personal experiences before, during, and after the Holocaust. Guided by renowned educators, documentary film-makers, and experts in archival technology, this project will collect videotaped interviews from all over the world to become the largest historical archive of its kind."[17]

The invitation not only noted the unforgettable personal details that witnesses would provide, but also the proprietary integrity of the enterprise: namely, after the living witnesses had died, the Shoah Foundation would preserve the sanctity and veracity of their testimonies: "Each videotaped interview will remain unedited, preserved exactly as it is told to the interviewer. The testimonies will be made available to museums and other non-profit organizations exclusively for historical and educational purposes." Thus a testimony would become a transgenerational inheritance (the "greatest gift a survivor can give to future generations"), and copies would become part of a "family archive." Finally, the promotional brochure emphasized the VHA's mission: to "honor the past, to ensure the future, so generations will remember, speak for those who never could . . . so others always will." Such discourses demonstrate the VHA's investment in the idea that audiovisual testimonies can enable the transfer of embodied traces of Holocaust memory—the physical resonance rather than actual living presence—to generations removed from the presence of living witnesses. However, while the VHA aimed to provide future generations with voices and faces of the Holocaust, it often positioned witnesses as exemplars and illustrations of an established historical narrative. Rather than interrogating or underscoring the multivocal qualities of Holocaust histories, this tendency reinforced, or fleshed out if you will, an already established rather than open account of the events.

Interview Methodology

The VHA's collection methods were by and large crafted to capture broad strokes of history, punctuated by viscerally charged personal details.[18] There was a strong emphasis on developing a standardized testimonial framework integrated throughout the VHA's extensive pre-interview protocol and aimed to position the archive as a monumental resource available to the greatest number of users.

As noted, *Schindler's List* both inspired Spielberg to embark on his archival endeavor and provided the narrative framework that shaped the VHA's interview protocols. At the heart of the VHA's mission was its aim to capture narratives in the words of those who lived through the Holocaust. Thus an early internal memorandum entitled "Techniques for Effectively Applying Interview Methodology" affirms as follows: "The goal of the interviewer is to elicit a *narrative* from the survivor. A good testimony is one in which the survivor has a chance to tell his story *in his own words*."[19] To advance that goal, interviewers were trained "not to engage in discussion," but rather to work as guides by "asking questions that pertain to the survivor's experience." It is unclear, however, how the interviewer was to select and present questions to a witness without necessarily serving as an active partner in dialogue. The goal of generating neutral and raw accounts represents a rhetorical discourse that attempts to efface the archive's own mediating presence, whereby the interviewer "must try to get the survivor [to tell] his story *without* [the interviewer] becoming a participant in the storytelling process."[20]

Ultimately, this conception of the interview methodology contains an underlying contradiction. The Shoah Foundation's internal memorandum, as well as the interview training protocol, states firmly that the interviewer is to "ask questions that will allow the survivor to recount his life's experiences within an ordered, properly sequenced, chronological framework." While the VHA sought to extract pure testimonial accounts, it also developed practices that shaped those remembrances into coherent and accessible narrative segments. These tensions permeate many aspects of collecting and transmitting testimony at the VHA—representing an effort both to project and to withhold the archive's authoring influence and thus affecting the ethical and epistemological interplay between interviewer and interviewee, and in turn between those witnesses and potential users. Certainly, different witnesses vary in their capabilities to tell their stories in front of the camera. So it is understandable that the Shoah Foundation would institute practices that attempt to facilitate user access and comprehension. Nonetheless, such practices have profound consequences, most notably the streamlining of more fragmentary and elusive testimonies in order to condense them into bits of coherent, usable information.

Consider a section of the training memorandum advising interviewers on "Eliciting Information": some survivors might be reticent in front of cameras, or might not be "good storytellers," while others might "jump from one topic to another, compromising the continuity and chronology of the story." Underlying this concern, it appears, is the foundation's investment in maintaining a form of narrative continuity reminiscent of the traditional Classical Hollywood Cinema paradigm. Accordingly, the memorandum describes how the testimony should unfold in order to achieve that aim. The interviewer should first establish "proper structure": "a good story, in addition to having a solid beginning, middle, and end, will also have well-developed characters and be rich in detail." Any good interview will present a "cast of characters," followed by a "description of setting or background in the opening scene," from which the story unfolds into a "number of acts, each with its own series of scenes."

Thus, far from eschewing the role of storyteller-participant, the VHA created an interview protocol that mirrors a three-act dramaturgical structure. To this end, an interviewer should draft a "structure outline" for the survivor's life before, during, and after the war, each period broken down into smaller temporal and topical sections: "The point is to have an organized and detailed, chronologically structured 'map' of the survivor's experience for immediate reference" during the interview. Indeed, the interviewer would present this outline to the interviewee at least one day before videotaping, in order to guide his or her memory of events that might otherwise not be "spontaneously recall[ed]" for the recording. In addition, this process will "show him the chronological pattern of his life experiences and will make him less likely to jump from one time frame to another." While archived testimonies always involve some form of rehearsal—whether it is initiated on the part of an institution supplying a pre-interview questionnaire or an individual witness gathering her thoughts in preparation—the VHA is highly invested in molding each aspect of the process. The VHA may have intended to cede to each subject agency in entering his or her story into the record. Nonetheless, it displayed considerable initiative in attempting to render that testimony into topical and coherent sequences.

Tension also arises between the litany of questions presented both before and during Shoah Foundation interviews and in the recommendation that interviewers think of their approach as a chess match in which silence allows a witness to contemplate his or her answer without distraction. Yet this prescription seems more geared to moving the interview along anticipated narrative paths than to engendering careful attention to the unanticipated and often tangential threads of memory.

Interview Training and Assessment

The Shoah Foundation created a systematized series of training and evaluation protocols to ensure that interviewers followed the archive's preferred, standardized methodology. It is important to note that in order to accommodate the demands of a project on this scale, interviewers were chosen from various backgrounds, with no requirement for previous experience in interviewing. Each volunteer went through twenty-five hours of training that included various assessment exercises.[21] After conducting a series of training interviews, interviewers received a "Quality Assurance Self-Assessment Form" on which they were asked to rank their own interview skills on a scale of one to ten, from the lowest to the highest level of performance. Interviewers were to base their ratings on a series of factors, in particular their ability to cover each of the three main narrative segments of witness experiences (before, during, and after the war), and the degree to which they provided guidance to the witness in conveying a coherent, chronologically linear account accompanied by appropriate silences and a "balance between facts and personal feelings."[22]

In addition to instruments for self-assessment, the VHA utilized a "quality assurance team" to review official, completed tapes and provide feedback to interviewers on various techniques. The VHA incorporated this information into training protocols in which trainees watched completed testimonies in order to identify the various strengths and weaknesses. Assessment criteria for the videos largely overlapped with the self-assessment standards, including issues such as whether or not the interviewer kept the testimony moving forward and allowed for constructive moments of silence. But the exercises also included deeper analysis, particularly concerning how the interviewer sought to clarify whether certain stories recounted by the witness were experienced firsthand or were told to them by others, either during or after the war. This line of questioning reflects the VHA's commitment to distinguishing between verified and unverified history and between personal experience and collective memory. To further this distinction, the quality-assurance report emphasized that interviewers should ask questions grounded in sensory memories—the sights, smells, and sounds that are embedded in a particular set of events.[23]

Role-playing sessions in which two trainees alternated as interviewer and interviewee also encouraged novices to ask detailed questions concerning everyday life, particularly queries that prompted witnesses to reconstruct an image of the economic, cultural, and religious milieu in their respective places of origin.[24] This emphasis on what the archive categorized as "sociological questions" extended to matters such as the following: "How much salary did you receive?" or "How much did bread cost?" Such questions were also analyzed in terms of an interviewer's skill in determining how a witness came to know particular information, in order to distinguish between firsthand and indirect experiences.

In other words, the Shoah Foundation's training procedures, like the pre-interview and interview protocol, were developed to verify and anchor subjective memories, thus grounding them in established historical and sociological data. Questions about the economic life of a particular town or the weather conditions on the day of a particular deportation transport seem designed not only to reconstruct the events, but also to establish the veracity of memory by cross-referencing it against more empirically objective information mentioned in other testimonies or in historical documents. This approach also informed the final segment of the interviews, during which witnesses showed such material evidence as photographs, memoirs, and personal effects, concluding with an opportunity for family members to join the witness on camera for closing remarks.

The procedures for handling those photographs and documents called for each item to be placed on a secure stand, cropped against a black backdrop. Furthermore, the interviewer was instructed to ask the witness to remain quiet during that portion of the interview for fear of compromising the authenticity and objectivity of the material evidence presented. Rather than integrating the sharing of such material objects into the testimony's narrative—for example, allowing a witness to hold and use a photograph or Star of David badge to illustrate his stories (as has often been the case in other archives)—those articles were set aside for the final five to ten minutes of the interview. During that time the interviewer was instructed to ask the witness to identify the name, place, and provenance of each item to be entered into the testimonial record.

Pre-Interview Preparation

The Shoah Foundation's pre-interview process reveals an equal dedication to reinforcing a preferred narrative framework for the recorded testimonies. Both the pre-interview form and subsequent interview methods were designed to "present a coherent story," one that enabled survivors to "maintain the chronological order of events," while also following the preferred scenario for how their testimony would unfold.[25] The pre-interview process, which began one week prior to the interview, was preferably conducted in person, or otherwise over the phone. In addition to addressing logistical issues, this procedure aimed to build rapport between survivors and interviewers, prepare witnesses for the interview, and assist them in gathering biographical and experience-related information for a pre-interview questionnaire (referred to by the Shoah Foundation as the PIQ) more than forty pages in length.[26] The foundation's training and interview guidelines almost exclusively used the term *survivor*, rather than *witness*, underscoring the extent to which the archive project and its interview methodology—notwithstanding its many non-survivor witnesses—is focused on survivors, particularly Jewish survivors, as its central identification category.[27]

Following completion of the pre-interview questionnaire, both parties reviewed the testimony format, including its separate segments covering events that occurred before, during, and after the war. Although no limit was set on the length of testimonies, interviewers were trained to break down those segments according to a respective 20:60:20 ratio. At the same time, witnesses were encouraged to feel that they could tell their own story: "Each survivor's testimony will be their narrative, but let them know you may occasionally interrupt for clarification, or to guide and keep them focused in the interview."[28] Interviewers were also trained to ask witnesses to use the period between the pre-interview and interview stages to consider what kind of message they wished to impart for future generations, as well as to consult with family members about joining them at the end of the interview.[29] As part of this final segment, witnesses were encouraged to bring in five to ten photographs, documents, and other ephemera that corresponded with events from before, during, and after the war.

For the recording of testimonies, interviewers were strongly encouraged to ask about famous or infamous people encountered during the Holocaust: "Often survivors forget to talk about encounters they may have had with people like Eichmann, Anne Frank, Leo Baeck, etc."[30] Yet caution might be indicated, for example, with regard to memories of the Auschwitz-Birkenau selections: "Keep in mind that many survivors from Auschwitz will say that they encountered Mengele. We are particularly interested in contact other than the initial separation process upon arrival."[31] Such moments as the selections overseen by Mengele had assumed so charged a status in collective memory that they might be unreliable as evidence of historical experience. "Additional Wartime Questions" asked interviewees if they were able to escape, in an effort to identify "those people who were actually in a round-up, camp, mass grave, etc., and who escaped from them."[32] These kinds of questions aimed to pinpoint the details of witnesses' experiences, rather than to engage in dialogue with the dynamics of individual and collective remembering. Other questions were intended to identify witnesses' roles in "investigating, discovering, or documenting the results of Nazi atrocities," in particular any prior participation as interviewees in oral history projects or as witnesses at a war crimes trial.[33] In other words, the Shoah Foundation protocols helped assert the authenticity and authority of each survivor, according to his or her place in the discourses of Holocaust suffering and testimony.

In addition to their evidentiary function, the pre-interview questionnaire moves toward broader social history with census-like questions about the witness's family members and community. Topics include family origins; languages spoken at home and in the town; political affiliations; extent of religious involvement and organizational affiliations; as well as education and military service.[34] These questions then influence how the interviewer will guide the testimony. One result of the VHA's laborious and extensive preparation is a bias toward forms of knowledge that the interviewee often cannot supply, such as the dates and nearest towns of death marches and places and dates of a loved one's death. Nonetheless, these inquiries position witnesses as informants of their own and others' experiences and thus shape how testimonies are catalogued, indexed, and accessed.

Before the recording, interviewers used the pre-interview forms to refine their own research preparation and to frame suggested lists of questions in accord with the age as well as the religious, social, and economic background of each witness.[35] Interviewers were also advised to monitor a witness to determine appropriate levels of intervention and guidance. If a witness is "eloquent, forthcoming, focused, and the testimony flows," the interviewer should "listen carefully and ask very few questions."[36] But intervention was called for when a witness was unfocused or went off track, thus keeping witnesses' memories on more desired paths.

Finally, on the day of the taping, the interviewer and videographer were asked to sit down with the witness to make him or her feel comfortable with the camera and lighting and to ensure the placement of photographs and other artifacts in chronological order. The interviewer was also instructed to provide moral support: "Let the survivor get to know you. Offer reassurance the interview will go well."[37] To keep the testimony material fresh, the interviewer's role included distracting the witness from thinking about the past before the taping began. To this end, he or she was advised as follows: "Clarify to the survivor that the purpose of this project is to gather authentic stories," which will then become part of a public record.[38] At the same time, the interviewer was urged to downplay the fact that witnesses would receive copies of their testimonies as family keepsakes, out of concern that they might hold back some recollections due to fear of how loved ones might react.[39] Finally, before the cameras rolled, each witness was required to sign a Survivor Release Form explaining the terms of use of each recording. The guidelines advised: "If the survivor resists, try to ease his or her fears by explaining the use of the form," and by assuring the survivor that he or she is not signing away his or her life story.[40]

The Interview

At the start of VHA videotapes the interviewer appears in a two-shot composition sitting alongside the witness, providing his or her name, the name of the witness, and the date, city, country, and language of the interview. The camera then cuts to a one-shot composition of the witness sitting alone, initially framed in a medium shot as it moves in and stays for a medium close-up (chest-high framing) throughout the main portion of the interview. The guidelines instruct the interviewer: "The camera will be focused on the survivor for the entire interview; you will be off-camera. Be sure to sit as close as possible to the lens, at eye-level with the camera" so that the witness looks toward the camera as much as possible.[41] Barring an emergency, the camera runs until tape changes are needed or until the scheduled pause before the segment when artifacts are shown and family members join the survivor: "Since this video is being used for historical documentation, it cannot be edited. If the survivor becomes too emotional or needs a moment to collect his or her thoughts, keep the camera rolling."[42] To make any cuts beyond those necessitated by a change in tape "challenges the historical validity of the testimony and should be avoided at all costs."[43]

These guidelines speak to the foundation's investment in the appearance of objective framing and editing practices. Interviewers were instructed to keep their comments to a minimum—a goal seemingly at odds with the extensive list of agreed-upon questions for the testimony. To compensate for their off-camera location, interviewers were told to maintain nonverbal connection with witnesses through consistent eye contact, hand gestures, and body positioning, thus achieving a silent yet present role in the process.[44] The guidelines explicitly mandated that interviewers not make new notes during the testimony; they might, however, take their prepared notes into the session. As much as the archive tried to structure the process, it provided suggested responses to unanticipated "what-if" scenarios.[45] For instance: "What if I know the survivor has said something historically inaccurate; for example, a date is different from what they told me previously?—Response: Gently try to verify the correct date. Be low-key and do not argue." If a survivor is "too emotional?—Response: "Do not comfort—*listen*. Your presence and silence have allowed the survivor to reach into his or her story."[46] Interviewers were thus asked to refrain from physical or verbal attempts to comfort survivors. A silent presence would avoid minimizing the witness's suffering with insufficient words. Finally, in the event that witnesses went off on tangents, particularly if non-chronological in nature, interviewers should guide them back to the pre-formatted scenario.[47]

One of the interviewer's primary responsibilities was to make the session as "smooth" as possible, ensuring a fluid and easy-to-follow narrative progression.

"Tips and Reminders" issued for interviewers in 1996 reveal concern within the foundation that many interviewers neglected the prewar portions of the testimony. In response, training protocols expanded questions on family life, education, religious practices, and experiences of antisemitism during those years. Following the three-act structure of Classical Hollywood Cinema that the interview format in many ways mirrored, the interviewer provided the exposition necessary to set up the inciting incident of the outbreak of war and persecution, followed by the central events of the Holocaust, and then leading to a sense of resolution through discussion of liberation or other postwar experiences. Offering the witnesses the opportunity to give lessons for future generations provided a way to create the sense of closure that the VHA found critically important.[48]

Yet there is fundamental friction in the Shoah Foundation's interview guidelines between ensuring both an uninterrupted interview and the preferred archival format. Even as the guidelines affirmed that interviewers must understand "the difference between guiding and interrupting"—indeed the VHA's "Tips and Reminders" preferred the former to the latter—the foundation's effort to ensure that testimonies adhered to the VHA's three-part format made interruptions structurally inevitable.[49] Interviewers were trained to preserve narrative flow, for example, by asking questions such as "And then what happened?"[50] Although the guidelines recommend that interruptions be as gentle as possible, their imposition of a preferred institutional framework on individual expressions of memory mandates a form of narrative intervention. Training and interview protocols reflect the temporal ideal of a two-hour interview, divided into three segments of twenty-four, seventy-two, and twenty-four minutes, covering events from before, during, and after the war (accommodations were made for allowing its testimonies to exceed two hours in duration—as they often did—though with the same three-part structure and ratio).[51] This sequencing of events conflicts in some ways with a recommendation in the VHA quality assurance guides: "*Do not be judgmental. Do not assume that you know what the survivor is going to say next.*"[52] Both the pre-interview questionnaire and the prescription of a three-part interview structure increased the likelihood that interviewers would attempt to anticipate the trajectory of a testimony and hence reinforce an assumption of what should come next in a witness's story.

Yet despite the discipline it imposed on the interview process and its intent to retrieve sociological data, the VHA also sought unique personal details: "We want balance—facts of historical events and emotional texture—so that it is not purely a linear account [to] which one cannot relate."[53] Thus the VHA sought to foster unique, singular expressions of memory at the same time that it developed approaches to fit its collections into a standardized set of protocols. This meant encouraging survivors to share their emotions, allowing them to spill forth in response to questions about the fate of family members or the brutality of perpetrators. In other words, the VHA attempted to guide testimonies to be at once historically grounded and viscerally charged.

To an even greater extent than the oral history program of the U.S. Holocaust Museum imposed restraints, the Shoah Foundation trained its interviewers to withhold their own voices or expressions of emotional involvement from the testimony. The guidelines distributed to interviewers and videographers were explicit on this point, for reasons going beyond the integrity of the interview. A section titled "Taking Care of Yourself" stressed the need to keep a distance between interviewers and the stories being shared in order to prevent their own psychic damage: "The histories you are exposed to may emotionally affect you. But be aware that most people that do this type of work have developed workable ways of separating themselves from the stories they are taping. This is not a matter of insensitivity but a necessity that will prevent burn-out."[54] To avert this danger of transference, which might put interviewers and videographers at risk of becoming surrogate Holocaust victims, the VHA encouraged them to adopt mental strategies that mixed "empathy, curiosity, and objectivity," for example: "Stay in the present moment; don't get swept up in the traumatic stories you may hear"; "Remind yourself that what you are hearing happened long ago, and the person recounting these horrors has survived"; "If you feel anxious, take a few slow, deep breaths." Videographers received additional tips: "Keep focused on the technical aspects of your job. This will help calm you."[55] The most illuminating aspect of these recommendations is the VHA's focus on the wellbeing of interviewers over that of witnesses, espousing the belief that survivors have managed to escape and transcend the horrors they experienced. The guidelines for conducting interviews seem to aim directly at containing the often shattering events that surface when testimonies are shared, suggesting somehow that participants in the testimony process can compartmentalize the technical, emotional, and historical streams of remembrance.

Although each VHA testimony varies in terms of the witness's identity and experience, interviews examined here always followed set types of questions. For the prewar period, each survivor is asked basic biographical information, such as current name (and its spelling), birth name (and its spelling) and any nicknames, as well as date and country/place of birth and current age.[56] In addition, witnesses are asked to provide the names (with spellings) of parents and siblings in birth order.[57] This line of questioning situates survivors within the historical, spatial, temporal, and familial fields of information that constitute the project's larger archival tapestry, which can be used to reconstruct a picture of certain communities prior to the war. Witnesses, both Jewish and non-Jewish, and particularly survivors, are asked to describe in detail not only their homes and their families' religious practices, but also the homes and religious rituals of their larger communities. Further questions address the class backgrounds of those living in their immediate neighborhoods, the kinds of currency used, the books taught in class, and the texture of "typical" everyday life.[58] Subsequent questions inquire about political issues, for example, experiences with antisemitism or knowledge of Hitler's *Mein Kampf,* in order to establish a transition to the next and longest section of the interview.[59]

That second section covers aspects of persecution, life in ghettos, or exposure to other harsh treatment, including pogroms.[60] These questions are as detailed as those in the prewar section. Thus witnesses are asked to describe the hours for ghetto curfews and the password system for entering and leaving. For a picture of living conditions, the interviewer often inquires about the following: "Describe your stay in the ghetto: size/how many people lived in one apartment/ room, etc. Describe furniture/number of windows, etc."[61] Questions about domestic space are paired with larger structural inquiries, such as those concerning the organizational setup of the Judenraete (Jewish councils).[62] Very few questions allow space for witnesses to reflect on how they felt or what they thought at the time, in keeping with an emphasis on generating what the archive deemed to be historically valuable information.

Questions become more personal once the interview moves on to discussions about a survivor's deportation to concentration camps, but they still maintain an emphasis on collective experiences, for example, by asking approximately how many people were assembled for their deportation, how many were placed into boxcars, and if they or other members of the transport knew their destination.[63] Questions such as "How do you know that? What time of year was it? What was the weather like?" help connect individual experiences with larger patterns of verifiable events.[64] Questions pertaining to arrival at a camp are equally detailed:

> Who made the selection? Did you know what it meant?; Did the person doing the selection ask you any questions? Describe your answers; How close was the camp to civilian populated areas?; Were you aware of the sequence of the Jewish calendar?; How did you keep track of the Jewish life cycle?; How were people murdered?; What happened to the dead bodies?; If they were buried, where?; Who buried them?; Do you know the names of the guards/officers/commandants of the camp?; Describe their appearance/uniform/insignia.[65]

Unlike more open-ended questions, especially those of the Fortunoff Archive, which allow for relatively more fluid stories, the interventionist nature of the vha protocol employs a more linear model of narration that asks witnesses to look back on their own pasts from the distant reaches of the present. Such exchanges do not necessarily exclude the emergence of deep memory, but the structuring of questions seems geared toward eliciting responses that fit into the record of common memory—information to be indexed into a larger testimonial catalogue. A number of questions, such as those pertaining to how people at a particular time and place were murdered and their bodies disposed of, would be difficult to answer by survivors who had no direct encounters with the killing machinery. While appropriate for witnesses with forced labor experience, such questions would seem to urge many other survivors to try to reconstruct precise details from which they were removed. This is reinforced in questions pertaining to mass killings, which inquire of survivors: "What did you think was happening to you? What was your last memory before the mass killing: Smell? Touch? Sound? After regaining consciousness, what was the first sense you experienced: Smell? Touch? Sound? What was your first thought?"[66] While these questions seem oriented toward the deep memory of a near-death experience, their specificity and detail seem framed to elicit the fullest image of events, rather than to engage with a particular survivor's efforts to piece together fragments that cannot be completely retrieved or reenacted for the camera.

Compared to the U.S. Holocaust Museum and Fortunoff Archive, however, the Shoah Foundation dedicates far more substantial portions of its interviews to mining the postwar experiences of its witnesses, in particular to soliciting personal reflections on the Holocaust and obtaining intrafamilial exchanges about the legacy of these events. Questions in the initial section of the postwar interview format ask witnesses to review the fates of loved ones, to provide names, as well as the number of those who passed and those who survived. Survivors are then often asked how, after liberation, others in their new communities responded to their survival or expressed interest, or did not show interest, in hearing their stories.[67] Many of the questions pertain to the subcategory of "reflections on the Holocaust," raising such issues as the following: "How often do you think about your Holocaust experiences? Do you have dreams/nightmares? How often? Describe in detail. Have your experiences affected how you raised your children?; Did your experiences affect you in other ways?"[68]

The vha's commitment to exploring the aftermath of the Holocaust is constrained, however, by an approach that asks witnesses to compartmentalize the various aspects of that legacy—to separate which aspects of their current life are affected by the Holocaust, rather than to look at the issues as entangled. The prescribed final question of each interview—usually some variation of "What would you like to tell future generations?"—suggests a dialogue about postmemory, but tends instead to project a redemptive, didactic role onto testimo-

Reframing Holocaust Testimony

nies. Open discussions of the process of memory are prompted only after the main body of the interview is completed, when photographs and artifacts are shared and families of witnesses sometimes appear on tape. The presence of survivors' spouses, children, and grandchildren often allows frank questions to be posed about the inheritances of the Holocaust, making it possible to mediate a difficult discourse on traumatic memory.

In this area, the guidelines list such questions as these: "Did you discuss the experiences with your children? If not, why? If yes, how did they react? What would you like to say to your children/grandchildren?"[69] And to children and grandchildren: "How much of your parents' wartime experiences did you know? If nothing, why? When was the first time you heard about your parents' wartime experiences? How did it affect your relationship with your parents?" and "Did your grandparents tell you what happened to them? If not, would you like to know more about your grandparents?"[70] In some of the testimonies explored for this book, survivors resist talking openly about discussions with their children and grandchildren; in other cases, this line of questioning generates discussion that until then had apparently been absent within the family. Some of the most illuminating moments in testimonies come precisely at the intersection between archival practice and intrafamilial dialogue.[71]

Like its pre-interview and interview instructions, the VHA's post-testimony procedures train interviewers to attend to both the informational and affective demands of the process. This includes verifying the correct spelling of names and filling in gaps from the pre-interview questionnaire to ensure a complete recording of the story, as well as alerting the witness to a forthcoming call to assess his or her psychological state. To aid the post-interview recovery, interviewees received a list of survivor-related resources, and interviewers who sensed that a witness might be depressed or upset were told to alert regional coordinators who could provide assistance. Equally important, as noted before, the archive encouraged interviewer and videographer to look after their own mental health: "Be sure to plan some time for yourself after the interview to relax. The process can be intense and exhausting."[72] They were also encouraged to speak about the experience with their families and with other interviewers, as well as to keep a personal journal, so long as confidential details of the interview were not compromised. In other words, the VHA both acknowledged and anticipated the shared emotional burdens of giving and receiving testimony, and provided recommendations for constructing an affective community sensitive to the psychic implications of traumatic memory. Indeed, the underlying assumption of emotional equivalence between interviewer and interviewee positioned the former as a surrogate witness who had internalized the aftereffects of the Holocaust.

Recording Testimonies

The technical specifications for VHA videographers mirror the protocol for interviewers in their shared aim of developing a consistent, standardized approach to the form and content of testimonies. While the guidelines make it clear that the interviewer is "responsible for the content, direction and length of the interview," the videographer is to ensure that the recordings "look and sound good."[73] All videotapes were created using a professional broadcast camera, complete with zoom lens, tripod, monitor, Lowell light kit, soft box, lavaliere, and boom microphone. The goal was a "soft ¾ key look" with a backlight to provide strong separation between the foreground and background of the frame and ensure a constant source of light on the eyes of each witness.[74] To help create this look, the archive trained its videographers to find a location inside the witness's house that would provide a substantial depth of field, avoiding flat walls and shooting with a longer lens and a wide open F-Stop in order to give a softened sense of the domestic surroundings and convey a "portrait" look.[75] As mentioned, after placing the interviewer and interviewee in a medium two shot during the lead-in to the interview, the videographer framed the witness in a medium shot, usually from the knees up. Placing the witness's chair in front of the camera gave a broader sense of the surroundings. The camera then was to carefully zoom in and settle on a "comfortable close shot" (medium close-up). The guidelines caution videographers not to move beyond that point unless they are otherwise instructed: "Be sure to avoid extreme close ups. Once the close shot has been established, do not zoom in or out. Such camera moves would add editorial comment to the testimony, thereby compromising its historical validity."[76]

In striving for authentic historical information, these production practices aim to record seemingly raw footage of traumatic memory. But they fail to consider that the use of videotape and the medium close-up themselves constitute "editorial commentary." The VHA envisions the camera less as a mediating presence than as a scientific instrument capable of capturing a direct encounter with the testimonial subject. Thus, as indicated earlier, cameras kept rolling, barring emergencies and changes of tape: "*The Shoah Foundation does not edit any interview. All interviews are raw, archival footage for historical documentation and cannot be edited.*"[77] The videographers were, however, allowed and even encouraged to zoom and pan the photographs and other artifacts presented at the close of the interview. Many VHA videographers employed the Ken Burns "pan-and-scan" approach to detailing objects, which carefully places them on secure stands against black backdrops, rather than in the hands of witnesses. The VHA guidelines did, however, call for an establishing shot before moving in for more detailed coverage: "Since the photographs will also be part of the archive, they must be established as being complete, unedited, untrimmed documents."[78]

Indexing, Cataloguing, and Accessing the VHA

At every step, the VHA aimed to present a consistent and historically authentic collection of testimonies.[79] Indexers viewed testimonies and used a note-taking procedure, based on the witness's words, which allowed considerable discretion in how to characterize individual segments of testimonies; they also provided a three-paragraph overview. This initial labor-intensive indexing and cataloguing protocol—with its quota of one testimony a week per indexer—would have taken more than fifty years to complete the catalogue. New cataloguing and indexing procedures adopted in 2001 used both the hard copy of the Pre-Interview Questionnaire *and* the recorded testimony. Perhaps most importantly, if those two sources contradicted each other, the testimony would not override the questionnaire; rather, the archive would use additional information as a *supplement*—further evidence of the investment in anchoring its audiovisual testimony to a written, standardized record.

After 2001, indexers—renamed "historical content analysts"—worked with an indexing interface alongside the recorded interview. For one-minute segments of each testimony, they entered in keywords from an established list, along with people and place names.[80] The list of keywords was based on an index generated from the initial 4,800 testimonies processed.[81] A "historical content supervisor" monitored the indexing.[82] Moreover, the quota for indexing was raised from the initial one a week to one-and-one-half testimonies per day. Altogether, these reforms greatly expanded access to the archive while reducing the layers of supervision and customization. Nearly all of the VHA testimonies had been fully indexed by 2006, more than 47,000 of which were completed under the new protocol.

By removing the note-taking approach, the new indexing process reduced the amount of historical reviewing and increased the importance of the keyword list, which served as a skeletal structure for conducting individual testimonies.[83] Thus the indexing and cataloguing protocol drove the interview process, not the other way around, often at the expense of the specificity of witnesses' experiences. The archive's reliance on the PIQ as an indexing framework also influenced the interviews by privileging a linear chronology. That is to say, a testimony that follows an anticipated agenda—notably the standard sequential 20:60:20 ratio of events—is easier for an indexer to track and verify than are the tangential or associative paths of a witness's memory. The predominance of keywords relating to wartime experience is one result.

The terms for accessing the archive's catalogued holdings are as codified as its recording and indexing protocols. Before the interview, a witness had to sign a "Survivor Release Agreement" stating that the Shoah Foundation, while not owning the rights to the witness's life story, nonetheless holds the global copyrights for the recorded testimony conducted by the VHA. It is important to note that while the VHA stresses the evidentiary integrity and objectivity of its testimonies—guaranteed in particular by the eschewing of any editing *during* the recording—its Survivor Release Agreement includes language that allows for such intervention by the Shoah Foundation *after* the testimonies have been archived: "We intend to make the archive available to museums and other nonprofit institutions throughout the world which are devoted to educational, historical or similar pursuits. Consistent with these purposes, we may use the interview edited or unedited, by itself or combined with other materials, in any medium including literary, print, audio, audio-visual, computer-based or any other medium now known or created in the future."[84] According to this agreement, then, the copyright also extends to the name, photograph, likeness, voice, personal photographs, and other objects as they appear on the videotaped interview. While each of the three archives featured in this book requires witness release agreements for their interviews, the Shoah Foundation's language is much more detailed and anticipatory in specifying potential future uses of interview footage. Furthermore, in contrast to the Fortunoff Archive (though not the USHMM), the VHA database makes both the first and last names of its witnesses available, thus enabling its collections to be searched for particular names of interviewees.

All of those practices reinforce the contention that the Shoah Foundation's primary mission was to record as many testimonies as possible in order to make a widely accessible archive. This emphasis on archival access as conceptualized by the VHA—and manifested most dramatically through its extensive indexing system—places primary focus on the archive's search capabilities at the potential expense of concerns regarding witness anonymity and intellectual rights to testimonies. It also raises issues about the infrastructures that were put in place to make the VHA accessible. In contrast to the holdings of the other two featured institutions the VHA's cataloguing system is not interoperable. In other words, the metadata of the holdings, while searchable using the VHA interface through Internet2, is not universally accessible through other interfaces and thus cannot be readily cross-referenced or linked with other holdings in any standardized way. Thus it is a much more proprietary, insulated system than the MARC standardized library language employed by the Fortunoff Archive and the USHMM, even though the Shoah Foundation has promoted the accessibility of its VHA.

The non-interoperability of the VHA holdings was a subject of discussion at a meeting of university representatives who participated with the Shoah Foundation in a 2004 grant from the Andrew W. Mellon Foundation to explore the archive's pedagogical potential. In 2005 the participating institutions, which then included the University of Southern California, Rice University, Yale University, and the University of Michigan, submitted a final grant report entitled "Pedagogical and Scholarly Implications of the Shoah Foundation Archive in Research Universities."[85] Representatives of the Yale University Library, which at the time housed both the Fortunoff collection and a bank of dedicated vha interface computer terminals, advocated for extending search capabilities across both archives in order to make their respective metadata interoperable. While the vha was heavily invested in digitizing its vast collection of testimonies, the Yale representatives expressed concern that the vha's digital standard was geared toward testimonial transmission at the expense of long-term preservation. They mentioned, for example, that the Fortunoff Archive was adopting a jpeg 2,000 format with a lossless compression ratio of 3:1, which they argued was better suited for preservation without compromising access.[86]

Despite the vha's stated commitment to preservation and access, its structure was criticized for its insularity. The Yale delegation, for example, described the challenges encountered by users who had to learn the vha's unique indexing terms, rather than working with established library standards. At the very least, they argued, the Shoah Foundation should provide a map of its metadata that would give a more schematic sense of the archive's contents. Even better, they suggested, the foundation should strive to create a multi-institution shared repository of other collections, including the Fortunoff Archive.

In a 2005 addendum to the final grant report, Yale's representatives stressed their own university library's established reputation and again promoted the idea of a "shared model such as a consortium of universities running a large multi-institutional repository."[87] This would enable the vha both to meet established scholarly standards and to focus more attention on access and preservation. While Yale's ideas were generally well received at the meeting, no agreement was reached on the vha's integration into a multi-university project. The vha's search interface thereby remains incompatible with general library metadata standards. This impasse speaks to the cultural tensions between the Fortunoff Archive and the Shoah Foundation in particular, with the former advocating for a more established, collaborative approach and the latter guided by its initial focus on collecting vast numbers of testimonies. Having recorded, indexed, and catalogued those testimonies according to its unique methods, the Shoah Foundation has since had to retool its search infrastructure retroactively in order to make those testimonies more easily accessible.

The Mellon Grant participants also disagreed on the design of the vha interface, in particular the complicated procedure for accessing testimonies, beginning with a web-based interface that was only fully accessible through a secure Internet2 connection. The current version of the interface offers access to a smaller collection of testimonies associated with the Rwandan genocide of 1994 and the Nanjing Massacre of 1937–1938, with the majority of the holdings focused on the Holocaust. For that event, five search links are presented: general keywords, "experience group," "index," "people," and "places." The keyword search uses "free text," including keywords, names, and interview codes. The experience search offers eleven areas, which include "Jewish Survivors," "Roma and Sinti Survivors," and "Homosexual Survivors." The index search allows for a more structured query, using an archive-specific list of indexed terms from the USC Shoah Foundation's thesaurus. The people search is straightforward, allowing testimonies to be located by witness names. Finally, the place search enables users to locate testimonies according to geographic locations, with the option of using Google Maps to refine the query.

Depending on the experience, subsequent pages refine the search according to national identity, camp or ghetto experience, and place name. The index search accommodates a broad investigation of concepts such as "pogroms," while the more specific search first offers a set of root words, such as "psychological, emotional, and cognitive experiences," which are then organized into narrower concepts, such as "feelings of abandonment" and "decisions regarding suicide." The index search draws from a list of terms associated with one-minute-long segments of testimonies. Rather than referencing exact transcription text from an interview, it thus requires some familiarity with the VHA's vast list of keywords.

The VHA also allows users to refine their search according to the gender of interviewees, the language of the interview, and experience group, along with other criteria, which then produces a row of linkable portrait images of survivors that match the terms of the query. Once a designation is made, a final "viewing screen" appears with the testimony, and the interview—if available on the cache—begins to play. Otherwise, the searcher can enter a request into the system. An updating function provides notification when the interview becomes available. A media player is located prominently near the center of the screen, with a toolbar for playing, stopping, and tracking back and forth through the interview. Beneath the media player are various segment and index links that allow the user to access points directly in the testimony by people, terms, and concepts, such as "Life before the War" or "Selections at the Camp." There is also a biography with basic information about the survivor's experiences before, during, and after the war. In addition, a toolbar minimizes and maximizes data and allows the viewer to move between segments and to store particular searches as files for future viewing. A map also appears to the right of the viewing monitor, marking the relevant locations of events covered within the testimony.

The Shoah Foundation responded to initial critiques about difficulties in using its interface by implementing a series of changes, in particular to increase its navigability.[88] Additional funding from the Leo Rosner Foundation supported development of the previously described keyword search, which allows users to enter any text rather than relying on a set list of search criteria: "By greatly simplifying testimony searches, users can now 'surf' the Shoah Foundation archive using Boolean data, much as they do when they implement a Google search online."[89] Nevertheless, as the Yale project team pointed out in its addendum to the final Mellon grant report in 2005, the VHA interface remains outside established catalogue searching structures. Thus the recommendation stands that the Shoah Foundation redesign the interface to correspond with familiar online catalogue models that have long been established across university libraries.[90] Furthermore, unlike the USHMM, which provides typed transcripts for many of its interviews, and the Fortunoff Archive, which makes available typed finding aids with brief testimony descriptions and related time codes for each of its holdings, the Shoah Foundation provides no such resource, instead giving brief keyword listings in the scrolling biographical and keyword portions of the VHA testimony window.

Exemplary, Unexemplary, and Widely Circulated Witnesses of the VHA

The Shoah Foundation's protocols for assessing particular interviews provide additional valuable insights regarding its preferred modes of testimonial performance. The foundation bases its internal process for rating the effectiveness of certain testimonies on a scale from one to four, with four being the most "exceptional." These ratings measure primarily a witness's storytelling skills, especially his or her ability to convey "particularly vivid" details; they also track educational utility and graphic content. The archive does not publicize this ratings system; however, some staff members have used it internally, in particular for providing consultation to those interested in using testimonies to develop education programs or provide footage for filmmaking.[91] Although I was not provided ratings for every VHA interview examined here, I did obtain access to a sampling of testimonies representing the two extremes of the 1-to-4 spectrum (from lowest to highest use value). The Shoah Foundation has not extensively delineated the basis for these ratings, although they generally correspond to notions of which material and which witness is deemed most dramatically compelling and charismatic. The VHA's ratings system provides a view into the Shoah Foundation's institutional preferences, embodying an idealized vision not only of its witnesses but also of its interview methodology.[92]

Olga K.: A Case Study of a Highly Rated Witness

Olga K., a Hungarian Jewish woman born in 1926, was accorded a "4" by the Shoah Foundation for her testimony recorded on 4 June 1995. The viewer first sees her sitting in a chair, framed in a medium close-up, in what appears to be a living room adorned with a painting and bookshelves. Olga has bright red hair and incredibly fair skin, and she wears a string of pearls set against a blue print blouse. Her Hungarian accent remains thick, but her English is articulate and her voice resonates with depth and determination.

Thus, from the beginning, the video reveals Olga to be a charismatic and capable performer of the testimonial form. She delivers her early accounts of life in Hungary with an eloquence and passion that contrasts with the more dispassionate and restrained demeanor of the interviewer, who—in keeping with training guidelines—remains engaged though analytically sober throughout most of the testimony. For example, Olga recalls how she returned to her hometown from Budapest, where her family had sent her for school, not knowing that deportations were imminent. When she says she does not regret her decision to return, the interviewer asks, "You decided to go home because you thought it would be safer?"[93] Olga replies: "I would bear an insurmountable guilt today had I not been part of the deportations with my parents . . . had I been saved from the experience, it would be horrendous feeling of guilt . . . and I don't want to survive guilt, because I stayed with them to the very end." This highly emotional moment when Olga reveals the extent of her devotion to her family is countered by the more removed interviewer, who avoids entangling herself with the emotional threads of the story, preferring instead a more objective distance.

She later recounts that local gendarmes had detained her father, grandfather, and other family members and subjected them to "horrendous torture," as revealed when they returned home: "Lacerations on their bodies. They could hardly walk." The testimony resumes after a tape change, with the question: "What happened after your family was released from the gendarmes." After responding that her father considered suicide, Olga shows great physical and emotional intensity, at one point choking up, pursing her lips, holding her nose and mouth, shaking her head from side to side, facing down and away from the camera, and eventually crying.

Olga responds similarly in recalling how her childhood piano teacher had collaborated with the Nazis and even conducted sadistic gynecological searches on victims before deportations. She confronted this man soon after the war, and as she recalls this on camera, with her hands held up in the air and her voice rising, she proclaims, "How worse, how more degenerated can they get?" A prolonged pause follows, and this time Olga stares directly into the camera with a penetrating gaze, then shakes her head from side to side while pursing her lips. The interviewer's silence allows the moment to resonate. Similarly, the interviewer asks fewer questions as Olga's story advances to the moment of her camp internment, as if allowing Olga to confront what the Shoah Foundation considers to be a core Holocaust experience—the now iconic moment of arrival at Auschwitz-Birkenau.

At other moments the interviewer does intervene, following the epistemological lines of the VHA training protocols, in order to clarify how Olga obtained knowledge during an event, in this case her internment. When Olga was asked whether she herself had directly experienced torture, she recalls that one particularly cruel block elder would force prisoners to hold up heavy bricks with their hands while kneeling down on pebbles. At this point, Olga reenacts the motion of lifting her hands in the air to raise the bricks, though the restricted camera framing of the interview limits a fuller range of expression. The emotional and dramatic intensity of the moment seems to account in part for the interview's high rating, at the same time that it shows the limits of traumatic reenactment through video testimony.

While Olga's performance of her memories exemplifies the Shoah Foundation's preference for how testimony is to be personified, it also reveals the frictions generated when the seemingly tangential paths taken by the witness diverge from the approved itinerary. This is particularly so when they interfere with the interviewer's task of establishing events for the record of common memory. Such tension occurs early in Olga's testimony, when she falters in responding to basic questions about her hometown and the names and spellings of family members. At one point, the interviewer asks, "Can you tell me about your childhood and your relations to your family?" At first, she easily complies, remarking, "It was a most happy childhood, filled with . . . I'm sorry." At this point, Olga turns her head from side to side, starts to cry, and stares at the ceiling. During the rather long progression of questions, her composure begins to wear down, although her passion is still very much in evidence. She concludes her comments by stating, "Filled with love and devotion. It was beautiful." At this moment, when the interview protocol calls for entering information into the record, the weight of the endeavor seems to press down on Olga, and she can no longer keep that past at a distance. In other words, the interviewer's agenda, with its focus on detailing a coherent and chronological account of events, ends up triggering the witness's more fluid journey through the past.

Another such moment occurs during Olga's discussion of her arrival at Auschwitz-Birkenau, which she remembers vividly: "We arrived in Auschwitz on the 15th of June. It was a Thursday." "Do you know what time of the day it was?" the interviewer inquires, following Shoah Foundation protocol, which

asks interviewers to press witnesses to anchor their memories with meteoro-
logical, temporal, or spatial markers. The question sparks Olga's intense interior and exterior reenactment of events. She becomes very animated, and using
wide, sweeping gestures, many of which are obscured by the limited range of
the camera, extends her hands outward to suggest a frame through which she
is picturing events in her mind's eye—including an image of a clock that she remembers from her arrival at the camp. At this point she openly acknowledges
on camera that her memory of this clock is not perfect, that she receives it only
in fragments. But her intense physical and vocal performance mirrors the fissures of this reenacted scene. She says to the interviewer: "There is an arch, you
see, it is so recognizable, how can you miss it? And near the arch was a station
mark as far as I remember it . . . I must have seen a clock. I believe . . . I can see
the clock but I cannot place it, where I saw it, that's the problem. But I believe it
showed 7:20 AM. I think. But I'm positive it was on the 15th of June, 1944." This
exchange reveals the extent to which Olga's memory of the events is marked by
an imperfect and self-aware process of reconstruction in the moment of her retelling. Yet this juncture in the interview marks her ability to pinpoint the date
of the event in question through that reconstruction. It demonstrates, in other
words, the VHA's epistemological framework, which attempts to link particular
details in an effort to reconstitute a larger picture of events. Olga's incomplete
memory of the clock is thus able to affirm her absolute conviction regarding
the date of her arrival. The visceral charge of Olga's account seems to elude the
interviewer's efforts to establish a progressive narrative that moves toward the
selections at Auschwitz-Birkenau. And yet some of the moments that stand out,
in part because Olga insists on repeating their significance, are those points in
the testimony when she asserts that her present recollection is inevitably interpenetrated by a mental journey back to the past.

When Olga's narrative reaches her separation from her family at Auschwitz-
Birkenau, she looks down toward her lap and says, "I can see them, they are all
here." She appears to be playing the scene before her, internally, and attempting to express it through voice and gesture. She turns her hands outward at one
point, but then closes her eyes and holds her hands to her face as she fights back
tears, seeming to recognize the impossibility of making such things knowable.
The memory is for her very much alive, as she recalls her father: "And that was
the last time we heard his voice." Again, the difficulty of this remembering is
evident as she buries her head in her hands and then wipes her nose with a tissue, while keeping her head turned down and away from the camera: "It's been
fifty-one years, but it's like yesterday." For Olga, the past does not seem to be
sequestered, but rather penetrates her present, for example in her inability to
encounter German shepherd dogs or trains without thinking about the trans-

ports: "And it goes on and on, the nightmares, the reoccurring . . . it's not even reoccurring, I live with them. They are always there. I just learn to live with them. I accepted them. So did my mother and my aunt. Otherwise you can't live with it. And you have to talk about it. But I don't talk about it unless I'm asked." Nonetheless, the conceptual and methodological frameworks of the Shoah Foundation attempt, through both the chronological segmentation of events and the frequent imposition of redemptive lines of questioning, to compartmentalize the temporal units of experience rather than emphasizing how they bleed through one another.

The formal composition of the witness establishes this segmentation from the beginning. Like other interviews, Olga's begins with a wider medium shot of the subject, with the camera remaining static as she gives her vital biographical information. Once these details have been locked down, so to speak, the interviewer can proceed to the core material: "I'd like to begin by asking you to tell us something about your life before the war." At this point the camera operator racks the lens to a medium close-up, which with the exception of a few moments will be held for the duration of the interview. Like the opening series of biographical questions, the accompanying medium shot serves to establish the space and setting of the interview as the witness provides the fundamental exposition of his or her narrative. Simultaneous with the change to a medium close-up, the interviewer asks Olga for the names and spellings of several relatives and to give an account of how many people lived in her hometown. As noted, Olga goes off-track with these basic questions and eventually veers from the intended linear trajectory. The interviewer restores the proper sequence with a query about Zionist activity in her hometown. Still, there is a recurring tension during this segment between the interviewer's interest in extrapolating from Olga's experiences and Olga's own focus on experiencing her singular memory of events. Thus the interviewer interrupts her warm recollections about the layout of her house: "Okay, so in this period during the '30s . . . you started to feel increased antisemitism in the town. What did you know, you and your family . . . about what was going on in Hungary at the time and in Europe more generally?"

In the closing segment, photographs and other artifacts from Olga's life are displayed on a fixed stand, cropped against a black backdrop. Her voice can be heard just off-camera, accommodating the interviewer's request to identify the provenance of each item, in addition to listing the names of each person appearing in the photographs. As she does this, the camera pans across each image, often zooming in on particular details. It is a revealing moment not only because it mimics a particular trope of documentary representation (the beforementioned Ken Burns effect), but also because it underscores the Shoah Foundation's historiographical approach to the interview process. While the fixed medium close-up is the preferred method of achieving an objective and standardized approach to recording the witness—appearing not to mediate and hence somehow to compromise the authenticity of how testimony is performed—the evidentiary qualities of the photographs are presumed, and therefore can be subjected to the zoom, pan, and scan. In other words, while the photographs and other material artifacts are taken for granted as uncontestable evidence for the historical record, there seems to be far more anxiety about the need to anchor and fix the living witnesses through a series of protocols and regimens established from the onset of the pre-interview process.

Richard K.: A Case Study of a Lower-Rated Witness

Richard K., one of the VHA's lowest rated witnesses (at "1") was born in Strasbourg in 1912. He was significantly older than Olga at the time of his taping (19 August 1996), and his more advanced age (eighty-four at the time of the recording) seems to account in part for his far less dynamic performance. In addition, Richard is framed in a less compelling visual style: his pale skin and gray hair are accentuated as he sits in a white chair in front of white blinds, a position that fades him into the background, contributing to a drab production value. His taciturn nature underscores the colorless setting, since Richard, when pressed to recall details from his past, does so dryly and with little elaboration. Thus he early on informs the interviewer: "Well, I don't remember much about my father. It was many years ago."[94]

But in several instances, the lack of elaboration is as much a function of the interview protocol that insists, particularly early on in the testimony, on establishing answers to a series of census-like biographical questions. When the interviewer asks the simple question, "When were you born?" Richard gives us a first glimpse of his emotive, less restrained side, revealing with warmth and sadness, in tone and facial expressions, his love and nostalgia for his long-departed mother. However, rather than allow Richard to follow that associative path back toward his mother—whom we later learn was one of his central losses stemming from the Holocaust—the interviewer returns to the chronological framework of the interview, asking him to recall his earliest memory of school and family. Thus his moment of deep memory is elided by the interviewer's persistence and obscured by the framing of the recording. For, as Richard recalls with tenderness the memory of his mother, his otherwise stoic face hints at a sudden twitch of a smile, which is soon overtaken by intense grief. A tighter close-up would have better captured that expression, but the medium close-up, like the more removed nature of the questioning, leaves that moment largely unexplored by the interview.

Many aspects of the interviewer's approach seem perfunctory or ill-prepared, such as the question concerning Richard's experiences of antisemitism as a young child. It is quite possible that Richard encountered persecution growing up in Strasbourg, an area of contested territory that was returned to France with the Treaty of Versailles. However, this question lacks the flexibility that could have tailored the standardized question to this witness and his specific cultural and national background. In addition, the frequent sound of rustling pages off-camera can be heard, as the interviewer presumably flips through her list of questions, without much attention to nuance or to unanticipated directions taken by the witness. Illustrating how the VHA's focus on detail-oriented questions discourages reflective responses to the interplay between past and present, the interviewer asks Richard to discuss his father's prior marriages, and to provide the date when his father and mother first met. These queries ask Richard to provide details that he does not know and end the possibility of any ensuing flow in the interview. At certain points the interviewer helps guide the witness to his answers, often through the use of leading questions, as Richard continues to relay very little information. We eventually learn that he was able to leave Strasbourg for Rotterdam, and from there escape to Brazil, before eventually settling in Kentucky. This life history might help account for the distant quality of the interview; namely, the fact that Richard left Europe before the onset of war removed him from immediate proximity to the Holocaust. And yet, his mother stayed behind and died while interned at Theresienstadt. Much like the previously discussed case of Kurt K., whose testimony was recorded for the U.S. Holocaust Memorial Museum and extracted for the film *Testimony*, the central aspect of Richard's experience of the Holocaust was not his direct victimization at the hands of the Nazis, but rather the pain of separation from and ultimate loss of his family.

Also like Kurt, Richard eventually returned to Europe as an American G.I. He recalls with somber intensity how his brother, who also served as a G.I., came very close to killing a German soldier after the war out of vengeance for murdered family members. Yet rather than encourage Richard to elaborate on the idea of vengeance or other emotional responses to the war, the interviewer asks him to state his rank in the American Army. The cataloguing framework of the interview drives the testimony here, not allowing smaller, more emotional details to rise to the surface.

All of this is to say that the preferred framework of this interview is not aligned with what appear to be the still lingering issues from Richard's own memories. Nowhere is this clearer than when the interviewer begins to wind down the testimony and asks Richard, "How do you think your experiences after the war affected your life afterwards?" Richard had already answered that query, albeit in less direct ways, throughout the interview, whether through his moment of mixed anguish and joy over his recollections of his mother or through his foray into issues of vengeance immediately after the war. Rather than cultivating those moments, the interviewer largely followed the predetermined format, except for resorting to explicit, and in certain cases, uncomfortable questions to mine the very issues that had been neglected. In response to the interviewer's question about the legacy of the war, Richard replies, "Well, I learned how to have patience." He smiles a bit, but appears to be very tired and, seeming to recognize that the interviewer is looking for more, comments: "Well, I don't know what to say there. What do you want me to say?" To which the interviewer responds, "About losing your mother, and other family." The answers to that question had, of course, already been given, though in terms perhaps too nuanced and not explicit enough to be fit into the standardized framework of the testimony.

As the interview concludes and Richard's wife joins him on camera, the interviewer asks about his children, in a gesture toward the more redemptive strains of Holocaust memory. Rather solemnly, Richard replies that his daughter is divorced and never remarried, and that his son has never found a wife. When it comes time to share photographs of his family, the handling of this segment is much more disorganized than is usually the case with VHA interviews. There is no black backdrop or fixed stand for the pictures, and we can hear Richard bickering with his wife about the whereabouts of certain photographs. At one point, he holds up a postcard written to him during his time in Brazil, but he cannot recall any information about its origins. When the interviewer asks if he has kept any of the letters sent to him from his mother after he left home, he replies, "Yeah, I got lots of letters down in the basement." His response here echoes the scattered quality of the interview as a whole—speaking to how Richard discovers both memories and material artifacts outside the standardized grid of the VHA protocol. The interviewer, sensing an opportunity to uncover the written correspondence between mother and son, asks, "And you were able to write to her also?" to which Richard replies, "Yes, but then it suddenly ended, you know." And at just that very moment, the screen and the interview abruptly cut to black, never to resume—underscoring the incomplete and fragmented nature of the recorded testimony. Thus the interview unexpectedly ends with Richard's reference to a central aspect of his Holocaust experience—the loss of his mother— a remembrance he seems primed to explore just as the camera stops running. Although this appears to be the result of a technical failure, it nonetheless illustrates how the archive's policy of handling photographs and artifacts only at the end of interviews prevents their integration into the larger body of the testimonial narrative.

Julia L.: A Case Study of a Widely Circulated Witness

The testimony of Julia L., a Romani woman born in Germany in 1926, illustrates how the VHA reveals its representational preferences, not just through its rating system, but also by how widely it circulates and features particular survivors. Staff members of the Shoah Foundation recommended Julia's interview to me for its compelling pedagogical value in 2004, when I was a teaching assistant at USC for Michael Renov's senior seminar "Representations of the Holocaust." We subsequently incorporated her testimony into our in-class discussions. The Shoah Foundation has edited Julia's interview, along with six others, into thirty-minute abridged testimonies that serve to highlight the foundation's approach and its mission. It makes these versions, as well as suggested lesson plans for teachers, accessible through its website.[95] An analysis of her original testimony can illuminate some of the preferences and tensions that mark the exchange between individual memory and institutional documentation.

Julia's testimony, recorded on 12 November 1995, was framed in much the same way as most of the other VHA testimonies examined thus far. Its main segment commences with her sitting in a chair in her living room, with the interviewer just off to her left and adjacent to the camera. Like Olga K., but in contrast to Richard K., Julia inhabits a colorful, warm space, represented by red flowers in the background and her bright red hair, earrings, and necklace, which are further accented by her sharply patterned dress and sharp blue eyes. Julia, also like Olga, is animated and charismatic in her demeanor, and she often makes strong gestures with her hands as she articulates various points. She talks with a sense of grandeur and joy about growing up as a "Gypsy" and living in a close-knit family. Julia is quick to laugh, particularly early in the interview, but is also prone to tears as her story progresses, and she becomes choked up at recalling her close relationship with her parents and their looming separation upon arrival in Auschwitz-Birkenau.

In reaching that moment in her experience of the Holocaust, Julia vividly recalls her arrival at the camp: "We got there at night, I tell you, and all those bright lights, lights from everywhere . . . and some of them [her fellow prisoners] went this way, and some of them that way."[96] She proceeds to describe the process of delousing, tattooing, shaving, and clothing collection, and how her parents were horrified by the experience. Julia tries to move forward in her story, but the interviewer asks her to take a step back to describe what had happened earlier. Throughout the interview, Julia appears to have a strong handle on the details of her experiences and the layout of the camp. She also provides a rich texture to the telling of her story. For example, she describes being interned with other women on one side of Birkenau, but also adds how she was able to peek over the wire to the other side of the camp where she could see and hear horrific things, such as the skin-and-bones appearance of other inmates and the "screaming going out." As Julia recounts an incident when she was caught stealing food and punished with a whipping, her gestures mimic the motions of her torturer, and she describes in detail the appearance of the implement used. Julia also has a strong memory of certain dates, recalling the exact day when officials brought her in to have her bloodlines checked prior to deportation. She requires very little guidance from the interviewer and for the most part keeps her narrative clear and well composed.

The interviewer maintains a sober engagement with Julia throughout the recording, asking for clarification on particular points of information rather than developing more directly personal lines of questioning. When asking Julia about one of the rites at Auschwitz, she poses the question in these terms: "Tell me about getting the tattoo. How long did that process take?" She proceeds to ask Julia to reveal the tattooed number on her left arm, and as she presents the marking, the camera zooms in to record it while the interviewer asks her to read the digits out loud. Julia accommodates, her finger pointing to each number as she explains the meaning behind their sequence. The interviewer is heavily invested in establishing the logistical details, asking: "How long did it take to put on the tattoo?"

Critical moments arise later in the testimony when the interviewer's focus on reconstructing the details of life in Auschwitz comes into tension with Julia's memory of events. The interviewer poses the question: "When did you find out about the gassings and the crematoria, was that right after you arrived, or were you sheltered?" Julia responds by spinning her hands in the air as she describes the smoke she saw billowing in the sky: "Oh yeah, our Dad told us about that. And of course you could be aware of the situation, you could be looking around and see smokestacks . . . there was just black smoke coming out twenty-four hours a day." The interviewer seeks clarification on how Julia acquired this knowledge: "So your father told you?" to which Julia responds, "Yeah, they told us, my Dad told us, and other people too." There is some slippage in her response: she fails to fully satisfy the interviewer's query—and the archive's preference— namely to pinpoint the precise source of her information, particularly to detail what Julia had witnessed firsthand. Here Julia comments on the inability of the interviewer to comprehend the scene: "You're living with five-hundred people in one block. Let me tell you something. It's like putting, visualize yourself, can you visualize five-hundred people in so much square foot there with the open toilets . . . with the smell . . . with the bodies piling up in the back?" At this moment, Julia looks forcefully at the interviewer, asserting the vividness of her memory and the existential paradox of the experience, "You adapt. You adapt. I don't mean you survive it, but you adapt."

Rather than asking Julia to elaborate on the relationship between "survival" and "adaptation," the interviewer presses for more details about what she learned from her father: "How did he tell you?" she asks. Julia replies by mimicking how her father used his hands to delineate the layout of the camp and describe the machinery of death:

> JULIA: He told us, there is where the gas chambers are, and you
> see that smoke over there, that's where the bodies are
> burned. And he was trying to tell us that there was some
> kind of conveyor system. I have never seen it. But he said
> that on the gas thing, they opened up, because so many were
> dying there they couldn't handle them all by hand, so they
> had kind of a conveyor system in there, I imagine. And they
> got rid of so many bodies.
> INTERVIEWER: Did you ever see the conveyor system?
> JULIA: (Shaking her head in confirmation) I'll tell you, I dreamt
> about it many times. Later in life, when I was out of the con-
> centration camp, I used to dream that I see this conveyor go-
> ing, and there was little men on that conveyor, and I used
> to go half up to it, and then slid off again. It was a terrible
> dream. But lately I haven't had it. I haven't had it for years.
> But I had it for a long time, that conveyor, that screaming go-
> ing up there.
> INTERVIEWER: But did you see it, or was it just from your dad
> talking?
> JULIA: (Shakes her head in confirmation) You see it, after, we see
> it . . . when you start going on the outside working . . . you
> work around crematoriums.

Throughout this intense exchange, Julia uses her hands to imitate the movement of the conveyor belt, describing the little men falling off the belt as they made their way out of the gas chambers.

There is certainly an oscillation between what Julia saw in her dream and what she actually witnessed in real life, and the interviewer ultimately insists on having Julia clarify the nature of what she saw firsthand, what she heard secondhand, and what she imagined in her mind's eye. For Julia, however, what she dreamt, heard, and saw "in the flesh" seem entangled. In her experience, at least, the conveyor belt was and remains structurally true to her experience even if she never saw it outside of her dreams. That is to say, regardless of the fact that no such conveyor belt existed, her image of it seems to have been a founda-

tional part of how Julia structured her experience at the time of her imprisonment, including her receiving of knowledge from her father, as well as critical to
her framing her identity as a survivor. It is an experience that appears central to
her personal history, but is not one that can be easily accommodated in an official history or archival project that aims to verify the facts as they happened in
the past. The VHA protocol, which attempts to establish how information was
gathered, and then to test that knowledge against other verified events, can fall
short when it encounters expressions such as these, which reside in the emotional experiences and dream lives of survivors. While perhaps the Shoah Foundation, like the United States Holocaust Museum, is attempting to preserve the
historical record in the face of Holocaust denial, the historiography of the Shoah
is certainly strong enough to endure such nefarious, fallacious claims without
archives placing added burden on witnesses.

Those limitations also pertain to the VHA's repackaging of its testimonies
for educational programming, as exemplified by the abridgement of Julia L.'s
original testimony, which ran more than two and a half hours in length, into
a half-hour segment featured alongside other edited testimonies on the Shoah
Foundation's website. It appears in the section entitled "Living Histories," which
presents testimonies edited to fit various topical and thematic categories, each
with a corresponding set of lesson plans, biographies, discussion questions, and
other materials intended for educational use. Julia's excerpted interview appears
under the heading "Deprivation and Perseverance," and the footage is structured
in accordance with those themes.

Julia's abridged testimony hews to a strong narrative structure, which opens
with the following caption: "A member of a large, close-knit Sinti and Roma
family, Julia Lentini recounts in her testimony the persecution she and her family
experienced at the hands of the Nazis and their collaborators. The lesson's theme,
'Deprivation and Perseverance,' reflects Julia's efforts to assert her humanity
and spirit in the midst of suffering and deprivation." From the outset, then, Julia's abridged interview is given a narrative and thematic anchor, later to be reinforced through subsequent captions and post-production editing that shape her
testimony in line with those itineraries. The dissolves, in particular, quicken the
pace of Julia's delivery, leaving little-to-no space for the moments of tension, silence, and reflection found in the original footage. The edited sequencing thus
serves to advance a highlights reel of plot points and themes, rather than including such illuminating, albeit fantastical moments as Julia's dreams and remembrances of the conveyor belt. Although that imagery from her original testimony footage speaks volumes about how Julia viewed her own plight caught
in the extremity of Auschwitz, it is omitted in favor of what she saw and heard
firsthand.

This editing strategy works in conjunction with the lesson plans and other linkable educational materials that accompany the abridged interview. Intended student objectives include the aim to "generate a list of ways the Nazis and their collaborators deprived Julia and her family." In keeping with that goal, one of the suggested student activity sheets presents a random list of quotations from her testimony, which students are asked to place in correct chronological sequence in order to "demonstrate how she and her family were systematically deprived of their trust of civic officials, home/possessions." This kind of lesson only reinforces the VHA's all-encompassing effort to make testimony legible as sequence rather than as associative process—or as content that can be rendered accessible through chronological, causal, thematic segments, rather than to acknowledge that it may follow diverging paths. Such an interview arc positions witnesses as exemplars of larger historical moments—as embodiments of broader themes, whether "deprivation and perseverance" or "power and resistance."[97]

The Limits and Potential of the Visual History Archive

With the end of its active recording of Holocaust testimonies, the Shoah Foundation faces the challenge of expanding access to its extensive holdings. In part, this requires finding ways to "package" and recycle these testimonies.[98] One consequence of this development has been a marked tension between the foundation's concern with the proprietary integrity of its holdings and its acknowledgment of the inevitability over time of what Douglas Greenberg, the former executive director, refers to as "fugitive uses" of VHA testimony—that is, uses that the foundation has not directly sanctioned or developed.[99] The foundation has attempted to anticipate and regulate such uses by expanding access to the archive among a growing number of subscribing institutions. Underlying these efforts seems to be anxiety over the flow of testimony beyond the reach of institutional framing and authorship, as well as a deep concern with protecting the integrity and sanctity of witnesses' stories. Technical improvements in transmitting testimonies through Internet2 have facilitated the expansion of VHA partnerships beyond the original four universities (Yale, USC, Rice, and Michigan). Moreover, secure interfaces now give participating institutions expanded points of network access beyond the earlier format of dedicated stations housed within particular on-campus locations. This improvement addresses an earlier critique by Mellon grantees: users' discomfort at viewing intensely personal testimonies in public, often distracting settings.

These issues of access speak to the earlier discussion of the Shoah Foundation's role as a proxy for survivors who have given testimonies. Filmmakers and academic institutions wishing to screen or integrate VHA testimony into their own media work must receive explicit consent for that usage from the interviewee through the foundation. Once consent has been granted, the highly secure nature of the VHA interface is designed to ensure that any fugitive uses of that testimony are carefully regulated.[100] The question remains, however, as to how that consent can be provided in the absence of living witnesses, when the Shoah Foundation is the only remaining, albeit surrogate, authority for making such determinations. This challenge is all the more pressing given the foundation's transition away from collecting testimonies and toward making them accessible. This change of direction fulfills both the foundation's goal of expanding the educational and scholarly uses of its holdings and its mission to use the testimonies to counter contemporary bigotry, intolerance, and the violation of human rights.[101]

When considering the interview protocols of the USC Shoah Foundation, I am reminded of Raul Hilberg's remarks in Claude Lanzmann's *Shoah* (1985): "In all of my work I have never begun by asking the big questions, because I was always afraid that I would come up with small answers; and I have preferred to address these things which are minutiae or details in order that I might then be able to put [them] together in a gestalt, a picture, if not an explanation, at least a description, a more full description, of what transpired."[102] On the surface, the VHA appears to represent elements of Hilberg's approach: its interview protocol starts with small personal and sociological questions that enable the interviewer and interviewee to partially reconstruct individual and collective events. The details captured in the vast store of testimonies represent an elaborate and rich commemorative tapestry that embodies the diversities and complexities of individual and social experience.

Yet the mode of questioning practiced by Hilberg as a scholar of the Holocaust is not necessarily constructive in its application to collecting and archiving audiovisual testimonies. I am not suggesting that the VHA's interviews or those of other visual history archives be spared the same rigorous scholarship that is applied to more traditional texts such as official institutional records. On the contrary, I embrace the notion that audiovisual testimonies, as evidenced in the work of Christopher Browning, can serve as essential historical sources, often providing information that is unavailable through more traditional documents. However, in order to engage with testimonies as historical evidence, we must never drift away from questions about the particular conditions and points of mediation that shape their production. While small questions might yield valuable historical data, when incorporated in an overly instrumentalizing database, they have the potential to obscure the textures of individual memories that often work in tension between past and present, witness self-authorship and institutional intention.

As many participants in the Mellon grant report have commented, one of the central strengths of the VHA is its ability to provide access to embodied, physically performed accounts that offer dimensions not present in exclusively textual (that is to say, written) versions of events. That underscores the importance of developing frameworks for conducting and interpreting these viscerally charged and analytically inscribed resources. These may rely on bigger, meta-discursive questions to spark reflection on the processes that enable traumatic memories to be expressed. The moments of rupture and excess that often mark Holocaust testimonies cannot easily be catalogued and integrated into a search database by abstracting them from the protracted and often unanticipated labor that unfolds during the preparation for and conducting of such interviews.

The VHA framework tends to position witnesses as avatars of an already established historical record, embodying particular events and lending them authority and authenticity, but not always framing them in ways that expand the dialogue between personal memory and history writ large. The implications of the VHA's institutional preferences become increasingly pressing as the archive develops new ways of packaging testimony and anticipating its potential fugitive uses. As the Shoah Foundation forges a new institutional identity, one based on scholarly, educational, and other forms of public access, it has explored such strategies as thirty-minute edited versions of exemplary testimonies that more directly capture what it sees as the essential value of the testimony experience. And it has developed the online resource "IWitness" to give educators and students access to particular, topic-based segments of testimonies that provide "engaging and customizable multimedia activities in which students can demonstrate their knowledge and express their personal connection to the topic."[103]

But what is left out in the process of editing down an interview and rendering it as topical or "customizable"? What are the criteria not only for designating one account as "common" or "representative," but also for extracting the essential elements from that testimony? The sheer size of the VHA's holdings makes it impossible to reduce this rich source of narratives into discrete and coherent packages. Moreover, focusing attention and resources on the segmentation of testimony evades larger issues such as cultivating archives as affective communities for future generations of users, not only for witnesses giving testimonies.

Walter Reich, a professor of psychiatry and the former director of the United States Holocaust Memorial Museum, has critiqued what he perceives to be a bias in American culture toward Holocaust testimonies that favor lessons of healing and forgiveness rather than those that portray the darker, more traumatic aftershocks of the Holocaust. Without directly invoking the Shoah Foundation, he has suggested that this tendency represents the "Schindlerization of Holocaust testimony."[104] Underlying this and similar critiques is an often-unwarranted skepticism toward more popular forms of Holocaust representation, arising in part out of a concern that the rigors and complexity of Holocaust history and the experiences of its victims will be compromised. Although this is an understandable concern in theory, the "Schindlerization of Holocaust testimony"—to use Reich's phrase—while operative in some parts of the Shoah Foundation's archival framework, is regularly challenged and evaded through the individual expressions of memory housed within its VHA. As Holocaust survivors pass from the scene and the Shoah Foundation assumes a growing role as a surrogate of living memories, the richness of those sources can be preserved, even as the boundaries for their popular transmission expand. To achieve this task, it is not enough to extract the essential historical details or the raw emotive resonances of the Holocaust, as is often the preference of the VHA; we must also train our eyes and ears to detect the dialogue between witnesses and the archive—the exchanges that challenge the imposition of closure and redemption by illuminating the often contested relationship between the form and content of testimonies.

FOUR

Telling and Retelling Holocaust Testimonies

The Fortunoff Archive, the United States Holocaust Memorial Museum, and the Shoah Foundation each contain diverse and substantial collections of Holocaust testimonies, yet they have developed their own particular approaches for attempting to shape the multiplicity of perspectives documented within their archives. That mediation does not imply that an archive's intentions and structures determine how meaning is interpreted from those sources. Rather, institutional practices constitute voices of testimonial co-authorship that act in conversation with those of interviewers and witnesses.

However, as argued throughout this book, moments that capture a sense of the dialogical, mutual labor involved in testimony are often consigned to the periphery rather than to the center of the archival process. And in relegating them to the margins, archives often obscure what Beate Müller describes as the "conflicting intentions and epistemological complexities" that interviewers and archivists bring to the testimony process.[1] Individual witnesses can nonetheless deliver testimonies that exceed the intentions and methodologies of archives. We must attend to the fleeting, ephemeral, and seemingly marginal elements that flicker across screens or are left on the cutting-room floor, but that nonetheless represent unexpected and essential traces of meaning. Developing testimonial literacy involves looking both within and outside the frame of videotaped interviews.

While the previous chapters have to a large extent focused on archival frameworks and practices, this chapter underscores the mediated, dialogical aspects of individual interviews. It does so by analyzing a number of the select category of "comparative testimonies," that is, interviews delivered by witnesses at each of the three featured archives. Although I was able to identify and analyze the testimonies of at least fourteen such subjects, I will focus here on five of the most illuminating sets of interviews.[2] These comparative testimonies not only present individual, singular textures of survivors' experiences, but also reveal the framing presence of the three archives, thus drawing attention to certain conditions and possibilities for testimonies to be delivered and received against the grain of archival mandates.

This group of witnesses is exceptional in the sense that they delivered audiovisual testimonies to each of the three archives examined in this book. However, in compiling this list of interviewees I came across larger numbers of survivors who gave their testimonies across two out of the three archives, and heard several accounts of witnesses discussing their experiences giving testimonies at other archives and at schools, community groups, and museums. In other words, while the comparative witnesses are unique, the fact that they gave testimonies several times is by no means uncommon based on the interviews I examined. The identification of these witnesses has provided a rare and crucial opportunity not simply to tease out the methodologies and parameters of particular archives, but also to help foreground how individual performances of testimonies can counter or least evade the approaches of archives and interviewers. The archival mediations of testimonies, while constituting important considerations, are among many others that include the formative backgrounds, cultures, and identities of interviewees that have shaped their lives both inside and outside the archive.[3]

Lily M.: "When I start to talk about Tosha, I lose myself"

The United States Holocaust Memorial Museum

Lily M., a Lithuanian Jew, was born in 1924 and thus survived the war as a young adult. Her testimony at the Holocaust Museum on 16 October 1990—the first of her three interviews in my study—brings to light many of the issues raised earlier regarding that institution's interviewing process. For example, the ways in which interviews engage or leave unaddressed the entanglements of common and deep memory derive from particular institutional methodologies and conceptual frameworks that inform the collection of video testimony. More specifically, they reflect the museum's oral history department's emphasis on silent, emotionally disengaged interviewers who yet are delegated to keep witnesses on track with their narrative progression.

In this first interview, Lily delivers her account with dramatic urgency, as if recognizing that her time before the camera is limited and there is much that she needs to tell. The first twenty-five minutes of her two-hour interview focus primarily on her remembrances of losing her mother before the war, and how bereft she felt: "I don't have nothing. I have nothing to live anymore."[4] But the museum's tripartite interview framework, which allocates more than 60 percent of testimony to the war years, leaves inadequate time and space for experiences such as Lily's, in particular when testimonies diverge from the museum's emphasis on historical chronology. Lily's interview also reveals the museum's epistemological biases, including its focus on what witnesses saw (rather than heard). For example, the interviewer asks about her experiences in hiding while Jews from Vilno were being transported to a nearby mass-killing site in Ponary:

> INTERVIEWER: When you were in the secret room, you told us
> about, that you heard people being taken to Ponary. Can you
> tell me what you actually saw?
> LILY: Well, I . . . Me and my sister, we were lying on the floor and
> there was just a little, a little opening. It was an attic and be-
> tween the old wood, there was a very small opening. . . . You
> really had to look with one eye because we were very afraid
> that we will be noticed. And when I heard this music, this
> fiddle playing, I, I got very excited. I didn't know what kind,
> what kind of fiddle playing, so I put my eye to it and I saw
> fiddler playing in the front, in the front of the column and
> men, women, and children were taken in columns, taken
> out through the streets of the ghetto, going toward the
> gates. And I with my own eyes heard, saw the people taken
> there. The women were carrying little children and they
> were playing.[5]

As she delivers this account, Lily squints as though witnessing events through a crack, and repeatedly places her hands to her right ear, to emphasize what she heard. For Lily, the aural and visual dimensions of that experience bleed into each other. The music is both her entry into the process of witnessing and something that still resonates with her after the war. But by stressing what Lily "actually saw," the interviewer misses the experiences revealed through both audio and visual cues. The interviewer then asks, "What happened to *you*?" thus trying to move Lily away from this critical moment of witnessing in order to emphasize her own experiences.[6] But that moment of witnessing is a deeply embedded, multisensory encounter that cannot be separated from what the museum understands as firsthand experiences.

Toward the conclusion of Lily's testimony, the challenge of distinguishing personal encounters from collective experience, common memory from deep memory, is again revealed as she recounts the horrific details of a death march she herself experienced in the last days of the war:

Many times in the night when I, I get up. I get up. I wake myself up screaming and I see those young girls, frozen, falling on the snow. This is something undescribable. The, here on the cheeks, they were red, and they were just sticks. This is something that whoever wasn't there cannot believe it. And when I talk to you I think I'm telling you something that happened to somebody else because I cannot believe that I went through it and lived to tell. It was March 11, 1945. We came to a place called Kruma.[7]

Starkly apparent in viewing and listening to this segment of her testimony is the lived nature of her memory—the way the past seems to mark her everyday life, surfacing at unanticipated moments. Lily's memories of the experiences of the march seem to be difficult for her to represent as a sober historical account. She herself does not fully grasp the after-images or the fact that she was subjected to such horrors. But while she does not transmit the full details of her memories, she conjures the labor of *attempting* to reconstruct the traces. As she describes the march, her eyes open wide and she places her hands on her face to empha-size the redness of the other women's cheeks, evidently trying to capture some element of the moment in her words and gestures. As she remarks, "I cannot be-lieve that I lived through it and am alive to tell," she leans forward in her chair, clutching her chest, urging both the interviewer and the audience to absorb what she is expressing.[8] Her recounting demonstrates not only how deep memories return in ways that are often resistant to narrative framing, but also how they can place the testimonial subject in a position that entangles past and present moments. She also speaks in a collective voice that represents those who are not present to bear witness.

That emergence of deep memory can also spark remembrance of the se-quence and location of experiences, enabling the transmission of common me-mory. For instance, Lily concludes her remarks on the death march: "It was March 11, 1945. We came to a place called Kruma." The transition between these two modes of delivering her testimony—between sharing the rupturing burden of her trauma and recollecting the precise date and location of stops along the death march—is fluid. The two impulses of memory in this segment are inter-twined, not discrete, as Lily recalls and reenacts her past. However, the muse-um's library database catalogues its testimonies primarily according to historical experiences, rather than considering the larger context of how such moments are recaptured in the present. The traces of deep memory are often effaced as pri-ority is given to the more readily indexed aspects of common memory.

Lily's articulation of collective voices comes to the surface on two other oc-casions in her Holocaust Museum video. The first occurs in her discussion of her life in the Vilno ghetto alongside other young women consigned to do labor. She speaks in a hushed, almost sentimental tone, acknowledging that while life in the ghetto was incredibly difficult, some vestiges of humanity were preserved: "There were theaters, and people really were trying to survive." At this juncture, she returns to a very specific memory of "a poem that was written by one of the girls that used to walk everyday with me to the Polo barrack, and if you wanted I can read it for you." She proceeds to bring out a piece of paper and read the poem in its original Yiddish, stopping to translate it for the interviewer: "It is enough. It is enough. We have no strength to walk in our shoes on those hard cobblestones." Lily has apparently prepared for this moment, having written out this brief poem in anticipation of delivering the lines on camera. And yet while the reading was prepared, its utterance triggers something seemingly more impromptu. As she reads the lines, her voice rises with excitement as she grows more animated. We learn of the affection that she had for the friend and how, for her and her other companions, the poem was one of their few sources of comfort during their hard labor. At one point, a German guard discovered them reciting the lines:

> So right away we took this piece of paper and we put it inside you know (clutching her breast), and we were afraid because they were, they were just beating us up for no reason. But somehow girls made copies of this poem and many times we used to walk, you know, to work a bit and we used to recite it. And so in 1948, when I had a little, I came a little bit to myself, the first thing what I did I remembered the story, it was like written down in my heart. I wrote it down and I said, let me remember this.

Lily's reading of the poem on camera thus represents multiple kinds of re-enactment—recapturing not only the poem from its wartime context but also from its salvaged form, reconstructed three years after the war. She had committed the poem to her heart and memory, but she chose to write it out to fulfill her vow to herself to remember and give voice to her companions. What had earlier been something to share only with her friends is in Lily's testimony brought to light and entered into the archival record. In performing the lines, she not only gives voice to the absent, but also sheds light on the process that brings that voice to the surface. Lily's recollection does not just preserve a discrete, perfect unit of memory—not that there is such a thing. Rather, it sparks an act of remembrance that is at once spontaneous and rehearsed, singular and yet collective. It is a laborious endeavor that exhausts her physically and emotionally, and in the process disorients her. The first interview tape ends as Lily finishes reading the poem, and we can see her exhaustion as she becomes conscious of the studio around her after having been consumed by the past: "I jump from place to place," she remarks, and the camera fades to black.

At another point, Lily tells of her deportation from the Vilno ghetto to a concentration camp. She recalls passing through the gates of the ghetto, catching one last glimpse of her family home and of her childhood innocence. Then suddenly, she hears the voice of her aunt singing a beautiful lullaby-like song. Lily then proceeds to sing the song in her own melodious voice, translating the words afterwards: "Dear Vilno. Our town that we are born. Our dreams and our desires all went . . . only have and say your names. When they only have your name on our lips, we have to cry. We are dreaming about you and we are thinking about you and we cannot forget old times." Just as the recitation of the poem enabled Lily to fulfill her obligation to remember and give voice to her companions, so her singing of her aunt's song takes her back to that moment of leaving the ghetto and in the process seems to restore some semblance of her human dignity.[9]

The emergence of deep memory also helps move the narrative of her story forward, as she makes the transition from the song to her experience of being herded into a boxcar and sent to the camp. During this moment in her testimony she uses her arms to convey the confined space of the boxcar, placing both arms to her sides to express enclosure. "We couldn't even squat," she remarks as she hunches down in her chair. Upon her arrival, she recalls a smell: "And I don't know if it was my imagination, but I smelled something burning [at this moment, she rubs her left hand on her nose, closes her eyes, and sniffs the air]. And in my imagination we were, I mean not my imagination, my mind, I felt that we are taking to the crematoria."[10] Lily seems immersed in the moment, revisiting not only the vision but also the feeling and smell of the events. There is slippage in her words between what she now imagines and what she thought at the time, though she is quick to clarify her statement. Her memory is embedded in the senses, conveying how what she "felt" at the time overlapped with what she thought and imagined later in life. The entanglement of her visceral and cognitive response to events is ultimately reenacted in front of the camera during her archived testimony. And yet it is the cognitive aspects that are given priority by the museum. As Lily's testimony moves forward to her recollection of liberation, the interviewer interjects: "We have one minute. Can you tell us just very briefly where you were taken?" With that, Lily must hurriedly wrap up her story, and is unable to discuss her postwar experiences since a third tape was not issued for her interview. The central experiences of Lily's testimony, as far as the interviewer was concerned, had been recorded, and those events that continued to resonate in the present are largely left unexplored by the Holocaust Museum.

Lily gave the second of her comparative testimonies to the Fortunoff Archive's affiliate program in New York on 13 November 1990, a little less than a month after her Holocaust Museum interview. As in that case, she is framed in a medium close-up, sitting in front of the fixed camera, with the two interviewers placed just adjacent to the lens. The two interviewers introduce themselves from behind camera, but are never seen on screen. Lily strikes a strong appearance, accentuated by prominent eyebrows and bright gold earrings.

Lily initiates her description of events before the outbreak of war by remarking that she must "continue with my memories," appearing here to be guided less by a strict narrative than by a recurring flash of sounds, images, and smells.[11] She still seems to grapple with the challenges and intensity of telling her story. This is particularly evident in her description of being confined in the Vilno ghetto. With squinting eyes, pursed lips, and hands held near her face, she struggles for words: "You know, um, um, when you take away from a person their pride, and their human, it is just one more step of an animal and this was done to us." The dehumanizing aspects of her experience are at the foreground, and are given immediacy by the emotional nature of her description. At one moment, she describes the small attic hiding space that her father built for the family. She tells of hearing and seeing Jews being taken away for deportation, and as she describes the scene she holds her hand to her ear and enacts the gesture of looking through a carved-out peephole in the boards of the hideout. Lily also recalls another moment with great intensity—the hearing of a fiddle being played as forced musical accompaniment to the deportations: "It is something that will stay always with me." Although she cannot recall the precise music being played, her emotional memory of the event still resonates: "They took the dignity from the Jewish people." Here, then, it is less the accuracy of the historical details—precisely what music played during that particular deportation—and more a matter of how she integrates the memory into the emotional contours of her experience.

During this second interview, Lily continues to reenact certain memories with the same intensity registered in her prior version. Take, for instance, her recollection of being discovered and deported from Vilno. She remembers her aunt, whom she regards as a "second mother," singing a song. As in the earlier interview, she asks the interviewers if she may sing and translate the piece. The interviewer agrees, and Lily proceeds to sing in a beautiful voice: "Vilno, Vilno. This is a beautiful city—I will always remember the narrow streets, the cobblestones, the hills and the valleys of my town." In one of the most animated moments in her Fortunoff testimony, the performance of the song functions as a memorial to both a lost loved one and of a beloved city. It paints a picture of a place, but one that ultimately remains confined within the subjective vision and hearing of the witness.

Lily's memories cannot be confined to the typed page of a transcript or finding aid, but rather are embedded in her multisensory memory. Thus she recollects the selection process before Jews were placed on the trains to the camps: "And if there is the smell of death, a smell of misery, a smell of blackness, there was something in the air, the sound, I mean, the sound of destruction, you could feel it, the air was so thick with the sound of destruction. You could cut it with a knife." In the course of giving this account, Lily periodically sniffs the air and insistently holds out her hands. Her intense reenactment of this scene has the effect of foregrounding the enmeshed sounds, smells, and textures of the events. She does not so much convey a narrative account as she reenacts the events in their multisensory texture. This is echoed in her recollection of death marches in freezing conditions that cause her fellow woman inmates to collapse in the snow: "As I am talking to you, I see it before you." As she utters these words, she holds her hands out in front of her so as to frame this picture.

The intensity and emotional layers of Lily's testimony are evident in both of her first two comparative testimonies. But whereas her account at the Holocaust Museum placed greater emphasis on mining the witness's experiences for historical details, in the Fortunoff testimony—in large part as a reflection of the agency the archive accords to witnesses—Lily is given more room to perform her memories on behalf of herself and others. She thus appears to deliver her accounts in a more associative, less confined manner, often at the expense of linear storytelling.

At the same time, both of Lily's first two comparative testimonies exhibit evident ruptures between common memory and deep memory, as well as between the agenda of the interviewer and that of the interviewee. The video-testimony collections of the Holocaust Museum and the Fortunoff Archive both place an emphasis on having witnesses deliver their accounts in terms that relate to their individual histories as opposed to serving as informants of larger historical developments or collective experiences. Yet this may be an impossible challenge for certain subjects whose individual fates were intertwined with those of others, and their role as witnesses is often as much about speaking for those who are now absent as it is a matter of portraying their own individual survival. Delivering Holocaust testimony is a collective act in that it involves documenting the traces of lost traditions, communities, and individuals.

That collective voice can be heard in Lily's Fortunoff interview when she recalls how her friend Tosha at the Dunawerke labor camp had written a song that for Lily embodied one of the few traces of humanity able to persist during the war. Lily asks her interviewer for permission to sing the song, and she does so with clear warmth and fondness but also with a sense of urgency in entering this ephemeral fragment into the record. She remarks that Tosha did not survive the war but that by singing her song, "I want to just pay homage to her." Here, Lily not only pays respects to her departed friend, but also gives presence to a now absent voice and reenacts the humanity that Tosha was able to create in the camp. In so doing, she also testifies to the fact that in the face of grave dehumanization, some semblance of humanity persisted then and remains after the events. At this point in the testimony, Lily is clearly absorbed in the memory of her friend and the feelings that it invokes. The interviewer, who has largely given Lily room to explore various paths of memory, retains responsibility for imposing some structure on the testimony, and attempts to move the account back on its sequential track, "So you were still in Dunawerke?" Lily seems slightly thrown off by the question and responds, "Um, when I start to talk about Tosha, I lose myself." There is a sense here that she is startled out of her intimate, deep memory of a close companion in order to trace the narrative development of her own experiences. Toward the conclusion of her Fortunoff interview, Lily will further underscore her sense of obligation to speak for others, even at the expense of the value she places on keeping to herself: "Six million people cannot talk. I have to talk for them. I am a very private person. It is very hard for me . . . just the idea that I have to spill my guts before strangers, I can't do it, but I have to do it." The labor of testimony by Lily appears to be neither comforting nor cathartic in this interview, but rather seems to function as a way of fulfilling an obligation to others and not only to one's individual experience.

The Visual History Archive of the USC Shoah Foundation

Lily recorded her third and final comparative testimony at her home for the Shoah Foundation on 4 May 1995, almost five years after her first two recordings. She is again physically expressive throughout the interview, at one point mimicking the gestures and voice she used to say goodbye to her father as he was loaded onto a truck for deportation. "When I think of my father, this is how I see him," she says, referring to that moment of separation.[12] She seems to be preoccupied by this memory until she glances over at the camera, realizing that she is getting signs that the tape is about to conclude and transition to the next one. "I'm sorry," she remarks, apologizing for having allowed her emotions to overtake her to the point of running past the allotted time for the tape. As with the Holocaust Museum, the Shoah Foundation training instilled emotional restraint in its interviewers. There is no dialogue about the flow of emotion here, but rather an attention to shaping testimony into its sequential segments. There are considerably fewer instances in this interview, as compared to her other two testimonies, in which Lily has sung or recited poems as acts of remembrance to those who passed away. She does, however, repeat the song she learned from her friend Tosha at Dunawerke, repeating what she had said in the prior interviews, "I want to pay homage to her." Here, as in the earlier testimonies, she honors through song her responsibility to remember, and recreates a sense of the camaraderie and love that she shared with the other women in the camp. However, in line with the VHA's emphasis on the details of what witnesses saw and did during the war, there is no discussion here of the larger issue of communal intimacy. The interviewer's follow-up to the song asks, "What did you do in the slave labor camp Dunawerke?"—thereby eliding the fundamental emotive and performative contours of Lily's remembrance.

As discussed, the VHA's mandate to record names, dates, places, and other historical information that can be inscribed in the record of common memory can challenge the delicate equilibrium that some witnesses have managed to create through protracted struggle. As with past testimonies, Lily describes to the Shoah Foundation interviewer her death march from Dunawerke, during which one of her friends was shot in the face. The interviewer asks Lily for the woman's name, but she appears to be stricken with anxiety as she reencounters the memory of her dead friend through the process of giving testimony: "No. I don't remember her name. I'm just too nervous now to tell her name. But I have nightmares about her and I always see her. It is something that will always stay with me." The events in question continue to echo with her, and it is precisely that resonance and the challenge of giving testimony on camera that make it more difficult to recount certain details.

Pronounced conflicts between VHA interviewers and witnesses over those very kinds of issues emerge in many testimonies. In this case, as Lily responds to a series of questions concerning life in the ghetto, she asks the interviewer: "Can I speak about my father?" She proceeds to speak with evident love and pride about her father, a pharmacist, and his role in the community. The interviewer eventually interjects, asking Lily where her father's pharmacy was located. Lily responds, "But if you give a chance, I can tell a little bit about my father, may I?" And the interviewer replies, "In a minute, I want to ask you a couple of questions before we digress." This is but one instance where the interviewer's investment in establishing exposition and moving the narrative forward competes with the witness's firm commitment to speak about someone close to her and his life in the community—comments that are deemed to be "digressive" or insufficiently informative to the storyline.

Leo B.: "If there is such a thing as a memory, that stench is still there"

The Fortunoff Video Archive for Holocaust Testimonies

The testimony of Leo B. (born in Vienna in 1921) was recorded at the Fortunoff affiliate in Baltimore, Maryland (Baltimore Jewish Council), on 5 February 1989, in what was his first interview across the three archives. He appears on screen, framed in a medium close-up with a warmly lit office with bright orange wallpaper as background. As is the usual practice for the Fortunoff Archive, he sits in front of the camera with the interviewers just off to the side of the lens. Leo is an impressive figure. He is dressed in a sharply fitting gray suit and has a head of bright white hair. He is composed and elegant in speech and manner, and appears to be generally at ease in front of the camera. As the interview progresses, the few questions that are posed seem to allow Leo the space to dig deeper into his memories. This is particularly evident when he recalls how after making his way to France, he courageously escaped from a boxcar destined from Drancy to Auschwitz-Birkenau. Using a rancid, urine-drenched rag from the overflowing communal waste-bucket, Leo was able to free himself from the train by loosening the metal bars on the window of the car. At this moment one can detect a physical shift in Leo: his eyes widen and he clutches his hands as if grabbing the bars of the window. After a prolonged pause, he stares straight ahead at the camera, remarking: "If there is such a thing as a memory, that stench is still there. It's powerful."[13] As he says this, he holds his nose and his speech begins to stammer. He appears to be absorbing the lingering scent of this memory, while also being repulsed. Like Lily M.'s, Leo's memory is largely embedded in its multisensory dimensions. His recollections, as hard as he might try to express them on camera, are ultimately confined to his interior experience.

And yet the Fortunoff Archive, rather than imposing a preexisting narrative trajectory onto Leo's interview, grants him a greater degree of latitude to wander through his thoughts, thus revealing moments while recollecting his multiple escapes from the Nazis, when there are intersections between common and deep memory. As he recalls his and his companions' decision to plan their escape from the train leaving Drancy, he comments: "And the memories are here. And they will live forever. And we decided if we don't do something about it now, who knows, and that decision was the decision of my life. The watershed." Leo fluidly transitions from reflections on his current memory process to recollecting a monumental decision he made in the past. He is transmitting not only the content of his experiences—those moments that represent the "key segments" or historical highlights of his time during the Holocaust—but also the form of his expression, the exhausting labor of testimony. Toward the conclusion of his interview, he remarks with evident physical and emotional exhaustion: "We're making a small effort, really, but this effort comes from experience, not from hearsay, not from 'I have read this here or there,' but it is vividly in our hearts and minds and it is emotionally straining and very exhausting."

At other moments, the labor associated with Leo's testimony is shown in impromptu, off-the-record traces that highlight the shift in tone between pre-interview and interview interactions. The very beginning of Leo's testimony illustrates such a dynamic. We see and hear him talking with the interviewer and camera operator before the interview officially begins. In a tone more befitting a Borsht Belt comic, Leo tells the following joke: "You know what a woman said to her husband over a cup of coffee in the morning? She asked him, 'Darling, now that I'm gray, do you still love me?' He said, 'I loved you through five different colors, why not gray?'" You can hear the people in the studio chuckling, but then rather effortlessly, Leo composes himself and without any audible prompting from anyone, dives right into the beginning of his testimony, "My name is Leo B., I was born in Vienna, Austria." I bring up this moment to demonstrate that a witness can be a consummate performer—someone who is comfortable in front of the camera and is so intimately familiar with certain memories that he can fluidly modulate between these various modes of address in the studio. In addition, his joke, with the resulting laughter, highlights the fact that there is always an audience in the studio, one that in partnership with the witness follows the various turns in the story.

That unintentionally recorded moment breaks down the preferred "fourth wall" of testimonial production. And in doing so, it underscores the process-oriented aspects of testimony, underscoring the notion that witnesses, in reenacting their experiences before the camera, are engaging with videographers, interviewers, and their anticipated audiences. Despite the Fortunoff Archive's emphasis on privileging the agency of witnesses, the process of delivering testimonies necessarily involves an ongoing set of conversations—ones that do not necessarily speak to the core concerns of the archive. The messiness and spontaneity of the process exposed in such "off-camera" moments are as revealing of the humanity of witnesses and the dynamic of the interview process as anything captured on the official record of the testimony. As Leo's subsequent testimonies will make evident, many of his stories may be repeated, but the nature of their telling and the protocols that shape them are not always the same.

The United States Holocaust Memorial Museum

Similar moments occur within Leo B's testimony at the United States Holocaust Museum, the second of his comparative interviews, recorded on two separate dates (31 July and 28 September) in 1989. The museum does not include "off-camera" exchanges in its typed transcripts of interviews, instead leaving them marked as "technical conversation" with no further explanation or description. What often gets left out of the official record, then, is not only the human texture of the witness but also the shared nature of the testimonial process on the part of the interviewer and interviewee.

Consider, for instance, when Leo's testimony comes to a close, and the interviewer, straying from the museum's usual approach of "silent empathy," can be heard sighing, as though exhibiting some degree of physical if not emotional engagement. Sensing this, Leo remarks: "You are out of breath and so am I," thus hinting at the shared burdens involved in generating his testimony.[14] When Leo then begins to reflect on his testimony, he reveals self-doubt and insecurity: "Did that go too long with me, maybe I . . . became too verbose?" The interviewer responds: "Don't worry about it, that's fine. I'm assuming the tape is off." But it quickly becomes apparent to her that the tape is in fact still rolling, recording this unofficial exchange. The cameraman hastily racks his zoom back and the screen cuts to black before any more conversation is documented. The interviewer and videographer recognize that there has been a breach in the protocol of silent engagement and anxiously cut the moment short, out of concern that it would be integrated into the official portion of the interview. The museum's interview policies prefer that witnesses like Leo speak just about memories, not about testimonial practices.

One of the more striking aspects of this particular testimony, especially of its iteration of Leo's escape narrative, is his repetition of certain terms that he had earlier used for the Fortunoff Archive, and that he will in turn employ in his later Shoah Foundation version. The recurring themes and senses that Leo expresses across all three archives include the olfactory resonance of the urine-soaked rag. As he repeats it for the Holocaust Museum: "The stench is still up here, and it's powerful." He accompanies this statement with the gesture of holding his nose.[15] Leo even comments that "I have repeated that [the story of his escape] so often, and I don't want to over-dramatize."[16] Leo is clearly conscious of the performative, repetitious aspects of the process of giving testimony. After all, his testimonies at three different archives make him an exceptional witness. This is not meant to suggest that his testimony is somehow less genuine. The repetitions, in addition to providing the witness an opportunity to engage the narrative that has helped him to grapple with the past, also show the breaks and nuances in the prepared or otherwise more familiar aspects of testimonies.

At the same time, and consistent with the Holocaust Museum's effort to focus on what it deems to be the "key segments" of survivor's experiences, the interviewer asks Leo to focus on his dramatic story of escaping from a boxcar en route to Auschwitz. Yet Leo resists casting himself as a hero in this testimony.

Thus the museum's emphasis on what Leo did, rather than on what he experienced or felt, only serves to inhibit his deeper penetration into what he himself has characterized as an oft-told tale. While the exceptional nature of his escape narrative is dramatically compelling and no doubt foundational to his experience of the Holocaust, its value cannot be extracted out of the larger context and spectrum of his testimonial performance. Leo repeatedly denies any acts of heroism on his part: "We are not heroes. I don't even exult in the word 'surviving' because it speaks of something so, so exclusive." Rather than engaging him on what it means to survive carrying the weight of his memory, the interviewer keeps pressing him about what he did, trying to elicit details of his exceptional escape. Leo ultimately gives that account, but resists the pressure to stick to the facts and talk about heroism: "You make a hero of somebody, but that person knew deep down that here was a lot of fear."

A similar divergence between the intentions of the archive and the interviewee occurs toward the end of the interview, during the segment set aside for displaying personal artifacts. Leo's items include copies of his family's deportation documents, which he describes with particular attention to the names of his mother and sisters. He remarks: "These are the three people closest to my heart." Yet the interview transcript preserves none of his comments during the artifact-sharing segment, not even marking them as "technical conversation"—the usual practice for moments designated as falling outside the official boundaries of the testimony. As evident in Leo's case, the sharing of personal effects—in particular, photographs—often sparks deeply intense reflections on loss. Although the museum records such objects on tape—and the objects themselves are in some cases donated or copied for its collections—they are not considered part of the interview. By consigning them to a special segment at the end of the recording, the museum fails to recognize their potential for both animating the memories of survivors and serving as material surrogates for those who did not survive.

The Visual History Archive of the USC Shoah Foundation

Leo recorded his third and final comparative testimony for the Shoah Foundation's VHA on 9 November 1995. Five years after his previous archival recordings, he shows his physical vigor and charisma, but is noticeably more constrained by the VHA interview format. For this interview, Leo describes many of the same experiences almost verbatim from earlier iterations, including expressions of the guilt he felt for having survived while his mother perished. He also recounts his escape from the boxcar. While these remain emotionally intense moments, they lack the earlier immediacy of expression, and the interview protocol allows no equivalent space for Leo to reenact his memories.

Take, for instance, his account of sleeping in a barn between two cows and their manure after he escaped the transport to Auschwitz-Birkenau. His language is almost identical to that in his two earlier accounts: "And even today, as we drive through the country, I love that odor, that manure is like a perfume to me, it brings back those olfactory senses that are always important when you think back on these little moments of danger."[17] At this moment, Leo, although he has told this story several times before, appears to inhabit the scene, holding his hands to his nose, his voice filled with evident joy in this memory. But rather than work to create a space where Leo can follow that associative path, the interviewer interjects, "What happened next?" The earlier, less densely formatted approaches of the two other archived testimonies, while limited in their respective ways, nonetheless capture the sense of Leo's overflowing memory of events, rather than attempting to contain them within a standardized narrative structure. Some of the most arresting moments in Leo's testimony are precisely those that do not happen "next," but rather flow from his tangential reflections on certain events.

As the VHA testimonies conclude with the artifact-sharing segments, we are reminded of how the material traces of the Holocaust often stand in for the absence of someone with whom the object was associated. Consistent with the VHA protocol, those objects are confined to a separate, final segment of the interview. At that point—removed from his fuller account of his experiences—Leo presents an assortment of photographs and artifacts, including a yellow Star of David marked with the French word *Juif*—"the original cloth star I wore"—Leo informs the interviewer. He continues: "It has special connotation. A distant relative sewed it on my lapel. She was on the same wagon as me. She and her husband went to Auschwitz and perished. And whenever I touch this star, I think of Toni [the relative who sewed it on his lapel]." For Leo, the Star of David is a material trace, not only of his subjugation and ultimate survival, but also of a tactile encounter with a murdered family member. The texture of the star rekindles his memory of that relative, but because the archive's protocol requires that it be presented on a fixed stand, set against a black backdrop, that encounter is not more organically integrated into his testimony.

Max "Amichai" H.: "I'm an escape artist"

The Fortunoff Video Archive for Holocaust Testimonies

The testimony of Max "Amichai" H., a Dutch Jew born in 1933, demonstrates the Fortunoff Archive's relatively more open approach to witness narratives, as illustrated in the latitude with which it allows witnesses to interact with their photographs and ephemera in the course of reenacting their memories. Amichai recorded the first of his three comparative testimonies at Fortunoff's Baltimore affiliate on 12 March 1989. As evident in this interview, the possibility of generating and interpreting testimonial meaning often depends on such small yet ultimately pivotal decisions as the framing of the camera or, in this case, an archive's approach to documenting the personal possessions of witnesses.

Amichai's testimony for the Fortunoff Archive includes moments when he incorporates certain artifacts directly into the main body of his testimony. In one notable instance, when he recalls being saved by Dutch farmers who sheltered him and his family, he pulls out a children's book that he read to the young children of his hosts. From a very young age Amichai had a fondness for reading to children. And as he holds up this precious "object survivor," we get a fuller sense of the affection and humanity that characterized the dynamic between Amichai and his rescuers. The Fortunoff Archive was fairly consistent in allowing witnesses to bring documents and photographs for the entire interview, thus fostering the emergence of more impromptu moments. By contrast, the other two featured institutions relegated such objects to the concluding moments. Amichai's later testimony at the Holocaust Museum in 1990, for example, concluded with a photo- and artifact-sharing session with objects that included a photograph of the family that sheltered him and a hat made by Scottish soldier liberators. Presented on a stand and cropped against a black backdrop, they were not integrated into the main interview. Some of these objects were later donated to the museum as "object survivors"—accessories to his testimony—and there is a sense that their introduction into the tape serves a more curatorial than testimonial function.[18] We never see Amichai handling the artifacts, and his off-screen discussion of them in the museum interview is largely limited to brief accounts of their provenance.

Further distinguishing Amichai's Fortunoff interview are the ways in which he is asked to reflect on the motivations for telling his story. Having survived the war as a young child, Amichai is considerably younger than the majority of witnesses analyzed from my comparative sample. Much of his testimony recalls his time hiding with his family in a Dutch chicken coop. Amichai is careful and deliberate, to the point of distinguishing between his more reliable memories and those events he has reconstructed through second-hand knowledge. Toward the end of the interview, however, he is asked, "Why do you think it was important for you to tell your story today?" This inquiry sparks Amichai to become more animated in his gestures, and he slips into a reflection on the nature of his self-professed dual identity as a past victim and as someone carrying on an everyday life in the present: "For a long time, I had a hard time integrating my two lives . . . I dealt with these obviously terrible memories by walling them off, by saying that was then, this is now . . . I realize that I can't wall it off, that [his past] is as much a part of my life as what I have here which on the surface looks like any other city dweller."[19]

Throughout this passage, he moves his two hands apart and then together, to illustrate the merger of those two selves. Amichai proceeds to thank the interviewer for giving him the opportunity to initiate the process of addressing the interwoven nature of his past and present experiences. It is only through dialogue with the interviewer that the testimony shows the challenges of isolating common memory from deep memory.

The United States Holocaust Memorial Museum

In sharp contrast to Amichai's testimony for the Fortunoff Archive, where the entanglements of common memory and deep memory are acknowledged and fostered, his later testimony for the Holocaust Museum (recorded on 1 February 1990) attempts to disentangle those interwoven threads of memory. At one point, Amichai recalls the deportations of Dutch Jews, but finds himself reflecting on his return to the Netherlands more than forty years after the war:

> I mean the Jews were deported and gassed, but the rest of the people had a very hard time as well. And after the war, you know, I, I went back to the Netherlands for about a half a year, and one of the interesting, for me, things that I did was I joined a therapy group because I'm having a hard time living all this stuff down. And I figured, in Dutch, on the scene that might help me quite a bit. And there was some people in there my age and when I raised that this was an issue for me, the subject completely switched from all the troubles they had at home and the troubles that they had at work, and they were completely there with me, talking about the experiences in the Netherlands, because no one came off free from it. But you know the early experiences that I had for example is that the Nazis, the Germans, hard to distinguish as I say, built a wall down the center of my school. One side for the Jewish kids, one side for the non-Jewish kids.[20]

In that moment, Amichai is only able to express his remembrances of the past by interweaving them with commentary on their challenging legacy. The difficulty of coming to terms with his past is triggered by his return to the physical site of trauma in Holland and then engaged through his entrance into therapy. The flow of his trauma is not discrete from his everyday life—as he says, he cannot "live all this stuff down." His discussion moves seamlessly from the deportations, to his return to Amsterdam, and back again to the Holocaust years with his description of his school. However, rather than engage Amichai on the challenges that continue to vex him, the interviewer presses back in time, remarking: "Can you tell me a little bit about the events leading up to your departure from Amsterdam?" And thus the interplay between past and present is left at the periphery of the testimonial exchange.

The Visual History Archive of the USC Shoah Foundation

Amichai's testimony for the Shoah Foundation (his third testimony, recorded on 6 October 1995), reveals the tensions and limitations of the VHA archival methodology, particularly when it presumes certain narrative throughlines or leaves the more self-reflective elements of testimony unaddressed. At one point, Amichai, with his composed and soft-spoken demeanor, mentions his grandfather's religious practice prior to the onset of the war. The interviewer follows up, "So your grandfather, I assume, was buried in a Jewish cemetery?"[21] To which Amichai, assertively and with glaring eyes, responds: "No, he was not, he was gassed at Sobibor." The interviewer then catches his mistake, and comments, "So that's a little ahead. Let's back up then." While the exchange could be explained as a personal lapse on the part of the interviewer, I would argue that it is more indicative of the VHA interview process, which in attempting to compartmentalize testimonies often disrupts the associative flows of memory. In this case, Amichai's reflections on his grandfather are presumed to belong in the prewar section because they are expressed early in the interview framework. As it turns out, they are firmly embedded in a loss stemming from the Holocaust era.

Later in the testimony, he recalls how his Dutch rescuers advised him to lie about his identity in the event he encountered outsiders: "Mainly I was taught to lie and act stupid." He comments that he had absorbed those lessons so well that he had applied them throughout his life, "And I'm an excellent liar, I'm an excellent dodger, even today." This compels us to consider his testimony in a different light, learning as we do that Amichai has trained himself to be able to evade certain aspects of his identity. This does not undermine the overall veracity of his experience, but rather informs the extent to which he is aware of how he comes across to others, and actively shapes his story accordingly. It also speaks to his postwar internalization of the survival instinct, which even affects how he enters buildings. As he remarks, when approaching any unfamiliar structure, he first gets a sense of its layout so that he always knows where the closest exit is located: "I'm an escape artist. And an excellent liar. And it's nothing particularly to be proud of." In positioning himself as an escape artist and a performer of sorts, he emphasizes the ways in which his role as a survivor giving testimony mirrors his strategies for surviving the war in hiding—as someone who at all times is conscious of how to construct a life narrative. Yet given the VHA's emphasis on the verifiability of testimony and the presentation of objective evidence, further discussion of Amichai's internalized role as a performer is marginal to his testimony rather than central to a dialogue, and thus sidelines a revealing moment of his testimony, one that relates to the mediated nature of witnessing. As with the testimony of Julia L., explored in chapter 3, the Shoah Foundation privileges objective history over subjective, self-reflexive commentary.

Chaim and Selma E.: Intertwined Testimonies

This final section extends the analysis of comparative testimonies even further, analyzing the exchanges between two closely connected witnesses. It explores interviews with a husband and wife who delivered separate testimonies across all three archives—as well as exchanges sparked between the two survivors' family members who join them on camera at the close of one of their interviews.

Chaim E.: "I see the picture in front of me; you have to imagine something."

The Fortunoff Video Archive for Holocaust Testimonies

Through its interview and training methodology, the Fortunoff Archive places greater emphasis than the Shoah Foundation and the Holocaust Museum on asking interviewers to achieve a balance between intervention and restraint in conducting testimonies. The interview with the Polish Jewish survivor Chaim E. (born 1916) is a particularly illuminating case: not only has he given comparative testimonies, but the Fortunoff Archive identified him as an exemplary witness and has selected and edited his testimony for external circulation. In addition, Lawrence Langer chose Chaim's interview with Fortunoff for analysis in providing consultation to the U.S. Holocaust Memorial Museum.

Chaim's testimony for the Fortunoff Archive, recorded on 12 May 1986, is the first of his comparative interviews; it also features Lawrence Langer as one of the two interviewers. The video shows Chaim seated on a yellow couch, against a black backdrop. Initially, he faces the camera in a medium shot from the knees up, but eventually the camera settles in on a medium close-up, with the two interviewers sitting just alongside the lens. The camera is mostly static, but it occasionally moves in for an extreme close-up. Perhaps because this is the earliest of his comparative recorded interviews, the testimony has a less polished and more spontaneous quality. His tone and manner convey a heightened sense of urgency, as does his apparent challenge of grappling with the mediated form of this encounter. One of the most illuminating aspects of this interview, as I will elaborate, is the dialogue between him and his interviewers on the labor of testimony. Chaim comes across as forthright and insistent, if not emboldened, in significant moments of his testimony, perhaps most clearly when he comes into tension with the archive's agenda.

The testimony starts not with a question (or litany of questions) from the interviewers, but rather with his own declaration: "My name is Chaim E."[22] He then jumps right into the events of his life before the war. He communicates in large part through gestures, using his hands to emphasize certain elements of his story and periodically turning his head upward to consider particular details. At moments such as during his discussion of the Nazi occupation of Poland, the camera tries to punctuate Chaim's recollections in line with his physical gestures. For example, it moves in for a tight close-up as he echoes Langer's notion of the "choiceless choice" facing victims of the Holocaust: "You didn't have any choices. You didn't think. You were just driven to do whatever you do. You're just driven."

Using expansive hand movements, Chaim proceeds to describe the Sobibor death camp, where he was interned as a slave laborer and from which he subsequently escaped during an uprising. His gestures lend immediacy to his description of the escape and his participation in killing one of the camp guards. These gestures also underscore the manner in which Chaim's recollection of those experiences represents a form of internal and external reenactment. One sees and hears him engaging with his vision of events—turning up his head, holding up his hands—as he reflects upon what happened, but also faces the challenge of making those experiences legible to the interviewers and the prospective audience. The challenge is greater in that he must speak in English, his non-native tongue, and in terms that must be made audibly and visually accessible.

At one point Chaim comments on the inadequacy of language to convey the meaning of his experiences: "The feeling is easy to tell but hard to bring over to someone, what it means." After covering what he considers to have been the main experiences of his life before, during, and after the Holocaust, Chaim addresses the interviewers: "So that is roughly the story. If you have any questions to talk more about, I would be glad to do it, I really wouldn't know more to tell." It is at this moment, an hour and a half into the testimony, that one of the central dynamics of the interview comes to the foreground. Responding to Chaim's invitation for questions, Langer asks about the psychological aspects of being a slave laborer at Sobibor while executions went on around him: "All the time you were there you knew what was going on in Lager III. How did you manage that? Did you just block that out?" To which Chaim replies, "That is what I am trying to tell you, there is nothing you can do." Pausing deliberately to consider his words, staring upward as if to visualize his recollections, and conveying through the intensity of his voice the enduring trauma, Chaim responds:

Reframing Holocaust Testimony

CHAIM: We knew about and were sad about, but doing, we couldn't do anything. Really, the story really cannot be told. If you ask ten people and listen to their story, and ask them to tell the story back, you will get back ten different stories. Why? Because I am not so strong in the language. But even someone who is strong in language can't tell it. Only the one who lived it through knows what happened. Because the feelings that are involved in the story are not the same, you cannot tell how I felt when I found the clothes of my brother. If you ask me what I was thinking, I wasn't thinking at all, I was horrified. It is more than the other story. It is the feelings that you cannot bring out.

LANGER: Are you saying that they are alive in you, but there is no language to explain to someone else?

CHAIM: No. I try in my best words to bring the picture out of it. But, you see, I see the picture in front of me. You have to imagine something. The one who listens has to imagine something. It has a different picture for me than for the person who imagines something.

As Chaim speaks of his individual experience of finding his brother's clothes as he sorts the effects of prisoners gassed on arrival at Sobibor, his reflections seem to speak to a larger issue in Holocaust testimony. Langer's question is incisive, in so far as it sparks Chaim to comment on his state of mind—the *how* rather than the strictly *what* aspects of his experience, as consistent with the emphasis of the Fortunoff Archive—but it nonetheless leads to a gently defiant response when Chaim proclaims that the "story can't be told." As expert and reflective as Langer is in engaging testimony, he is nonetheless asking Chaim to distill what cannot be fully conveyed. Chaim asserts that his story is woven of both visceral and cognitive threads—he learns of things, like his brother's death, through a process of discovery that is deeply emotional and impossible for someone else to comprehend. He further contests the notion that even the most polished witness can possibly convey the fundamental experiences of the Holocaust. It is not only an inability to transmit experiences in verbal terms, Chaim argues, but also a limitation of reenactment: "I see the picture in front of me. You have to imagine something." This moment clearly resonated with Langer, as he later highlighted this particular section of Chaim's testimony in his book *Holocaust Testimonies: The Ruins of Memory*, contending that it represents a form of "anguished memory" that "reveals the limits of memory's ability to recreate that past."[23]

The closest we can approach that picture is in our imagining of what Chaim visualizes in his mind's eye, combined with a vision of Chaim in front of the camera as he attempts to reenact his memory through verbal and physical language. In other words, we bear witness to his process of witnessing—we are shown the traces of his memory work—but we will always remain outside his experience. One of Langer's correspondences with the Holocaust Museum's director Michael Berenbaum includes a letter regarding another testimony, though it reflects his perception of a broader similarity among survivor testimonies: "The importance of these testimonies is that if we watch enough of them, we become part of his [the witness's] intuitively understanding audience, not perhaps in the same way as authentic former victims, but close enough to move into the subtext of his and their narratives."[24] I would add to Langer's comment that the subtext of witness narratives emerges not only when we function as an "intuitively understanding audience," but also in those moments when our intuition, including that of Langer, fails, and the witness resists our particular itinerary for the interview. Langer's encounter with Chaim clearly reveals the challenges of spoken language for the witness, but also the difficulty of opening up a window into his personal landscape of memory.

Chaim's Fortunoff testimony on finding his brother's clothes also underscores how the interplay between common memory and deep memory intersects with the relationship between collective and individual memory. Up to that point, Chaim had barely mentioned his brother, and he did so only in the context of their transport together. When Langer asks him when he found out what had happened to others in his transport, Chaim continues to discuss his work sorting clothes: "Those were the clothes from the people on our transport who went to the gas chambers." Langer interjects, "Do you remember when you found out what happened to those people, did someone tell you, or did you just suddenly realize it?" Chaim rather pointedly interrupts Langer here, asserting: "Alright, you will find out in a minute how I found out." He then proceeds to describe his process of discovery: "When I came to work and started to separate the clothes, I found my brother's clothes and his pictures and everything he had with him. . . . I found the clothes of my brother and so I know what happened."[25]

In this exchange, Chaim had initially tried to follow a more circuitous route to the memory of his brother, until being interrupted. There is an intense dynamic here between interviewer and interviewee as Langer urges him toward the pivotal juncture. However, it is ultimately through delay and indirection that Chaim reaches that point, all the while speaking about his everyday tasks as a way of building up and coming to terms with what was to be discovered. Later, in his role as consultant to the Holocaust Museum's oral history department, Langer cites this section of Chaim's testimony as having been notable:

He [Chaim] insists that: "The only one what's lived it through knows what happened." Not merely a problem of language, but of not being able to share feelings that have no common basis. His example is that we couldn't possibly know what he felt when he recognized his brother's clothes. But as he tells about it, it sounds like another story, not what really happened. "I see the picture in front of me," he says. "You have to imagine something."[26]

Yet this exchange between Lawrence Langer and Chaim E. was not included in the book adaptation of the documentary *Witness: Voices from the Holocaust*. As mentioned in the earlier discussion of the ways the Fortunoff Archive excerpted testimony for the book, few of the interviewers' words, whether comments or questions, made their way into the volume. Instead, the book follows a thematic organization, using portions of each witness's story to illustrate particular concepts. Chaim's testimony, for example, is featured prominently in a chapter entitled "It Started with Dreams: Aftermath," under the heading "Escaped from Sobibor."[27] The published excerpts from his Fortunoff testimony provide scant evidence of the tension that emerges in the dialogue between Chaim E. and Langer. Instead, they are employed to illustrate the anti-redemptive and nonheroic aspects of Holocaust experience and memory that Langer emphasizes. In the course of adapting the testimony for its published format, the book's editors left out the very process that generates powerful testimonial meaning in this archived account.

The United States Holocaust Memorial Museum

Chaim's testimony for the Holocaust Museum, recorded in July 1990, is his second account across the three archives. In the four years since his Fortunoff interview, Chaim has aged considerably, and his slower, quieter speech requires the audience to pay even closer attention to his testimony. Also, the museum's use of a fixed medium close-up, as opposed to the less disciplined, roving camera for his Fortunoff interview, greatly limits coverage of his gestures. Compared to his earlier testimony, Chaim's tone here is more distant and controlled as he lists his experiences in sequence, using an "and then" repetition and transition that suggest the more sober realm of common memory. It not only shows Chaim's sense of familiarity with telling his story, but also picks up on his sense of removal from the intensely experiential and sensory dimensions of his account.

On more careful review of his testimony, however, we can sense certain breaches in his narration and perhaps detect the emergence of deep memory. At one point in the interview, when recalling his work as one of the few inmate laborers at Sobibor, where he cut the hair of soon-to-be-executed prisoners and processed their belongings, Chaim echoes his earlier words from the Fortunoff testimony on the difficulty of channeling these events: "It's, it's unbelievable how it takes to tell that. Whoever didn't see it cannot describe it how that really looks or feeling it."[28] At this point Chaim returns to visually embedded images, as is apparent in his description of a large transport that he had to process:

> There was a big transport and there was a lot of people, half-dead, dead, no clothes. Terrible, I never saw something like that. It's just unbelievable, half-skeletons. The people looked just unbelievable. . . . So they said all the bodies we had to throw on, on this to take it to the Camp III. And there were half-live people. We just had to throw them together with the, with the live people, with the dead people together. So I see an old lady, a gentle face and things like that and it is on top of all these bodies. It was horrible, horrible. I don't have words for it. You cannot, you cannot tell a story, no matter how good words you find for it, it still cannot give you the right picture what it is.

On one level, the limits of Chaim's recollection are caused by the linguistic barrier that is common to most of the testimonies examined in this book. Because these survivors are recounting their stories in English, their recall of events is more labored. However, even if Chaim had been speaking in his native tongue, the central dilemma would remain: how to translate his experiences from intensely visual, sensory, interior encounters into an externalized form. Yet that moment of disruption—when Chaim realizes that he cannot adequately express in words what he inhabits in the depths of his memory—reveals less about the historical content he recounts than his manner of recounting it. His reenactment of these past events, coupled with his inability to represent them fully, underscores not only the content but also the form of personal history, inscribing his testimony with the resonances of trauma without suggesting its full or direct representation. However, the Holocaust Museum's oral history methodology places limits on Chaim's performance of testimony. The restricted framing of the camera blocks off his arms and obscures the physical labor of his memory work, which plays out through his gestures. Additionally, the interviewer's failure to listen carefully or to intervene gently means that Chaim's penetrating remarks are unaddressed. The memory of the old woman with the gentle face clearly continues to resonate with Chaim, but the interviewer does not ask for elaboration or reflection.

Finally, toward the end of the interview, after having recounted his escape from Sobibor and his subsequent hiding in the Polish countryside, Chaim refers to his journey from Poland to Holland with his wife Selma and their infant child:

Reframing Holocaust Testimony

So we're on the boat and crossed my fingers that everything, already we go. And on the sea the child, probably Selma told the story, the child got sick from food poisoning. They gave it, this, this powdered milk or whatever, was too strong or whatever, and then the stomach and there was no medication, nothing. So the child died on the boat. Probably Selma told more private, more about than I, so that's basically the way we ended up in Holland.

As I will discuss shortly, Selma had attempted to describe this experience in her own testimony at the Holocaust Museum, which had occurred earlier on the day of Chaim's interview. However, the time limit for each testimony, coupled with the focus on wartime events, ultimately prevented a more detailed recording of that story. Chaim is clearly less comfortable talking about the loss of their first child, noting that Selma would probably be more inclined to discuss the "private" details. As I will later show, Selma had passed on that responsibility to Chaim, and because his interviewer did not ask him for further elaborations, this central experience for both survivors remains unexplored across their testimonies at the museum.

The Visual History Archive of the USC Shoah Foundation

Chaim E. recorded an interview with the Shoah Foundation's Visual History Archive in the fall of 1995. Upon analyzing that testimony and that of his wife Selma E., I learned that they had both re-recorded their testimonies for the VHA three years later. While I have yet to discover the precise reasons underlying the decision to conduct second interviews at the VHA, their first testimonies at that venue are marked by tension and evident irritation on the part of Selma and Chaim.

Chaim's initial VHA interview—his third of four across the three archives—took place nine years after his Fortunoff interview and five years after the one for the USHMM. His first VHA interview is far more routine than those earlier testimonies. The somewhat formulaic quality hints that he has mastered many of the tropes of his narrative account, and he uses some exact phrases from prior interviews with, however, less urgency. When Chaim does exhibit moments of animation, as in his recollection of stabbing a guard at Sobibor during the mass revolt and escape, the VHA's more constrained medium close-up, in contrast to the less fixed camera of the earlier Fortunoff tape, restricts more varied coverage of his physical description of events.

The interview protocol is still too densely packed to allow the kinds of unanticipated moments that emerged during his first testimony at Yale. The VHA positions Chaim as an informant to a historical experience, not as a subject reflecting on the process of how he encounters his memories. Its initial interview underscores the extent to which this site's dense format for conducting testimonies contributes to the account's detached, more clinical feel. In many ways, the interviewer demonstrates how the emphasis on objectivity in VHA training puts him at a remove from the rhythms and openings presented by Chaim during the course of his testimony. Take, for instance, the section relating to his time as a slave laborer at Sobibor. In a rather perfunctory manner, the interviewer asks, "What was the first work you were made to do?"[29] During Chaim's earlier Fortunoff testimony, this topic initiated an exchange between him and his interviewer on the nature of testimony and the impossibility of making another person privy to one's interior sense memory of an event. In this VHA testimony, however, both the interviewer's demeanor and the narrative and methodological parameters of the interview process inhibit such a dialogue. In responding to the question about work, Chaim explains how he was forced to sort through the clothes of victims who had just arrived with him on the transport: "While I was separating the clothes, I found the clothes of my brother." The interviewer takes this as an opportunity to probe further on what Chaim did to work and survive, rather than to create a space for him to reflect further on the process of discovery—a process in which knowledge of his loved ones' fate appeared concretely in the material traces he was left to sort.

Soon after this moment, the interviewer attempts to steer the discussion of hardship in Sobibor in a more romantic direction as he inquires about Chaim's first encounter with a transport of Dutch Jews, suggesting that Chaim's future wife Selma (who is from the Netherlands) was among the group: "Can you describe the first time that the Dutch Jews arrived and you saw Selma? Can you describe that night?" Chaim informs the interviewer that Selma was not among that first transport. This information complicates the effort to place the story in a more melodramatic light, as he adds: "It was always a sad experience when you saw a new transport of Dutch Jews. It was always a sad experience."

The contest between the imperatives of the interviewer and the archive, on the one hand, and the witness, on the other hand, is strikingly evident in Chaim's discussion of his life after the war. One particular exchange concerns the issue that was left unaddressed in his earlier testimonies: the loss of Selma and Chaim's child. To a question about what life was like on the ship, Chaim quietly and tentatively responds: "Ah, on the ship, Selma was, well first of all, the child died on the boat . . . ," and he proceeds to talk about the loss of his first child, who was buried at sea. The interviewer appears to be thrown off by this revelation, perhaps suggesting that this detail had not come up in the pre-interview questionnaire. Rather than follow up on this story, the interviewer keeps the narrative moving forward, resorting to logistical questions such as, "Where did the boat land next?"

Chaim's second vHA testimony, three years later, was handled more gently, as the interviewer allowed more detail than his predecessor. At the same time, it echoes many of the limitations of the prior testimony, particularly on the issue of Chaim's and Selma's child, which the interviewer again moves past without much elaboration. However, a revealing exchange occurs during the photograph-sharing session, when the camera records an image of Chaim, along with his brother and father, standing at the grave of Chaim's mother in Poland. The interviewer asks how he acquired the photograph, and Chaim responds, "I found it, I sorted through the clothes and found this picture with his [his brother's] clothes."[30] In his earlier remarks, during the main body of the testimony on the discovery of his brother's clothes, Chaim is given little time to reflect on the impact of that incident. Here, however, at the conclusion, the picture surfaces as a powerful material trace of that moment. He then proceeds to describe how one of his granddaughters had seen that picture, and when she traveled to Poland she took another photograph of the same gravesite to provide what Chaim refers to as "proof" of what she found. In this juncture, the photograph from Chaim's past is salvaged not only to reveal something about his time in Sobibor and the loss of his family, but also to spark a discussion of the transmission of memory to future generations, which often, as in this instance, is restaged through a return by survivors and their progeny to the topography of destruction. This moment provides a powerful commentary on the obligations of postmemory, issues that are openly explored as Chaim and Selma are later joined on camera by their daughter and granddaughter to discuss their past.

Selma E.: "So tell Chaim . . . to tell that story."

The Fortunoff Video Archive for Holocaust Testimonies

Selma gave her testimony to the Fortunoff Archive in March 1980, six years before Chaim's and at an early point in the development of the archive.[31] A Dutch Jew born in 1922, she delivers this first of her four recorded testimonies with both insistency and restraint. In keeping with the less standardized production practices of the early Fortunoff interviews, the camera alternates between various forms of composition, frequently moving in from a medium close-up to a tight close-up that captures details of her face and hands. The use of the latter in the earlier part of her testimony accentuates Selma's penetrating gaze, particularly when she looks straight at the camera while remarking as follows: "In Holland, you could never believe that something could happen."[32] The urgency with which she performs her testimony is intensified when she describes her arrival at Sobibor. Perhaps because this is the first of her testimonies in this context, Selma's performance of testimony appears to be more energized than subsequent versions. Her hand gestures have an urgent quality as she describes her arrival at the camp: "The train ride was very horrible, something unbelievable and then we came to Sobibor with all the screaming, and the whips, and throwing in old people and they went right away to the gas chambers." She proceeds to mimic the screaming voice of a mother who is separated from her infant upon arrival—and still seems troubled by that sound. Later, when Selma recounts the moment when she first encountered Chaim: "A minute was a day. I couldn't tell you what every minute was what happened in my life. Then I remember one thing. We went to work and then we came back. And a big fire was burning and the smell of hair and bone, and the music for the evening was playing. And we had to dance. And I danced with the young man who is now my husband." Selma's memory of the incident, while viscerally charged, is not firmly grounded in a precise recollection of events. In contrast to the methods employed by the Holocaust Museum (particularly in its first stages of collection) and the Shoah Foundation, the Fortunoff interviewers do not press Selma as extensively on the historical details, but rather allow her to linger on the moment without asking her to fit her experiences into a preexisting format. The interview technique used here and by the Fortunoff Archive generally remains more critically aware of the challenges and ruptures of testimony. Like Chaim in his testimony, Selma reflects on the difficulties of telling her story: "Something that I really can't tell. Something that you can only really tell the people who know what happened. But, can we stop, a little bit?" At this point, the testimony is officially put on hold, though the camera remains rolling and zooms in for a tight close-up of her hands.

This moment, a liminal juncture of the interview, is facilitated by a more open discussion in this testimony and by the archive in general, about the challenging processes of the testimonial endeavor. At the same time, the interviewers for this testimony seem overly invested in teasing out the difficult aspects of Selma's story. Laurel Vlock, one of two interviewers, asks Selma in a rather cloying tone: "I know this will be hard for you. But you were dancing in the camp with your [future] husband. What were you thinking?" At this and other moments in the testimony, Vlock, a cofounder of the archive as well as a television producer, shifts the testimony in an emotionally charged direction. Still, the interview's more fluid, conversational, and less formally structured dynamic seems to reveal the interpenetration of Selma's past and present experiences. For example, in describing how a Sobibor guard named Wagner used a shovel to split open the head of one inmate, Selma uses her hands to mimic the splitting motion, recreating a detail of an event that still vividly resonates with her: "I saw that Wagner, with a shovel, just split a man's head in two. And I see that man still standing in front of me. You know, I have to go out tonight. I don't want to go out anymore." At this point, she smiles and laughs at the morbidity of that statement, recognizing the contrasts between the graphic nature of her recollection and the comparatively mundane details of her plans for the evening. Selma appears comfortable enough in the interview to relay that kind of expression, and the less structured interview allows the conversation to flow with ease.

Although this interview, and those of the Fortunoff Archive and its affiliates more generally, are not as tightly formatted as those of the other two archives, they nonetheless tend to dedicate relatively less attention to survivors' postwar experiences. That, coupled with an early tendency to keep interviews to less than two hours (a practice that was eventually discontinued), had the effect of limiting Selma's discussion of an event that proved to have considerable importance in her future interviews. Thus, when the two-hour limit nears, Selma makes repeated passing references to having given birth to a baby in Poland not long after the war. She mentions her loneliness when left with her infant son while Chaim was on the road working. Selma and Chaim then decided to relocate to Holland, traveling by ship, with a stop in Odessa along the way. Selma describes how en route, they struggled to get clean water for their son, who eventually fell ill. Her pace quickens as she describes the ordeal: "The middle of the night, the transport went farther and we went to Odessa. . . . I remember we run to get some clean diapers for the baby." At this point, the interview abruptly cuts off, never to resume. The details of her son's death remain a source of contestation between Selma and her interlocutors, as both parties are constrained by the temporal limits and interview methods imposed by the archive. This detail—although so clearly a central part of Selma and Chaim's story—simply falls outside the boundaries of wartime experience. Thus, key events in Selma and Chaim's postwar lives are missing from their Fortunoff testimonies, which instead focus on Sobibor and other Holocaust-related places and events.

The United States Holocaust Memorial Museum

In terms of production quality and methodological approach, Selma's testimony for the Holocaust Museum in 1990, recorded a decade after her Fortunoff interview, is considerably more standardized and structured. As is customary for the museum's testimony collection, she is videotaped in a fixed medium close-up and sitting in front of a black backdrop. In contrast to the Fortunoff Archive's earlier practice, the camera does not move in to capture such details as Selma's hands, and the range for capturing the witness's gestural expressions is far more limited. As I have described, a major motivation for the museum to create its oral history department was the need to generate exhibition and program content; thus, the more standardized approach to composition can be viewed as an effort to facilitate a consistent aesthetic style for integration in museum exhibitions. But it is also important to recall that Selma's earlier testimony at the Fortunoff

Archive was conducted at a very early stage in the emergence of video Holocaust testimony projects in the United States. Not surprisingly, her subsequent testimonies lack the sense of impromptu performance in front of a camera. This is not to suggest that Selma's interview for the Holocaust Museum lacks urgency. Still, a decade later, even though her advancing age has not diminished her vibrancy, she has had time to reflect on the details of her story, and she delivers her information in a far more rote manner.

At moments, however, the visceral charge from her previous testimony rises to the surface, especially when she discusses her arrival at Sobibor and describes the whipping and beating that she and her fellow inmates endured: "They opened the doors and then we heard screaming and with the whips throwing, and we heard 'Raus! Raus! Raus!' That we had to go out of the train with whips and, and hitting us already, and, and, and everybody stumbled over each other."[33] Although the camera captures only a very restricted range of Selma's gestures, we can see her mimicking the blows and whips. These are vocal and physical expressions of a moment that still seems to have a strong impact on Selma— an impact that cannot be captured in the transcripts that often are utilized as sources without use of the audiovisual record. The Holocaust Museum's typed transcripts, like the finding aids of the Fortunoff Archive and the keyword and segment lists of the Shoah Foundation, focus primarily on locating the informational aspects of testimony rather than their experientially charged, labored, and physical traces. At certain points, the museum interviewer's concern with quantifying or pinpointing the details of Selma's experiences in Sobibor conflict with her way of recalling events, as when she describes how she and others experienced the selections in that camp:

> We saw all the people passing by. We saw the, I think the women went first, and then the men went at last. But I don't remember exactly. I remember, saw them walking already that side to the gas chamber, that they had to take their clothes off. And I remember that also that I, we heard them speaking to the group of us standing there and say, "you came to Sobibor, and everything will be okay," and "here is a little card. You can write home that you are here in Sobibor . . . you go to a work camp." And we have to take a shower because the, it's "better for you that you take a shower, so we can, we will give you other clothes." That I remember, that they were talking to them. What, what they say exactly, I perhaps remember what I read later about it. But I remember that they talking to them, that they say, "Here is a card, you can write to Holland." For us, we were standing on the side and they brought us to Camp One. Sobibor was divided.

In this passage of her testimony, Selma very clearly recalls the deception that was so crucial to the machinery of death at Sobibor. The outcome of that deception is apparent to her, though the precise details of exactly how long and in what exact fashion the process unfolded are unclear. After Selma's remark that "Sobibor was divided," the interviewer asks her "How long did you stand on the side like that?" Selma cannot answer that question in strict temporal terms, but nonetheless conveys a vivid, melancholic assessment: "So long that the people came and they were gone. So the men was on the right side, of the men went first, and then that was nobody there. Was nobody there anymore."

Pressing further for an understanding of the logistics, the interviewer asks, "Where did they all go? All the . . . ?" Before he can complete the question, Selma replies: "We couldn't see it. We were standing on a spot that I, they were already going to the gas chamber, because Sobibor was a death camp. They, everybody went straight to the gas chamber."

This exchange is revealing on several levels. First, it captures the impossibility that survivors would be able to penetrate the interior core of the Nazi's genocidal machinery. As close as Selma was to the extermination process as a slave laborer, her experience differed from that of the majority of those deported to Sobibor. Furthermore, the dialogue with the interviewer underscores the challenge of quantifying the compartmentalized conditions of the selection process. Finally, Selma's remarks foreground the slippages that emerge between individual and collective experience. Note, for instance, the moment in which Selma transitions from the *we* to the *I* pronoun while describing her position in the selection line, and then catches herself and shifts to *they* when recalling the inmates' path to the gas chamber. Although she was among the group processed, she was one of the few spared extermination and was instead forced to do labor. Selma's recollection captures her proximity to the extermination process, but ultimately reinforces the impenetrable boundary that separated her from the gas chamber.

On other occasions, her testimony reveals not only what Selma cannot witness, but also what she chooses not to witness. Thus she describes in detail a collective punishment that was imposed on the slave laborers of Sobibor:

> And again Chaim and I were standing next to each other; and they took a bunch of people and we had to stand 10 or 20 people, I don't remember the amount, and they had to stand farther up, and they will shoot them. They were planned to shoot them. My system was always, I never looked, so they shoot these 10 people. We had to stay all on roll call together, the whole camp; and we had to look what will happen to you when you do things like and they all shoot them.

I didn't look. I saw them later that the Germans went again and shoot them again, that I remember, but I didn't see them falling. I remember one person seeing falling of that, that's what I think I saw.

In this instance, the "system" that Selma adopts in order to survive her experiences complicates fundamental aims of all three archives in this study, which are geared to record what witnesses saw with their own eyes. Selma deliberately obscures her vision of the shooting, and when she does see what occurred firsthand, as was the case with the selection process, her view is largely limited to the end result of the events she describes. The interviewer, in keeping with the testimony methodology of the museum, considers Selma's recollection of this incident incomplete as it fails to provide first-hand visible evidence of the execution. Yet her remembrance implies that Selma must have *heard* the shots if she and others were forced to stand in line during the executions. The fact that this point is never explored speaks to the primacy all three archives give to visual rather than aural and audiovisual aspects of traumatic memory. The implied resonance of the execution gunshots are not easily integrated into interview formats that typically ask witnesses to register visually embedded accounts of their experiences.

Perhaps the most glaring instance of friction between Selma and the Holocaust Museum's archival practice is found in the closing minutes of her interview. With approximately two minutes remaining in the second and final tape of her interview, she is asked: "When did you come to the United States?" This question marks a significant disruption in the trajectory of Selma's testimony. Moving from her and Chaim's experience surviving in the Polish woods after their escape from Sobibor, straight to their immigration to the United States, bypasses their interim postwar lives in Poland, the loss of their first child, and their time living in both Holland and Israel. Selma appears to be a bit thrown off by the question, since it indicates that her interview will conclude before she can delve into these immediate postwar experiences. She starts to rush through her story of the journey to Holland, only to be interrupted by the interviewer, who sees that she is moving back rather than forward in her story: "How did you get to Israel?" Before having a chance to address that question, the interviewer interjects again to notify her that, "Okay, that's the tape. That's the end." Selma then throws up her hands and remarks with evident dissatisfaction and frustration: "That's the end of the story?" The interviewer confirms that the interview has, in fact, come to a close: "The second tape is over." Selma again responds with evident irritation: "So tell Chaim [to] tell that story. That's very interesting. The baby died on the way to, to Holland, on the boat. When we went on the boat, the baby died on the boat from food poisoning and died and was buried at sea." As I indicated in my analysis of Chaim's Holocaust Museum interview, this very central moment in their lives ends up at the margins of their testimonies, which focus largely on their exceptional wartime escape from Sobibor.

At this point, the official portion of Selma's interview has come to a halt. An unofficial exchange continues on the videotape, and is deleted from the transcript though marked there as "technical conversation." During this "technical" discourse, Selma presses the interviewer on how he could have failed to anticipate the end of the tape. She purses her lips and extends her right index finger, all the while gazing at the interviewer with a look of disbelief as she remarks with clear disappointment and resentment: "Oh, you didn't know how much time was left?" It is an incredibly tense moment, as the interviewer seems to be at a loss for words. He then consults the oral history director Linda Kuzmack, who is located off-camera: "Linda, are we going to do a third tape?" Meanwhile, Selma awaits word on whether she will be able to continue her story. She inquires: "They do?" to which the interviewer replies rather sheepishly, "No, they, they're finished." And with that, the testimony comes to a close.

It is often precisely at such seemingly "peripheral" moments that some of the most urgent and fundamental aspects of survivor experiences come to the fore. As noted, the Holocaust Museum's interview methodology attempts to keep at bay the more contested or emotionally charged moments of testimonies in order to reinforce a sense of sober objectivity. While the transcript disguises such exchanges, they are available through careful engagement with the margins of the audiovisual record.

The Visual History Archive of the USC Shoah Foundation

Selma's first testimony at the VHA, delivered in October 1995, has many of the same limitations that were associated with Chaim's first interview for that archive. Specifically, Selma is allowed little space to reflect on her memories, as the interviewer moves through questions fairly quickly, often interjecting new lines of inquiries before Selma has fully responded to prior ones. Consistent with VHA practice, she is framed by the camera for most of the interview in a medium close-up, sitting in a domestic setting with family photographs placed behind her. The interviewer is located just off the left side of the camera. Dressed in a sharp red blouse and prominent glasses, Selma strikes an elegant presence, enhanced by the soft lighting that is VHA's standardized setup. The stream of questions that ask Selma to describe the familial and sociological details of her prewar milieu in Holland seem to stifle the flow of the testimony, but Selma's strength as a witness, her animated and forceful delivery, is usually able to transcend the challenges presented by the framework of this first interview for the Shoah Foundation.

Nevertheless, at moments, in spite of Selma's eloquent expression of memory, both the interviewer's feedback and the interview's predetermined framework inhibit her ability to form her testimony as she wishes. Several times, as Selma answers questions, we hear sighs and other nonverbal expressions coming from the interviewer as he moves the testimony forward, quickly jumping from one question to the next. Selma is noticeably thrown off by the barrage of questions and as a result is often unable to provide particular dates and sequencing, so that at one point she remarks, "I am a little confused by all the talking."[34]

Furthermore, the interviewer, having prepared the session from the pre-interview protocol, often loads his questions with information that should have been left to the witness to address on her own terms, for example, the events related to the loss of her son. Rather than ask about that journey in broad terms, the interviewer frames the question: "You had the baby with you, his name was Emiel?" This is the first time, in any of Chaim's or Selma's interviews, that we learn the name of their son. The topic of the baby was either left out of the interviews or referred to indirectly. Selma is noticeably irritated by the question, replying rather sharply, "Of course we had the baby with us." This exchange reveals how the extensive preparation of the pre-interview process can often lead the interviewer to engage the witness on obvious or pre-established points, rather than taking a more restrained approach that creates opportunities for the witness to arrive at moments on her or his own terms. In this instance, the child's name is an extremely delicate subject, particularly after previous testimonies in which exploration of that topic had been curtailed in deference to wartime events. While the VHA format allows relatively more space for covering postwar events, they are often explored through dense and highly structured exchanges. The issue of Emiel's death raises intimate and painful issues for Selma. She explains that on the ship "I didn't have any milk, I went to the kitchen and I got some milk, and I think it was too heavy milk, and I gave the milk to the baby and the baby got sick and the baby died twenty-four hours later. So we thought we were free. . . ." Note how Selma uses the term *baby* three times rather than referring to her son's name or gender. Understandably, this memory remains intensely difficult for her to confront, and Selma is much less inclined to directly approach the details in the same manner as the interviewer. Upon careful viewing it also appears that Selma is distracted by something the interviewer is doing off-camera, suggesting even more tension over how this particular element of her experience is being received.

That friction carries over into the closing moments of the testimony when the interviewer asks Selma about the lessons of the Holocaust: "Being that there are only a few survivors left of Sobibor, do you think that it's important for teachers to teach about resistance and the uprising?" This is clearly a leading question, but Selma is unwilling to answer it in the affirmative. "No," she replies emphatically, and then describes how the circumstances of Sobibor were unique: it was isolated in the woods; it was relatively small; the forced laborers were better fed. In other words, for her, no simple, universal lesson can be extrapolated from Sobibor. Selma further challenges the interviewer's pedagogical agenda with her declaration: "I am not a scholar, I am not a scholar from the Holocaust, so I don't know." Selma does, however, embrace her role as a witness who can speak to younger generations about her experiences. This point comes out when the interviewer asks her to comment on her children, at which point she responds by describing how they "live very much their own life," and that as a result she and Chaim often speak to children at schools in order to transmit their experiences.

The interview concludes with the photo-sharing segment, which includes pictures of Selma as an infant and a teenager, as well as her and Chaim's marriage license. Standing out among the images and documents is their son Emiel, captured in a photograph taken in Odessa when they were en route to Holland: "This is the little baby, our baby, and here's me and Chaim." It is a brief moment, located on the outer boundaries of the interview, but the photographic trace nonetheless captures an intimacy and warmth that was less cultivated during the main body of the testimony. However, each of the three archives fails to tend to the gendered ways in which Chaim and Selma remember and discuss Emiel's death. In Selma's case, most of the interviewers fail to create a space where she can more fully reflect on how the loss of Emiel shapes both her past and present experiences as a woman and mother.[35]

Selma's second VHA interview, like Chaim's, was recorded three years after her first, in October 1998. Selma shows her advancing age, but remains quick on her feet. While the second interviewer is far more patient with presenting questions and absorbing answers, the interview format remains densely packed with the standardized sets of questions concerning familial and sociological data, particularly in the opening tape. Consequently, substantial personal and historical detail is included in the early moments, but there is very little room for reflection on and exploration of the experiential rather than informational aspects of Selma's experience.

In keeping with the VHA's three-act structure, the interviewer first has Selma establish the fundamental details of her prewar life, but then transitions to the second part of the interview and asks a question that the archive commonly employs in order to approach what in screenwriting is often referred to as the "inciting incident." In this instance, in order to set the main body (or second act) of the story into motion, the interviewer asks Selma: "When did things start to change?," probing for a concrete marker to differentiate the "before" from the "wartime" aspects of Selma's life.[36] Selma says that 1940 was a critical year in that regard, but she does not recall the exact dates when restrictions started to be set in place for Jews living in Holland. The interviewer proceeds through another series of questions concerning Selma's experience of the German occupation, leading her to discuss her time as a teenager in hiding and her eventual imprisonment after capture by the Nazis.

In the midst of this conversation, Selma mentions that prior to her own imprisonment, her mother, as well as her brothers and sisters-in-law, had been deported from Holland to Auschwitz. She recalls her determination to travel to Poland to find her family and perhaps to help them. And she describes how along the way Germans or German-language speakers would make advances on her. At this point in the interview, the following exchange takes place:

> INTERVIEWER: Would they make advances on you? What are you
> saying? What happened when you said no?
> SELMA: I didn't say no, I just shied away. I was really, I was raped
> in the hotel once. Yeah. And I was very sick from that and I
> couldn't tell anyone and I really don't know what happened
> after that. I was at the doctor's and my family was whisper-
> ing what was going on . . . I was nineteen. Yeah, and I really
> didn't know what a man was."

Thus, in Selma's telling of her encounters with Germans who made advances on her during the war on her journey to Poland, she moves back to an earlier experience of having been raped at a hotel owned by her family in Holland. Her recollection of that earlier event informs her account of the subsequent experience, but the interviewer has difficulty integrating further discussion of her sexual assault since it emerges out of chronological order and broaches the taboo of rape. Furthermore, Selma had never mentioned this particular incident in any of her three earlier testimonies. Yet she is emotionally expressive at this point in the interview—her voice is noticeably more quiet and unsteady, even trembling as she wipes tears from her face. That particular interview tape comes to a close with this story, and the next tape begins with a discussion of Selma's initial encounter with a concentration camp, without further elaboration on camera of this critical, newly uncovered detail in Selma's experience.

When the discussion shifts to Selma's first deportation to the transport camp Westerbork and from there her transfer to Sobibor, the line of questioning remains largely logistical and informational rather than reflective: "What was the barrack like at Westerbork?"; in regards to the deportation and imprisonment at Sobibor, "Could you sit on the train?"; "Were there ever any days off?"; "Were there religious Jews there?" These are questions designed to reconstruct particular details about people and places—the historical content of her memory, rather than deeper reflections.

As in her earlier testimony for the VHA, Selma comments again about having lost her first child en route to Holland. As in the previous interview, she refers to her child as a "baby." And again it is only during the separate photo-sharing section of the testimony that Selma can present a photograph of her son, whom she then identifies by his name, Emiel. During the main portion of the interview, however, as Selma discusses the struggles of caring for one of her children while Chaim was working in Poland, we can see her look off-camera, indicating that she is turning to her husband for support or clarification as he sits in the interview room, out of frame. It is a compelling moment in that it provides a glimpse into the dialogue that takes place not only between interviewer and interviewee, but also between fellow witnesses who often share responsibility for their experiences and memories. Selma and Chaim may not appear on camera together for most of their testimonies at the three archives, but their respective interviews are very much in conversation with each other—as demonstrated by the way Selma and Chaim often defer responsibility to each other for relaying certain details in testimonies.

Toward the close of the main portion of the second VHA interview, prior to the photo-sharing session, the interviewer asks Selma: "I know you tell your story a lot. Why do you tell your story a lot"? Selma replies, "Very important that the children know about Sobibor and how my family got killed and how all the Jews . . ." Before she can finish this thought, she breaks into tears, barely able to speak the words, "that's the reason they should know." In contrast to Selma's testimony for the Fortunoff Archive and Holocaust Museum, her recordings for the VHA, as consistent with its methodology, provide comparatively significant space for commenting not only on her immediate postwar experiences, but also on her status as a survivor in the contemporary moment of her interview.

Testimony and the Prospects of Transmitting Cross-Generational Memory

At the conclusion of Chaim E.'s second testimony for the Shoah Foundation, he and Selma appear together on camera in a medium shot, sitting at a table and joined by their middle-aged daughter Alida and their teenage granddaughter Tagan. Early in this portion of the testimony, the interviewer asks Alida: "You are sitting here with your parents who are both survivors. What has it meant for you to be the child of survivors?"[37] This question sparks Alida's reflection on the formative, if ambivalent legacy of her parents' experiences: "I think it's been hard on many levels, but I think there are also some things that I have gotten as gifts from them. The hard thing is just knowing the pain and grief that they've gone through and that certainly affects who I am and what I think and how I feel." Aspects of familial dynamics emerge, including an allusion to some tension surrounding Alida's and Selma's frustration with moving to the United States from Israel due to Chaim's growing dissatisfaction about living there. It is clear that Alida longs for Israel, and she expresses some resentment at having had to leave. She talks about having managed to attend graduate school, achieve professional success, and raise her children on her own after a failed marriage.

However, despite Alida's satisfaction with her accomplishments, her parents' experiences have extracted psychic costs from her. In that respect, Alida represents the challenges frequently associated with members of the second-generation survivor community. She remarks: "Now I'm at a place where there's a lot of peace. I was in therapy for a long, long, long, long time. But now I'm at the other end of a lot of that. But it clearly impacted who I was and how I was a parent." Alida reflects on the aspects of her parents' strong character that enabled her to better grapple with her own struggles, but only after facing the difficulty of living in the shadow of such intense suffering. She elaborates on her experiences in therapy, for example, reflecting on the various anxieties she had to face, including "the fear of a Gestapo soldier coming to get me," even though she herself had never been in danger of that actual experience. Upon hearing her daughter say this, Selma turns to her and says, "Where did you see that?," to which Alida replies, "It was just an image that was in me, something to be scared of, and I was afraid to look . . . and one day I saw what the fear was and the fear was gone."

This exchange leads to an on-camera discussion of the ideas underlying the concept of postmemory. More specifically, it captures what Marianne Hirsch has described as "retrospective witnessing by adoption," that is, "adopting the traumatic experiences—and thus also the memories of others—as experiences oneself might have had."[38] This transmission of postmemory is rendered even more clearly by Alida's daughter Tagan, who enters the discussion by recalling a recent journey she made to Poland to visit Holocaust-related sites, including places associated with the experience of her grandparents. She eloquently describes this trip:

> The images that had not directly been put out, but that had been there, I had studied about the Holocaust in college and I had spoken to my Oma and Opa [her grandparents] a lot about things that my mom had no idea about since grandchildren often have the safety and freedom to ask questions that the children can't. And when I went to Poland, there were all these images that came up to me, and I was on a train going to Poland, and I felt terrified because I had all these images of Jews in boxcars going to camps.[39]

As Tagan characterizes it, the legacy of the Holocaust is inscribed in both the stories transmitted to her by her grandparents and through the iconic images of the events.

Yet for Tagan, the journey to the topography of terror creates an opportunity to activate in more viscerally charged terms her familial and educational explorations of the Holocaust. Her own upbringing had already been indelibly affected by the legacy of the events absorbed by her mother and now, in turn, shaping how she was nurtured. However, as Tagan mentions, being the granddaughter rather than the daughter of survivors gave her a degree of insulation and protection from the kind of psychic scarring experienced by her mother. Tagan's journey to Poland then seems to represent an effort to break through that insulation and assume a position in closer proximity to the landscape of events that have structured much of her family life. Tagan proceeds to read from the diary that she kept during the trip, recalling her journey by train: "I can imagine no joy here. As I pass boxcars and old crumbling buildings . . . I can only think of one thing. Images rooted deeply in my existence. . . . And as I stare out this window . . . I wonder what it will be like when I take my first step off this train." As Tagan reads this passage, Selma is clearly moved, and asks Chaim to get her a tissue to help wipe away her tears.

Rather than representing a moment of tension, which often permeated the dynamics among Selma, Chaim, and their various interviewers at all three archives, the VHA's format, particularly concerning postwar experiences, can nonetheless facilitate a more multilayered, less standardized dialogue on postmemory, as captured in this portion of Chaim's final interview. Throughout the main portions of both Selma's and Chaim's testimonies for the VHA, the interviewers largely privileged historical content. However, the substantial space created for postwar discussion, including the opportunity for witnesses to join family members on camera, has the potential to generate a more substantive and reflective discussion of the personal labor involved in transmitting testimony.

The interview captures Tagan's trip to Poland as part of an interfamilial, cross-generational postmemory investigation. Tagan has seemingly internalized the visceral charge that is carried in the embodied traces of the Holocaust, but—having acknowledged her more mediated access—she recognizes that she occupies a distinct outside position. Her encounter with postmemory is neither wholly redemptive nor anti-redemptive: she feels blessed that her grandparents have survived and endured, but also notes the pain that accompanies their legacy.

A question remains, however. To what extent can testimonial exchanges such as the ones with Tagan and her family be ethically, perhaps even politically, constructive? The media scholar Alison Landsberg contends that the transference of memory from the authentic, living body of the Holocaust survivor to subjects who have no direct link to that historical past—this includes museum patrons, film spectators, new media users, and students—can be productive in terms of developing social consciousness. Living survivors occupy a unique position in Holocaust remembrance and their eventual absence will alter the resonance of their recorded testimonies. At the same time, Landsberg emphasizes that mass cultural sites such as the United States Holocaust Memorial Museum will make available venues where what she refers to as "prosthetic memory" is generated in those who did not live through the original historical event.[40]

This emphasis on developing transferential commemorative sites in spaces of mass culture marks a shift away from a narrow and particularistic form of identity politics toward a more inclusive model that allows for diverse communities and subjects to be brought together at archives, museums, and classrooms through the shared encounter with memories that originate from outside their own personal and historical experiences. The affective and experiential aspects are vital to this exchange since cognitive understanding of the events is insufficient and must be coupled with bodily and visceral familiarity in order for it to be tied to political action.

Crucial to that notion of prosthetic memory, then, is the claim that Holocaust survivors, while providing the necessary firsthand accounts of the events, are part of a broader representational chain of Holocaust remembrance. While that conception of memory acknowledges that survivors' live and recorded stories serve as a form of referential anchorage, it emphasizes that priority should be given to the ways in which those traces of voice and body are ultimately transferred via technologies of memories, including museum installations, films, and other visual representations.

While the VHA methodology and interface have certain limitations, they do have significant potential to foster more substantial exploration of the postwar experiences of witnesses, including encounters with their families about the legacy of the Holocaust. The VHA interview format and the framework of its database often privilege a pre-established historical record and can inhibit the generation of unanticipated, associative, and less chronological accounts. However, in its attempt to sequester and contain the various elements of Holocaust memory, the Shoah Foundation's testimonies have the potential to illuminate the ruptures that can emerge when institutional preferences come into conflict with often dissenting witness testimony.

Moments such as the conclusion of Chaim's testimony, where three generations of his family meet on camera, illustrate how the separate itineraries of witness and archive can nevertheless converge at certain points. Such moments create spaces where both interviewer and interviewee appear to be directly engaged in a conversation about the interpenetration of past and present. By creating a

Reframing Holocaust Testimony

stage for Chaim and Selma to have a dialogue with family members, the archive has helped to enact a constructive strain of postmemory. Tagan, while bound to her grandparents by family ties, nonetheless serves as a kind of proxy for future users of archived testimonies. She helps position them as inheritors of the images and stories of the Holocaust, and suggests that they can embrace that role with an open recognition of its mediated and more self-conscious manifestations.

The legacy of the Holocaust that is inscribed in the immense collections of the Fortunoff Archive, Shoah Foundation, U.S. Holocaust Memorial Museum, and other audiovisual archives can be valued not just according to these sources' fidelity to a verified historical record, but for their rhetorical, performed, and cultural expressions. To place a burden of total historical veracity on survivors like Chaim and Selma E., as well as on future generations who express their and other survivors' stories as part of a performed representational tradition, is to lose sight of the more textured, imperfect, and often contested dimensions of how testimonies are produced. By reflecting upon or sparking conversation on the processes that help frame testimonies, archives can better position their users to work ethically and critically with the richness of these interviews and with the prospects of engaging witness accounts of other genocides.

Conclusion

Documenting Genocide through the Lens of the Holocaust

The labor of testimony is not simply a matter of retrieving the past, but also of recording the ways by which one reenacts that past. Interviewers, archivists, and those who access these sources encounter the challenge of engaging how testimony is generated and performed as part of a mutual, contingent process—one that is embedded in both personal and institutional practices and which does not reveal a static or infallible notion of memory. While the work of recording interviews with Holocaust survivors has largely wound down, the opportunity still exists to shape how their testimonies can be used. Such an endeavor requires practitioners, scholars, and users to develop a testimonial literacy that refines their sensitivity to survivors' lived, physical experiences as well as to their mediated encounters with archives. The honing of that literacy not only applies to preserving histories and memories of the Holocaust, but also to documenting other genocides.

There is a legitimate concern, however, that through various modes of Holocaust representation, the events themselves have served as a universalizing standard by which we measure the destruction of any other community. Certainly, the emphasis on transmitting personal stories of trauma as shared collective and individual experiences (prosthetic, postmemory, or otherwise)—as a visceral foundation for understanding the events in question—is constructive in terms of envisioning new boundaries of political solidarity. Nonetheless, it can potentially obscure the fundamental ethical connection that should be forged between those who give and receive testimony. In other words, it is crucial to remember that the work of testimony originates in a primary interpersonal encounter and not only as a media by-product. While social responsibility should ultimately be directed beyond the interpersonal encounter between interviewer and interviewees that is at the foundation of the original testimonial exchange, that dynamic still provides an ethical grounding for developing and extending our attention to the suffering of others. Some of the archives that I examine in this book not only focus on documenting events from the Holocaust but also carry a mandate to alert our attention to other genocides. Fundamental questions thereby remain about the limits of reinforcing the Holocaust as a historical and methodological paradigm for documenting other histories.

The Shoah Foundation beyond the Shoah

Those issues have become more concrete as Holocaust archives and museums continue to explore ways to circulate their existing testimonies in the public sphere and to address other historical traumas. The Shoah Foundation has been particularly active in that regard: after completing its collection of Holocaust testimonies, it has shifted its attention to making those sources accessible to students, researchers, and the general public across a wide array of digital platforms. Furthermore, it has begun to facilitate and consult on the documentation of other genocides, and has started to house testimony collections of other projects within its Visual History Archive, all the while exporting its Holocaust testimony template to other contexts.[1]

The Shoah Foundation's work consulting on the documentation of the Cambodian genocide is a particularly useful case study of that shift, underscoring the limits and possibilities of documenting genocides through the historical and conceptual lenses of the Holocaust. It raises a pressing question: How are the cultural, historical, and site-specific aspects of Cambodian genocide documentation influenced by the importation of a set of often contested interview methods and narrative structures originally developed for the collection of Holocaust audiovisual testimonies?

The Cambodian genocide, perpetrated by the Khmer Rouge between 1975 and 1979, took the lives of approximately 1.7 million people.[2] Those crimes have been subject to criminal prosecution under the jurisdiction of the Extraordinary Chambers in the Courts of Cambodia (ECCC) since 2003 and have been widely archived by the Documentation Center of Cambodia (DC-Cam), an independent research institute based out of Phnom Penh. The DC-Cam has acted as a central organization for compiling written records, photographs, and video testimonies of the Cambodian genocide for the ECCC. And while a more extensive institutional history of the DC-Cam falls outside the parameters of this conclusion, it is critical to underscore the central tenets of the center's mission—its dual emphasis on compiling a history of the Cambodian genocide for subsequent generations and on collecting data and testimonial accounts for legal trials. In short, to cite the words of its mission statement, the DC-Cam has a fundamental investment in "memory and justice."[3] To that end, the center has catalogued approximately

155,000 pages of primary documents and more than 6,000 photographs from the genocide, and has helped map 189 prisons and 19,403 mass graves.[4] These collected documents have not only advanced efforts to expand education and commemoration, but have also provided invaluable documentation for legal efforts to prosecute the perpetrators of the Cambodian genocide under the jurisdiction of the ECCC.[5]

In 2009 the Shoah Foundation hosted three DC-Cam staff members for a three-month internship and training program to assist in their efforts to record and preserve audiovisual testimonies of the Cambodian genocide.[6] This program offered guidance in all aspects of the testimony process, from video production, cataloguing, and indexing to digitization, preservation, and dissemination. In addition, the Shoah Foundation agreed to house and preserve the testimonies produced by the DC-Cam staff. The training sessions centered on the development of pre-interview questionnaire closely adapted from the Foundation's own Holocaust-related PIQ, which is intended to serve as a structure for conducting DC-Cam interviews.

The "Khmer Rouge Regime Survivor Questionnaire"—at forty-three pages—is virtually identical to the forty-four-page "Survivor Pre-Interview Questionnaire" used for the Foundation's Visual History Archive of Holocaust testimonies. Each survey includes three largely parallel sections—for Cambodia, covering periods before, during, and after the Khmer Rouge regime, with similar categories that had been previously used to document the Holocaust. Examples include "General Interview Details" and "Survivor Information," with census-like data; "Before the Khmer Rouge" (vs. the VHA's "Prewar Life"); the Khmer Rouge regime (vs. "Wartime"), which elicits experiences on "evacuation" (vs. "ghettos") and "cooperative units" (vs. "camps"). Both documents also have "after" sections and a family background space where interviewees can provide information on their parents, siblings, spouses, children, and extended family.[7]

In addition to organizing interviews according to the same chronological, 20:60:20 format as the VHA, the PIQ developed with the DC-Cam provides an outline for the performance of testimony (linear story structure, clear causality, reflections on aftermath, etc.). And they both have a census-like format, inquiring about interviewees' proximity to the largest city, their affiliation with a particular religious denomination, and patterns of migration and movement, in an effort to create a format for mapping and cross-listing interviewee experiences. Because the two questionnaires value informative over performative aspects of testimonies, they privilege the transcribable content of interviews rather than their gestural, vocal, and corporeal resonances that cannot be reduced to a catalogue or index.[8]

At the same time, the Shoah Foundation's exportation of its testimonial template to the DC-Cam also offers the potential for allowing genocide survivors to assert the very identities effaced by the Khmer Rouge regime. Michelle Caswell advances this argument in contending that the DC-Cam collections—by creating terms that include ethnic, racial, and religious identity—have helped the Cambodian atrocities to meet UN conventions' criteria for genocide.[9] Thus, Caswell argues that the DC-Cam can serve an ethical role by cataloguing and indexing categories of suffering that earlier documentation efforts might have designated as peripheral to the Cambodian events. Despite the limitations of the shared pre-interview framework, notably the privileging of linear, chronological, and redemptive storytelling over the associative and tangential paths of memory, its census-like aspects encourage the recording of accounts and data in previously marginalized categories such as race. Such archival practices can, at the very least, help create new models for collecting, cataloguing, and circulating memories of genocide in ways that suit the particular textures of collective and individual traumas.

The pilot interviews that the DC-Cam staff conducted at the Shoah Foundation are currently unavailable. And so it remains a fundamental question as to how those video interviews represent the particular remembrances and subjectivities of their witnesses. Nonetheless, the role of the pre-interview questionnaire in the DC-Cam testimonies strongly indicates an attempt on the part of the Shoah Foundation, working with the DC-Cam, to create an interview approach heavily oriented toward verifying the historical facts of the Cambodian genocide. That can often work at the disservice of attending to the traumatic aspects of testimonies. As the legal scholar Martha Minow argues, attempts to address memory, justice, and reconciliation in post-genocide communities—efforts that inevitably encourage narrative frameworks for understanding genocide—should go beyond a "plain statement of facts" to include "emotional and bodily responses" conveyed in the recounting and reception of traumatic narratives.[10]

I approach all of these issues not as a historian of comparative genocide, but rather as a scholar deeply engaged in transnational memory and media studies. That being said, the task remains for anthropologists, historians, jurists, and other specialists working on the Cambodian genocide to examine particular implications of the DC-Cam's interview methods and other important documentation efforts.[11] Given the fact that many of the projects documenting the Cambodian and Rwandan genocides are relatively nascent compared to those of the Holocaust, there is a compelling opportunity to examine how pre-interview, interview, and other testimonial elements associated with the Shoah shape the prospects for documenting other genocides in ways that neglect or tend to the historical, cultural, and individual specificities of events and witnesses.

The Limits of Multidirectional Testimonies of the Holocaust

A constructive conversation between the universalistic and the particularistic aspects of documenting genocides can transcend what Michael Rothberg has aptly critiqued as "competitive memory" or a "real-estate development" model of memory. In positing finite space for sites of remembrance, such a model implies that the commemoration of one event comes at the expense of memorializing another.[12] By contrast, Rothberg's notion of "multidirectional memory" illuminates the unanticipated paths and frictions that are created when different histories come into conversation with one another, continually in the process of flux and reinterpretation, sometimes in reactionary ways, sometimes in progressive ways, but always transcending a singular, linear, and predictable path.[13] As he sees it, these multidirectional paths can connect the Holocaust and other traumas. In his conception, the Holocaust not only affects the representation of other extreme events but in turn is affected by memories of other genocides, histories of colonialism, and other abuses and thereby moves beyond more conservative positions on the uniqueness of the Holocaust.[14]

Rothberg's concept of multidirectional memory acknowledges that certain memories of the Holocaust have the potential to be reactionary or competitive, to perpetuate hierarchies of knowledge and power rather than calling them into question. Nonetheless, such memories can represent radical potential when mediated and remediated by individuals with diverse interests. For Rothberg, tracing multidirectional memory involves looking across multiple archives, "cross-referencing" various sites, cultures, and discourses, and making new "imaginative links" between different histories and memories. Strict historical accuracy or ideological purity fails to account for all of the intertwined threads between memories; they generate imaginative and poetic connections, not simply positivistic linkages.[15]

I agree with Rothberg's critique that scholarship on Holocaust testimony has been too focused on the dyadic, psychoanalytical dynamic of testimonial production; indeed, it should pay more attention to circulations of testimonies as they move into public spheres.[16] However, I would argue that the relational encounter between interviewer and interviewee nonetheless provides a potential foundation for fostering critically reflective, nonappropriative encounters with the suffering of others. Rothberg's concept of multidirectional memory can assist in activating Holocaust testimony for this purpose, but only when it is paired with an investigation of the specific institutional histories, practices, and economies of archived witness interviews. As evident in the consultation between the Shoah Foundation and the DC-Cam, that dynamic not only shapes the contours of Holocaust testimonies but also increasingly affects testimonies and scholarship directed toward other genocides. In addition to its archival efforts, the Shoah Foundation has expanded its global academic reach through the creation, in 2014, of the Center for Advanced Genocide Research. That center states that its approach to fostering research in Holocaust and genocides studies "not be set out as the work of various disciplines working together, but rather the transcendence of differentiated disciplines to bring innovative understanding as well as a global approach."[17]

However, as nongovernmental bodies such as the Shoah Foundation assume a growing role in collecting, disseminating, and researching experiences of genocide and other human rights issues, we must continue to engage with such questions as how documentation methodologies and "global approaches" to scholarship imported from afar, which developed to address a particular history, can engage other culturally specific forms of suffering. And so this book concludes by initiating a conversation with those scholars who have keenly critiqued the risks associated with the "baggage one carries" in conducting research on trauma and memory across national boundaries.[18] That conversation involves interrogating the very utility and potential damage of adopting those specific terms and models of trauma, memory, and testimony in the first place when examining particular cultural contexts of extremity. It is essential to examine how various modes and traditions of storytelling and documentation, as well as conceptions of suffering and trauma, including those operative in video testimony projects, originate both from within and outside particular national spaces. For better and for worse, those testimonial and narrative discourses have become increasingly globalized and entangled in shaping archives of genocide. Ultimately, regardless of the context, the work of documenting genocide testimonies is never perfectly enacted by interviewers working on behalf of archives. Rather, the process is marked by often diverging intentions and agendas on the part of witnesses and those who are attempting to mold their remembrances. The resulting dissonances may perhaps prick our ears and open our eyes and other senses to the productive tensions and gaps that mark the reframing of testimonies.

NOTES

Preface

1. Although this testimony was recorded in the home of a cameraman, most of the testimonies collected for the Holocaust Museum during its earlier stages of development in the late 1980s and early 1990s were conducted in a dedicated studio. I am grateful to Joan Ringelheim for allowing me to observe this interview in my capacity as a Charles H. Revson Fellow for Archival Research at the United States Holocaust Memorial Museum's Jack, Joseph and Morton Mandel Center for Advanced Holocaust Studies from late 2006 to early 2007.

2. This figure combines the testimonial holdings of the Fortunoff Video Archive for Holocaust Testimonies, the United States Holocaust Memorial Museum, and the USC Shoah Foundation. As this book addresses only testimonies recorded by archives based in the United States, it does not account for the large number of video interviews collected by other institutions such as Yad Vashem in Israel. For a history of Holocaust interviews conducted after World War II, see Alan Rosen, *The Wonder of Their Voices: The 1946 Holocaust Interviews of David Boder* (New York: Oxford University Press, 2010).

3. The "Americanization" of the Holocaust has been extensively explored in works such as: Hilene Flanzbaum, ed., *The Americanization of the Holocaust* (Baltimore: Johns Hopkins University Press, 1999); Peter Novick, *The Holocaust in American Life* (New York: Houghton Mifflin, 1999); Michael Berenbaum in *After Tragedy and Triumph: Essays in Modern Jewish Thought and the American Experience* (Cambridge: Cambridge University Press, 2009); and. Alvin H. Rosenfeld, *The End of the Holocaust* (Bloomington: Indiana University Press, 2011).

4. James E. Young, *The Texture of Memory: Holocaust Memorials and Meaning* (New Haven, Conn.: Yale University Press, 1993), 283.

5. James E. Young, "America's Holocaust: Memory and the Politics of Identity," in *The Americanization of the Holocaust*, 69.

6. For further discussion on the impact of language in testimony, with reference to pioneering interviewers conducted by David Boder, see Rosen, *The Wonder of Their Voices*, 202–226.

Introduction

1. Oren Stier, *Committed to Memory: Cultural Mediations of the Holocaust* (Amherst: University of Massachusetts Press, 2003), explores mediations of audiovisual testimo-

nies beyond the narrative lines of interpretation examined by Lawrence Langer. At the same time, Stier—in his critique of Langer and in his own exploration of the framing contexts of testimony—examines just a handful of interviews and does not comprehensively explore the institutional cultures and methodologies that affect their production and reception.

2. Geoffrey Hartman, "The Humanities of Testimony: An Introduction," *Poetics Today* 27, no. 2 (Summer 2006): 250.

3. My examination of the infrastructures of testimony intersects with Zoë Waxman's discussion of the "socio-political economy of testimony" in "Testimonies as Sacred Texts: The Sanctification of Holocaust Writing," *Past and Present* 206: suppl 5 (2010): 335.

4. In Beate Müller, "Trauma, Historiography and Polyphony: Adult Voices in the CJHC's Early Postwar Child Holocaust Testimonies," *History & Memory* 24, no. 2 (Fall/Winter 2012): 157–195, the author examines similar sets of questions with regard to child Holocaust testimonies of the Central Jewish Historical Commission in Poland. And while those are distinct from my own sample of testimonies, they similarly involve a set of debates regarding positivistic historiography, testimonial performance, and the role of interlocutors in the narrative framing of interviews.

5. Marianne Hirsch and Irene Kacandes, "Introduction," in *Teaching the Representation of the Holocaust*, edited by Marianne Hirsch and Irene Kacandes (New York: MLA, 2004), 2.

6. Ibid., 7.

7. Marianne Hirsch, "Surviving Images: Holocaust Photographs and the Work of Postmemory," in *Visual Culture and the Holocaust*, edited by Barbie Zelizer (New Brunswick, N.J.: Rutgers University Press, 2001), 218. For further discussion of postmemory, see Marianne Hirsch, *The Generation of Postmemory: Writing and Visual Culture after the Holocaust* (New York: Columbia University Press, 2012).

8. Hirsch, "Surviving Images," 221.

9. Ibid., 218.

10. Hirsch, *The Generation of Postmemory*, 12. For an insightful analysis of the experiences of engaging Holocaust testimonies online see Caroline Wake, "Regarding the Recording: The Viewer of Video Testimony, the Complexity of Copresence and the Possibility of Tertiary Witnessing," *History and Memory* 25, no. 1 (Spring/Summer 2013): 111–144.

11. Some noteworthy examples include James E. Young, *Writing and Rewriting the Holocaust: Narrative and the Consequences of Interpretation* (Bloomington: Indiana University Press, 1988); Lawrence Langer, *Holocaust Testimonies: The Ruins of Memory* (New Haven, Conn.: Yale University Press, 1991); Shoshana Felman and Dori Laub, *Testimony: Crises of Witnessing in Literature, Psychoanalysis and History* (New York: Routledge, 1992); Geoffrey Hartman, *The Longest Shadow: In the Aftermath of the Holocaust* (New York: Palgrave Macmillan, 2002); and Henry Greenspan, *On Listening to Holocaust Survivors: Recounting and Life History* (Westport, Conn.: Praeger, 1998) and *On Listening to Holocaust Survivors: Beyond Testimony* (St. Paul, Minn.: Paragon House, 2010). Although formative

works, when examining testimony they primarily address the exchanges between interviewer and interviewee, and rarely explore in a comprehensive fashion, the ways in which testimonies are framed by institutional, cultural, and technical practices. Although Hartman's work on testimony does initiate a vital discussion of the ways in which testimonies are mediated, it does not address institutional and technical issues in-depth, nor does it address a substantial portion of testimonies.

12. See, for example, Dominick LaCapra, *History and Memory after Auschwitz* (Ithaca, N.Y.: Cornell University Press, 1998). The oral historian Steven High has made a compelling argument that those who record interviews should first examine what to do with testimonies once they have been archived. Steven High, "Telling Stories: A Reflection on Oral History and New Media," *Oral History* 38, no. 1 (2010): 101–112.

13. In addition to this book that literature includes the following: Gary Weissman, *Fantasies of Witnessing: Postwar Efforts to Experience the Holocaust* (Ithaca, N.Y.: Cornell University Press, 2004); Zoë Waxman, *Writing the Holocaust: Identity, Testimony, Representation* (New York: Oxford University Press, 2006); Annette Wieviorka, *The Era of the Witness* (Ithaca, N.Y.: Cornell University Press, 2006); Aaron Beim and Gary Alan Fine, "Trust in Testimony: The Institutional Embeddedness of Holocaust Survivor Narratives," *European Journal of Sociology* 48, no. 1 (2007): 55–75; Noah Shenker, "Embodied Memory: The Formation of Archived Audiovisual Holocaust Testimony in the United States," Ph.D. diss., University of Southern California, 2009; Noah Shenker, "Embodied Memory: The Institutional Mediation of Survivor Testimony in the United States Holocaust Memorial Museum," in *Documentary Testimonies: Global Archives of Suffering,* edited by Bhaskar Sarkar and Janet Walker, 35–58 (New York: Routledge, 2009); Amit Pinchevski, "The Audiovisual Unconscious: Media and Trauma in the Video Archive for Holocaust Testimonies," *Critical Inquiry* 39, no. 1 (Autumn 2012): 142–166; Wake, "Regarding the Recording"; Thomas Trezise, *Witnessing Witnessing: On the Reception of Holocaust Survivor Testimony* (New York: Fordham University Press, 2013); Jeffrey Shandler, "Holocaust Survivors on *Schindler's List;* or, Reading a Digital Archive against the Grain," *American Literature* 85, no. 4 (2013): 813–814 and the corresponding online Scalar project and accompanying PDF version at http://scalar.usc.edu/anvc/schindlers-list -on-vha/index (accessed 25 June 2014). This book diverges from those other works by providing a more comprehensive, comparative analysis of multiple archives and interviews, focusing on both institutional debates and video testimonies.

14. I refer to Michael Renov's discussion of *embodied memory* in reference to Holocaust testimony. I first came across his work in that area in "The Work of Memory in the Age of Digital Reproduction" (paper presented at the Visible Evidence XI Conference, Bristol, UK, 16–19 December 2003). Renov employs that term to describe how the individual texture of testimonial subjects can often counteract the more universalizing dimensions of an interview protocol. Applied to the context of traumatic testimony, that term is also invoked in Marianne Hirsch and Leo Spitzer, "The Witness in the Archive: Holocaust Studies/Memory Studies," *Memory Studies* 2, no. 151 (2009): 158.

15. Michael Renov, "Introduction: The Truth About Non-Fiction," in *Theorizing Documentary,* edited by Michael Renov (New York: Routledge, 1993), 6.

16. For a debate concerning the narrative mediations of testimony, see Gary Weissman and his critique of Lawrence Langer in Weissman, *Fantasies of Witnessing*, 89–139.

17. Geoffrey Hartman, "Introduction: On Closure," in *The Longest Shadow: In the Aftermath of the Holocaust* (New York: Palgrave Macmillan, 2002), 12.

18. Geoffrey Hartman, "The Humanities of Testimony: An Introduction," *Poetics Today* 27, no. 2 (Summer 2006): 255.

19. Ibid., 257.

20. Tony Kushner, for instance, wants to explore ways to preserve the "disjunction and confusion" of Holocaust testimony, while still making it available to a public audience. As a new strategy for conducting testimony, he suggests, for example, recording fewer survivors and interviewing them in a more self-reflexive mode that preserves the contradictions and gaps in the work of testimony. Tony Kushner, "Holocaust Testimony, Ethics, and the Problem of Representation," *Poetics Today* 27, no. 2 (Summer 2006): 291–292.

21. The quote on "received history" comes from James E. Young, *At Memory's Edge: After-Images of the Holocaust in Contemporary Art and Architecture* (New Haven, Conn.: Yale University Press, 2000), 15. I explore the notion of "reading against the grain" of Holocaust testimonies in Noah Shenker, "Embodied Memory" (Ph.D. diss.), 14. Those terms are also invoked in Müller, "Trauma, Historiography and Polyphony,"185–186. See also Shandler, "Holocaust Survivors on *Schindler's List;* or, Reading a Digital Archive against the Grain," 4–5. Each of these works makes the case that interpreting testimonies "against the grain" illuminates the contexts in which those sources were created.

22. Langer, *Holocaust Testimonies*, 5–6.

23. Saul Friedländer, "Trauma, Memory, and Transference," in *Holocaust Remembrance: The Shapes of Memory*, edited by Geoffrey Hartman (Oxford and Cambridge, Mass.: Blackwell, 1994), 254. On the prospects for exploring the audiovisual preservation of deep memory, see Shenker, "Embodied Memory" (Ph.D. diss.), 22–23, as well as Pinchevski, "The Audiovisual Unconscious," 154–156.

24. Langer, *Holocaust Testimonies*, 172.

25. Patricia Yaeger, "Testimony without Intimacy," *Poetics Today* 27, no. 2 (Summer 2006): 402. In the fall of 2002 Yale University hosted the conference, "The Contribution of Oral Testimony to Holocaust and Genocide Studies" to mark the Fortunoff Archive's twentieth anniversary at the school. The conference brought together prominent scholars from a wide range of disciplines to discuss not only the Fortunoff project, but also the overall prospects for Holocaust testimony archives. Several participants in that conference, including Patricia Yaeger, subsequently contributed essays on the subject to a volume entitled *The Humanities of Testimony*, published in a special issue of *Poetics Today* in 2006.

26. Yaeger, "Testimony without Intimacy," 402.

27. Ibid., 410.

28. Aleida Assmann, "History, Memory, and the Genre of Testimony," *Poetics Today* 27, no. 2 (Summer 2006): 264.

29. Ibid.

30. Ibid., 267.

31. Ibid., 270–271.

32. For an examination of testimony archives as "affective communities" see Hartman, *The Longest Shadow*, 153; and Pinchevski, "The Audiovisual Unconscious," 149.

33. Alan Mintz, *Popular Culture and the Shaping of Holocaust Memory in America* (Seattle: University of Washington Press, 2001), 23–27.

34. Annette Wieviorka, "The Witness in History," *Poetics Today* 27, no. 2 (Summer 2006): 388–389. Scholars such as Alan Rosen in *The Wonder of Their Voices* and Zoë Waxman in *Writing the Holocaust* provide a wider historical trajectory compared to Wieviorka's article here and to her book *The Era of the Witness*. However, I agree with Wieviorka's contention in both works that the Eichmann trial was central to rendering Holocaust survivor testimonies in official and popular forms.

35. Wieviorka, "The Witness in History," 389. For more depth and breadth on the question of Holocaust documentation, commemoration, and witnessing both during and after World War II, see Hasia Diner, *We Remember with Reverence and Love: American Jews and the Myth of Silence after the Holocaust, 1945–1962* (New York: New York University Press, 2009); and Laura Jockusch, *Collect and Record! Jewish Holocaust Documentation in Early Postwar Europe* (Oxford: Oxford University Press, 2012).

36. Wieviorka, "The Witness in History," 390.

37. Ibid., 392–393.

38. Scholars such as Peter Novick, *The Holocaust in American Life* (New York: Houghton Mifflin Company, 2000), 201, argue that since the 1970s Jewish culture in the United States has turned toward a focus on victimization during the Holocaust as a source for communal renewal, at the same time positioning survivors as the primary educators and interpreters of Holocaust history. Novick contends that survivors' embodiment of Jewish suffering, endurance, and memory encourages a homogenizing rather than a diversified vision of the Jewish community. He would use survivor testimonies more as evocative texts than as rigorous historical sources. Tim Cole makes similar arguments in *Selling the Holocaust: From Auschwitz to Schindler; How History Is Bought, Packaged, and Sold* (New York: Routledge, 2000), 14, contending that the Americanization of the Holocaust has reinforced a tendency to use past events to seek tidy resolution and redemption, in the process keeping contemporary suffering at a distance. Cole further argues that "Americanizing" films and archives such as *Schindler's List* and the Shoah Foundation are invested in precisely that kind of redemptive project, manifested in what he sees as troubling forms of experiential, visceral modes of representation.

39. Waxman, *Writing the Holocaust*, 158–159, offers a compelling critique of how Holocaust survivor accounts can be homogenized by dominant conceptions of cultural memory.

40. Hartman, "Introduction: On Closure," 7.

41. Ibid., 10.

42. Janet Walker, *Trauma Cinema: Documenting Incest and the Holocaust* (Berkeley: University of California Press, 2005), xviii.

43. Ibid., 11.

44. Alessandro Portelli, "Oral History as Genre," in *Narrative and Genre: Contexts and Types of Communication,* edited by Mary Chamberlain and Paul Thompson (New Brunswick, N.J.: Transaction Publishers, 2009), 23; and *The Death of Luigi Trastulli and Other Stories: Form and Meaning in Oral History* (Albany: State University of New York Press, 1991), ix. Portelli has provided a strong critical armature for understanding the co-authorship of oral history in general rather than in regards to the Holocaust in particular.

45. Walker, *Trauma Cinema,* 22.

46. See Christopher Browning, both *Collected Memories: Holocaust History and Postwar Testimony* (Madison: University of Wisconsin Press, 2003) and *Remembering Survival: Inside a Nazi Slave-Labor Camp* (New York: W.W. Norton, 2010).

47. Dori Laub, "Bearing Witness or the Vicissitudes of Listening," in *Testimony: Crises of Witnessing in Literature, Psychoanalysis, and History,* by Shoshana Felman and Dori Laub (New York: Routledge, 1992), 57–59.

48. For further discussion of the limits of these terms, see Henry Greenspan and Sidney Bolkosky, "When Is an Interview an Interview? Notes from Listening to Holocaust Survivors," *Poetics Today* 27, no. 2 (Summer 2006): 432. Greenspan and Bolkosky consciously avoid using the term *testimony,* which they contend suggests a monological rather than dialogical endeavor. However, I feel that this term captures the ethical and historiographical aspects of the debates concerning these sources without jettisoning the important fact that there are those who give as well as receive testimonies through a process that involves both conversation and contestation.

49. For an examination of how certain cultural preferences and ideals render victims as exemplary, see Carolyn Dean, "Minimalism and Victim Testimony," *History and Theory,* Theme Issue 49 (December 2010): 85–99.

50. Although I identified a small grouping of witnesses who had given testimonies across each of this book's three featured archives, many more individuals gave testimonies at two of the three sites, or gave multiple testimonies at other archives and venues, including Yad Vashem, which are not covered in this study. There are, in other words, what Henry Greenspan and Sidney Bolkosky refer to as "veteran" interviewees. See Greenspan and Bolkosky, "When Is an Interview an Interview?," 438. Also see both editions of Henry Greenspan, *On Listening to Holocaust Survivors,* in which the author writes of his sustained encounter with a group of Holocaust survivors over many years. While I did not interview survivors for this book, and thus was unable to attain the familiarity and intimacy that Greenspan fostered with interviewees, my comparative group of recorded witnesses nonetheless provides insights into how interviews change over time, with the added dimension of multiple archival contexts. For a compelling example of research conducted by multiple Holocaust scholars adopting different perspectives to analyzing one particular survivor (Helen "Zippi" Tichauer"), see Jurgen Matthäus, *Approaching an Auschwitz Survivor: Holocaust Testimony and Its Transformations* (New York: Oxford University Press, 2009).

51. For one exploration of gender in Holocaust testimony see Zoë Waxman, "Unheard Testimony, Untold Stories: The Representation of Women's Holocaust experiences," *Women's History Review* 12, no. 4 (2003): 661–677.

52. Michael Frisch's concept of *shared authority* has provided insights on the dynamic, collaborative aspects of recording oral history, which are in many ways applicable to the context of Holocaust testimony. Michael Frisch, *A Shared Authority: Essays on the Craft and Meaning of Oral History and Public History* (Albany: State University of New York Press, 1990). The shared aspects and the idea of "labor" associated with the interview process are keenly examined in Greenspan and Bolkosky, "When Is an Interview an Interview?," 432; 439.

53. Edward Linenthal, *Preserving Memory: The Struggle to Create America's Holocaust Museum* (New York: Columbia University Press, 2001) is the definitive, comprehensive history of the U.S. Holocaust Museum; it served as an invaluable reference in helping me to navigate the museum's vast institutional archives during my research fellowship at the USHMM. It was during that fellowship that I compiled the research used in this study. *Preserving Memory* intends to provide a wide-ranging chronicle of the museum's development; issues related to collecting testimony are of secondary concern, and it contains little in the way of analysis of individual testimonies or in-depth discussion of testimony protocols, preferences, and methodologies.

54. Public Law 96-388, Enacted by the 96th United States Congress, 7 October 1980, cited in "Responding to the Future: Work Plan 2000," 3 May 2000. U.S. Holocaust Memorial Museum [hereafter USHMM]; Institutional Archives; Director's Office; Records of the Museum Director-Jeshajahu "Shaike" Weinberg; 1979–1995; 1997-014; Box 22; Committee: Conscience.

55. For a more detailed examination of how the U.S. Holocaust Memorial Museum is integrated into the landscape of American commemorative culture, see Linenthal, *Preserving Memory*.

56. *Oral History Interview Guidelines* (USHMM: Washington, D.C., 2007), ii.

57. Press Release, undated (prior to opening), "The Assault (1933–39), The Holocaust (1939–45), and Bearing Witness (1945–Present): The Permanent Exhibition of the United States Holocaust Memorial Museum," pp. 1–2. USHMM; Institutional Archives; Records of Raye Farr Relating to the Segment Development of the Permanent Exhibition; CA 1990–1994; Box 13; Oral History.

1. Testimonies from the Grassroots

1. Geoffrey Hartman, quoted in Michael Rothberg and Jared Stark, "After the Witness: A Report from the Twentieth Anniversary Conference of the Fortunoff Video Archive for Holocaust Testimonies at Yale," *History and Memory* 15, no. 1 (Spring 2003): 94–95.

2. Ibid., 93.

3. I am thankful to Joanne Rudof for agreeing to numerous interviews and for providing her history (cited here) of the Fortunoff Archive: Joanne Weiner Rudof, "A Yale University and New Haven Community Project: From Local to Global," Fortunoff

Video Archive for Holocaust Testimonies Article (October 2012):1–2, http://www.library
.yale.edu/testimonies/publications/Local_to_Global.pdf (accessed 13 November 2014).

4. Ibid., 10.

5. Ibid., 2.

6. Ibid., 4.

7. Ibid., 5.

8. Ibid., 7.

9. Joanne Rudof, Archivist, Fortunoff Video Archive for Holocaust Testimonies,
email correspondence with author, 15 May 2014.

10. Geoffrey Hartman, "About the Yale Archive," in *Witness: Voices from the Holocaust,* edited by Joshua M. Greene and Shiva Kumar (New York: Touchstone, 2000),
252–253.

11. Ibid., 253.

12. Ibid.

13. The Fortunoff Archive is, however, in the process of digitizing its entire testimony collection, with plans for finalizing that process in 2014. Once that process is
complete, it will introduce a controlled, remote-access platform for universities and
Holocaust museums located across the globe. Joanne Rudof, Archivist, Fortunoff Video
Archive for Holocaust Testimonies, email correspondence with author, 15 May 2014.

14. Geoffrey Hartman, "About the Yale Archive," 254.

15. Joanne Rudof, Archivist, Fortunoff Video Archive for Holocaust Testimonies,
interview by author, 30 March 2006, New Haven, Conn., Yale University.

16. Rothberg and Stark, "After the Witness," 86.

17. Ibid., 88.

18. Ibid. Note that the conference report attributes the notion of the "Schinderliza-
tion" of testimony to Walter Reich.

19. Letter from Geoffrey Hartman to volunteer interviewers for the Fortunoff Archive, 15 January 1993; Fortunoff Video Archive for Holocaust Testimonies [hereafter
FVA] Internal Papers. This and other FVA archival materials were generously provided
to me by Joanne Rudof, Archivist, Fortunoff Video Archive for Holocaust Testimonies,
Yale University.

20. Ibid.

21. Langer, *Holocaust Testimonies,* 26.

22. Lawrence Langer, "Hearing the Holocaust," *Poetics Today* 27, no. 2 (Summer
2006): 305.

23. Correspondence and Analysis of Fortunoff Archive Testimonies from Lawrence
Langer to Michael Berenbaum, 4 April 1991. USHMM; Institutional Archives; Research
Institute; Subject Files of the Director Michael Berenbaum; 1989–1997; 1988-011; Box 20;
Lawrence Langer. Emphasis in original.

24. Ibid.

25. Ibid.

26. Ibid.

27. Ibid.

28. Ibid.

29. Ibid.

30. Ibid. Emphasis in original.

31. Rudof, "A Yale University and New Haven Community Project," 18.

32. "Toward an Understanding of Media-Based Testimony," Undated Training Documents; FVA Internal Papers.

33. Ibid.

34. Ibid.

35. Ibid.

36. Ibid.

37. Ibid.

38. Rudof, interviews by author, 15 December 2006 and 10 July 2007.

39. Rudof, interview by author, 10 July 2007.

40. Rothberg and Stark, "After the Witness," 88.

41. Rudof, interview by author, 30 March 2006.

42. Ibid.

43. Hartman, "About the Yale Archive," 253.

44. Rudof, interview by author, 30 March 2006.

45. Handwritten and Undated Notes on Fortunoff Video Archive Testimonies; FVA Internal Papers.

46. Outline for interviewer training held in New York City, 5 February 1990; FVA Internal Papers.

47. Letter from Geoffrey Hartman to volunteer interviewers for the Fortunoff Archive; 15 January 1993; FVA Internal Papers.

48. Notes for first session of "refresher course" (for training interviewers); undated; FVA Internal Papers.

49. Ibid.

50. Handwritten and Undated Notes on FVA Testimonies; FVA Internal Papers.

51. Ibid.; Fred O. Holocaust Testimony (HVT-943), 18 November 1987. Fortunoff Video Archive for Holocaust Testimonies, Yale University Library.

52. Fred O. Holocaust Testimony (HVT-943).

53. Ibid.

54. Handwritten and Undated Notes on FVA Testimonies; FVA Internal Papers.

55. List of sample questions, specifically those that interviewers should seek to avoid; FVA Internal Papers.

56. Ibid.

57. Rudof, interview by author, 22 August 2006.

58. Rudof, interview by author, 30 March 2006.

59. Handwritten and Undated Notes on FVA Testimonies; FVA Internal Papers.

60. Rudof, "Research Use of Holocaust Testimonies," 458.

61. *Those Who Were There*, VHS. Promotional video shown to American Gathering of Holocaust Survivors in 1983.

62. Ibid.

63. Ibid.

64. Joshua M. Greene, "Editor's Introduction" to *Witness*, xxiii.

65. Ibid.

66. Ibid., xxviii.

67. Ibid., xxiv.

68. *Witness: Voices from the Holocaust*, v hs. Directed by Joshua M. Greene and Shiva Kumar; v hs released 2001.

69. That observation is based on the author's research visit to the Anne Frank House museum in Amsterdam in June of 2006.

70. Lawrence Langer examines this particular moment in the testimony of John S., in *Holocaust Testimonies*, 30–33. Langer comments that there is an "immediacy of introspection" in the witness's testimony, as he is "confronted by the interviewer" through a particular line of questioning (31). The richness of that exchange is absent from *Witness*.

71. Greene, "Editor's Introduction," xxiii.

72. *Witness*, v hs.

73. Abraham P. Holocaust Testimony (h v t-738). f va, Yale University Library.

74. For further analysis of the testimony of Abraham P. and the dynamic that is forged between him and interviewers, see the following: Greenspan, *On Listening to Holocaust Survivors: Beyond Testimony*, xv–xvi; 98–101; 238–248; Langer, *Holocaust Testimonies*, 185–187; Langer, *Admitting the Holocaust: Collected Essays* (New York: Oxford University Press, 1995), 29–30; and throughout Sidney M. Bolkosky, *Searching for Meaning in the Holocaust* (Westport, Conn.: Greenwood, 2002).

75. Rudof, interview by author, 20 July 2006.

76. Correspondence and Analysis of Fortunoff Archive Testimonies from Lawrence Langer to Michael Berenbaum, 4 April 1991. u s h m m; Institutional Archives; Research Institute; Subject Files of the Director Michael Berenbaum; 1989–1997; 1988-011; Box 20; Lawrence Langer.

77. Rudof, interview by author, 20 July 2006.

78. Eva B. Holocaust Testimony (h v t-1). f va, Yale University Library.

79. Ibid. Note that while the h v t number for the 1979 and 1983 testimonies is the same, this footnote refers to the testimony from 1979.

80. Ibid., 1983.

81. Ibid.

82. Eva B. Holocaust Testimony (h v t-1101). f va, Yale University Library.

83. f va, Excerpts; Rabbi Baruch G., http://www.library.yale.edu/testimonies /excerpts/index.html (accessed 8 April 2009).

84. Rabbi Baruch G. Holocaust Testimony (h v t-295). f va, Yale University Library.

85. Outline for interviewer training held in New York City, 5 February 1990; f va Internal Papers.

86. Langer, *Holocaust Testimonies*, 22–24; Correspondence and Analysis of Fortunoff Archive Testimonies from Lawrence Langer to Michael Berenbaum, 4 April 1991. u s h m m; Institutional Archives; Research Institute; Subject Files of the Director Michael Berenbaum; 1989–1997; 1988-011; Box 20; Lawrence Langer. I reference Langer's

correspondence with Berenbaum, in addition to citing *Holocaust Testimonies,* in order to underscore that Langer has provided a scholarly as well as a practical archival intervention on issues of Holocaust testimonies.

87. Correspondence and Analysis of Fortunoff Archive Testimonies from Lawrence Langer to Michael Berenbaum, 4 April 1991.

88. Ibid.

89. Greene and Kumar, eds., *Witness,* 249–250.

90. Rabbi Baruch G. Holocaust Testimony (HVT-295). FVA, Yale University Library.

91. Hartman, "Learning from Survivors: The Yale Testimony Project," in *The Longest Shadow: In the Aftermath of the Holocaust* (New York: Palgrave Macmillan, 2002), 133.

92. Langer, "Foreword" to *Witness,* xii.

93. Ibid., xv.

94. Greene, "Editor's Introduction," xxv.

95. Rabbi Baruch G. Holocaust Testimony (HVT-295). FVA, Yale University Library.

96. Correspondence and Analysis of Fortunoff Archive Testimonies from Lawrence Langer to Michael Berenbaum, 4 April 1991. USHMM; Institutional Archives; Research Institute; Subject Files of the Director Michael Berenbaum; 1989–1997; 1988-011; Box 20; Lawrence Langer. Langer offers a similar analysis of Barbara T. in *Holocaust Testimonies,* 18–19.

97. Correspondence and Analysis of Fortunoff Archive Testimonies from Lawrence Langer to Michael Berenbaum, 4 April 1991.

98. Rothberg and Stark, "After the Witness," 86.

99. Ibid.

100. Ibid., 91.

2. Centralizing Holocaust Testimony

1. Oral History Interview Guidelines, USHMM. Written by Oral History Staff, Revised 2007, i.

2. "A Unique Institution: The United States Holocaust Memorial Museum," undated press release issued prior to the opening of the Holocaust Museum. USHMM; Institutional Archives; Records of Raye Farr Relating to the Segment Development of the Permanent Exhibition; CA 1990–1994; 1998-038.2; Box 13; Oral History; and Linenthal, *Preserving Memory,* xxiii.

3. For a more detailed examination of how the U.S. Holocaust Memorial Museum is integrated into the landscape of American commemorative culture, see Linenthal, *Preserving Memory.*

4. U.S. Holocaust Memorial Museum; Institutional Archives; Exhibitions; Permanent Exhibition-Development Files; 1990–1994; 1998-038; Box 13; Oral History.

5. Linenthal, *Preserving Memory,* 28.

6. Ibid., 32.

7. Ibid., 152–154.

8. "About the National Registry," introduction by Benjamin Meed, 1983. USHMM; Institutional Archives; Director's Office; Records of the Museum Director Jeshajahu

"Shaike" Weinberg; 1979–1995; 1997-014; Box 4; American Gathering of Jewish Holocaust Survivors.

9. Ibid.

10. "An Appeal for Information about Materials for the National Holocaust Memorial Museum," undated (circa 1988). USHMM; Institutional Archives; Research Institute, Directors Office; Michael Berenbaum's Committee Memoranda and Reports, 1986–1996; 1997-016.1; Box 2; Content Committee—28 September 1988. Emphasis in original.

11. A Mass Fundraising Letter from Benjamin Meed to Unspecified Recipients on Behalf of the American Gathering of Jewish Holocaust Survivors, November 1990. USHMM; Institutional Archives; Research Institute; Subject Files of the Director Michael Berenbaum; 1989–1997; 1988-011; Box 1; American Gathering-Federation of Jewish Holocaust Survivors.

12. "Resolution by the National Leadership Board Meeting, American Gathering of Jewish Holocaust Survivors," 20 February 1989. USHMM; Institutional Archives; Research Institute; Subject Files of the Director Michael Berenbaum; 1989–1997; 1988-011; Box 1; American Gathering-Federation of Jewish Holocaust Survivors.

13. Ibid.

14. Chairman's Guidelines for the Content Committee, assisted by historian Eli Pfefferkorn, 12 August 1985, p. 1. USHMM; Institutional Archives; Records of the Chairperson—Elie Wiesel, 1978–1986; 1997-013; Box 22, Museum Content Committee I.

15. Elie Wiesel, "Trivializing the Holocaust: Semi-Fact and Semi-Fiction," *The New York Times*, 16 April 1978.

16. Chairman's Guidelines for the Content Committee, 12 August 1985.

17. Ibid.

18. Ibid.

19. Ibid.

20. Typed transcript from Museum Concept Planning Committee, 6 November 1985, p. 173. USHMM; Institutional Archives; Records of the Chairperson—Elie Wiesel, 1978–1986; 1997-013; Box 21; Museum Concept Planning Committee Minutes, 11/6/85.

21. Press Release, undated (prior to opening), "The Assault (1933–39), The Holocaust (1939–45), and Bearing Witness (1945–Present): The Permanent Exhibition of the United States Holocaust Memorial Museum," pp. 1–2. USHMM; Institutional Archives; Records of Raye Farr Relating to the Segment Development of the Permanent Exhibition; CA 1990–1994; Box 13; Oral History.

22. Ibid.

23. "To Bear Witness, To Remember, and to Learn," by Anna Cohn and David Altshuler, 28 February 1984. USHMM; Director's Office; Records of the Museum Director Jeshajahu "Shaike" Weinberg; 1979–1995; 1997-014; Box 23; Concept Outline-Weinberg (2 Folders) [The "Red Book"—a report titled "To Bear Witness, to Remember, and to Learn," by Anna Cohn and David Altshuler, 28 February 1984].

24. Ibid., 12–14.

25. Ibid., 13.

26. Ibid., 14.

27. Memorandum to Museum Staff, Re: Attached Article, 13 July 1991, p. 1. USHMM; Institutional Archives; Director's Office; Records of the Museum Director Jeshajahu "Shaike" Weinberg; 1979–1995; 1997-014; Box 23; Concept Outline.

28. U.S. Holocaust Memorial Museum; Institutional Archives; Research Institute; Records of the Director Michael Berenbaum; 1986–1994; 1997-006; Box 93; Hillel Levine, Report on "Remembering and Memorializing the Holocaust: Psychological and Educational Dimensions."

29. Minutes of the Meeting of the Museum Content Committee, 21 October 1987. USHMM; Institutional Archives; Research Institute; Michael Berenbaum's Committee Memoranda and Reports Dates: 1986–1996; 1997-016.1; Box 1; Content Committee—21 October 1987.

30. "Proposed Gift List from Museum at Auschwitz to USHMM," undated. USHMM; Institutional Archives; Director's Office; Records of the Museum Director Jeshajahu "Shaike" Weinberg; 1979–1995; 1997-014; Box 56; Donations: Objects.

31. For further discussion of the Holocaust Museum as a site of organic memory, see Alison Landsberg, *Prosthetic Memory: The Transformation of American Remembrance in the Age of Mass Culture* (New York: Columbia University Press, 2004), 129–139. Although her section on the Holocaust Museum extensively covers issues related to what she calls "living" and "prosthetic" memory and provides rich analysis of the museum's Permanent Exhibition, it only marginally focuses on matters of testimony.

32. Press Release, undated (prior to opening), "The Assault (1933–39), The Holocaust (1939–45), and Bearing Witness (1945–Present): The Permanent Exhibition of the United States Holocaust Memorial Museum," pp. 1–2. USHMM; Institutional Archives; Records of Raye Farr Relating to the Segment Development of the Permanent Exhibition; CA 1990–1994; 1998-038.2; Box 13; Oral History.

33. "Proposed Concept Outline for the United States Holocaust Memorial Museum," Washington, D.C., May 1985. USHMM; Institutional Archives; Director's Office; Records of the Museum Director Jeshajahu "Shaike" Weinberg; 1979–1995; 1997-014; Box 23; Concept Outline—Weinberg (2 Folders) [The "Red Book"—a report titled "To Bear Witness, to Remember, and to Learn," by Anna Cohn and David Altshuler, 28 February 1984].

34. Memorandum from Eli Pfefferkorn, Director of Research Development, to USHMC Members, Regarding Print and Visual Materials for Exhibit Model, 3 December 1986. USHMM; Institutional Archives; Director's Office; Records of the Museum Director Jeshajahu "Shaike" Weinberg; 1979–1995; 1997-014; Box 120; Pfefferkorn, Eli.

35. Linenthal, *Preserving Memory*, 116.

36. Minutes of the Meeting of the Museum Content Committee, 28 September 1988, p. 2. USHMM; Institutional Archives; Research Institute; Michael Berenbaum's Committee Memoranda and Reports Dates: 1986–1996; 1997-016.1; Box 2; Content Committee—28 September 1988.

37. Ibid.

38. Ibid., 5.

39. Ibid.

40. "A Working Response to the Question of Explicit Imagery Including 'The Pornography of Murder,' Nudity and Violence in a Museum," Prepared by Michael Berenbaum, Alice Greenwald, and Shomer Zwelling on behalf of the Content Team, 26 February 1988. USHMM; Institutional Archives; Research Institute; Michael Berenbaum's Committee Memoranda and Reports Dates: 1986–1996; 1997-016.1; Box 1; Miscellaneous.

41. Minutes of the Meeting of the Museum Content Committee, 29 February 1988. USHMM; Institutional Archives; Research Institute; Michael Berenbaum's Committee Memoranda and Reports Dates: 1986–1996; 1997-016.1; Box 1; Content Committee—29 February 1988.

42. Minutes of the Meeting of the Museum Content Committee, 15 November 1988.

43. Ibid.

44. Ibid.

45. The museum label accompanying the boxcar on display in the Permanent Exhibition explains that it was "of the kind" used for deportations.

46. Memorandum from Cindy Miller to Ralph Appelbaum, Martin Smith, Shaike Weinberg, and Michael Berenbaum on 27 April 1989. USHMM; Institutional Archives; Research Institute; Subject Files of the Director Michael Berenbaum; 1989–1997; 1988-011; Box 29; Railroad Car.

47. Remarks of Dr. Michael Berenbaum to Joint Meeting of the Museum Development Committee and Content Committee, 20 January 2008. USHMM; Institutional Archives; Research Institute; Michael Berenbaum's Committee Memoranda and Reports, 1986–1996; 1997-016.1; Content Committee Records; Box 1; Content Committee —20 January 1988.

48. Agreement between the State Museum at Majdanek in Poland and the USHMM, 7 March 1989. USHMM; Institutional Archives; Research Institute; Subject Files of the Director Michael Berenbaum; 1989–1997; 1998-011; Box 28; Poland—Agreements and Collections Assessment.

49. Interoffice Memo from Susan Morgenstern to Shaike Weinberg, Martin Goldman, Martin Smith, Re: Attached Conservator's Report on Shoes, 2 February 1990. USHMM; Institutional Archives; Research Institute; Subject Files of the Director Michael Berenbaum; 1989–1997; 1998-011; Box 32; Shoes.

50. Interoffice Memo from Martin Smith to Susan Morgenstern, Regarding "The Shoes," 13 February 1990. USHMM; Institutional Archives; Research Institute; Subject Files of the Director Michael Berenbaum; 1989–1997; 1998-011; Box 32; Shoes.

51. "Proposed Gift List from Museum at Auschwitz to USHMM," undated. USHMM; Institutional Archives; Director's Office; Records of the Museum Director Jeshajahu "Shaike" Weinberg; 1979–1995; 1997-014; Box 56; Donations: Objects.

52. "Visit Regarding Schindler Ceremony," 30 November 1993. USHMM; Institutional Archives; Records of Raye Farr Relating to the Segment Development of the Permanent Exhibition; CA 1990–1994; 1998-038.2; Box 16, *Schindler's List*.

53. Ibid.

54. Ibid.

55. Ibid.

56. Memorandum to Museum Staff, Re: Attached Article, 13 July 1991, p. 1. USHMM; Institutional Archives; Director's Office; Records of the Museum Director Jeshajahu "Shaike" Weinberg; 1979–1995; 1997-014; Box 23; Concept Outline.

57. Raye Farr, Director, Film and Video, Collections Division, USHMM. Interview by author, 20 November 2006, Washington, D.C., USHMM.

58. Linenthal, *Preserving Memory,* xiv–xv.

59. Letter from Hadassah Rosensaft to Michael Berenbaum on 16 April 1988. USHMM; Institutional Archives; Research Institute; Subject Files of the Director Michael Berenbaum; 1989–1997; 1988-011; Box 16; Hair. My emphasis added.

60. Ibid. Emphasis in original.

61. I elaborate on my analysis of Landsberg's *Prosthetic Memory* in Chapter 4.

62. Letter from Hadassah Rosensaft to Michael Berenbaum, 16 April 1988.

63. Linenthal, *Preserving Memory,* 210–216, extensively chronicles the debate concerning the display of hair. That is where I first learned of this controversy—and was directed toward USHMM institutional archives documenting the debate.

64. Minutes of the Meeting of the Museum Content Committee, 13 February 1990, USHMM; Institutional Archives; Research Institute; Michael Berenbaum's Committee Memoranda and Reports, 1986–1996; 1997-016.1; Content Committee Records; Box 2; Content Committee—13 February 1990.

65. Ibid.

66. Ibid.

67. Ibid.

68. Ibid.

69. U.S. Holocaust Memorial Museum, Department of Oral History, *Oral History Interview Guidelines* (Washington, D.C.: 1998), ii.

70. "Oral History Report: An Overview of the Process and Initial Steps," 20 August 1988. USHMM; Institutional Archives; Research Institute; Subject Files of the Director Michael Berenbaum; 1989–1997; 1988-011; Box 26; Oral History.

71. Ibid.

72. Ibid.

73. Notes by Benjamin Meed, Re: USHMM National Registry, 3 January 1991, p. 3. USHMM; Institutional Archives; Research Institute; Subject Files of the Director Michael Berenbaum; 1989–1997; 1988-011; Box 33; Survivors Registry. Ben Meed lived to see a little more than a decade of the Museum's existence; he died in 2006. http://www.nytimes.com/2006/10/26/obituaries/26meed.html?_r=0 (accessed 21 May 2014).

74. Notes by Benjamin Meed, Re: USHMM National Registry, 3 January 1991, p. 3.

75. Survey distributed to American Gathering of Jewish Holocaust Survivors, Los Angeles, 19 April 1991. USHMM; Institutional Archives; Records of Raye Farr Relating to the Segment Development of the Permanent Exhibition; CA 1990–1994; 1998-038.2; Box 13; Oral History.

76. Memorandum from Linda Kuzmack to Michael Berenbaum, Re: Oral History Project Plans, 11 November 1988; and USHMM-Oral History Department—Description for Michael Berenbaum, 9 February 1990. USHMM; Institutional Archives; Records

of Raye Farr Relating to the Segment Development of the Permanent Exhibition; CA 1990–1994; 1998-038.2; Box 13; Oral History. My emphasis added.

77. Memorandum from Linda Kuzmack to Shaike Weinberg, Michael Berenbaum, Martin Smith, and Martin Goldman, Re: Yale's Proposed Agreement, 6 August 1990. USHMM; Institutional Archives; Research Institute; Subject Files of the Director Michael Berenbaum; 1989–1997; 1998-011; Box 26; Oral History-Fortunoff Archives-Yale.

78. Memorandum from Linda Kuzmack to Shaike Weinberg, Re: "Creating Oral History Affiliates," 13 April 1990. USHMM; Institutional Archives; Research Institute; Subject Files of the Director Michael Berenbaum; 1989–1997; 1998-011; Box 26; Oral History-Fortunoff Archives-Yale.

79. Memorandum from Kuzmack to Weinberg, Berenbaum, Smith, Goldman, Re: Yale's Proposed Agreement, 6 August 1990.

80. Memorandum from Martin Smith to Linda Kuzmack, November 1988. USHMM; Institutional Archives; Records of Raye Farr Relating to the Segment Development of the Permanent Exhibition; CA 1990–1994; 1998-038.2; Box 13; Oral History.

81. Ibid.

82. Memorandum from Martin Smith to Linda Kuzmack, 16 October 1989. USHMM; Institutional Archives; Records of Raye Farr Relating to the Segment Development of the Permanent Exhibition; CA 1990–1994; 1998-038.2; Box 13; Oral History.

83. Memorandum from Martin Smith to Linda Kuzmack, 24 June 1989. USHMM; Institutional Archives; Records of Raye Farr Relating to the Segment Development of the Permanent Exhibition; CA 1990–1994; 1998-038.2; Box 13; Oral History.

84. Memorandum from Martin Smith to Linda Kuzmack, November 1988.

85. Memorandum from Martin Smith to Linda Kuzmack, 16 October 1989.

86. Memorandum from Linda Kuzmack to Martin Smith, 18 October 1989. USHMM; Institutional Archives; Records of Raye Farr Relating to the Segment Development of the Permanent Exhibition; CA 1990–1994; 1998-038.2; Box 13; Oral History.

87. Report from Linda Kuzmack to Michael Berenbaum, 14 December 1988. USHMM; Institutional Archives; Records of Raye Farr Relating to the Segment Development of the Permanent Exhibition; CA 1990–1994; 1998-038.2; Box 13; Oral History.

88. "Oral History Report: An Overview of the Process and Initial Steps," 20 September 1988. USHMM; Institutional Archives; Records of Raye Farr Relating to the Segment Development of the Permanent Exhibition; CA 1990–1994; 1998-038.2; Box 13; Oral History.

89. Ibid.

90. Memorandum from Linda Kuzmack to Shaike Weinberg, Michael Berenbaum, and Martin Smith, Re: Videotestimony in the Exhibition, 13 July 1989. USHMM; Institutional Archives; Research Institute; Subject Files of the Director Michael Berenbaum; 1989–1997; 1998-011; Box 26; Oral History.

91. Ibid.

92. Memorandum from Linda Kuzmack to Shaike Weinberg, Michael Berenbaum, Martin Smith, Ralph Appelbaum, and Cindy Miller, 21 November 1989. USHMM; Institu-

tional Archives; Records of Raye Farr Relating to the Segment Development of the Permanent Exhibition; CA 1990–1994; 1998-038.2; Box 13; Oral History.

93. Summaries of Completed USHMM Oral Histories, undated. USHMM; Institutional Archives; Research Institute; Subject Files of the Director Michael Berenbaum; 1989–1997; 1988-011; Box 26; Oral History.

94. Oral History Interviewee Release Form. USHMM; Institutional Archives; Records of Raye Farr Relating to the Segment Development of the Permanent Exhibition; CA 1990–1994; 1998-038.2; Box 13; Oral History.

95. Memorandum from Linda Kuzmack to Michael Berenbaum, Re: Oral History Project Plans, 11 November 1988; USHMM; Institutional Archives; Records of Raye Farr Relating to the Segment Development of the Permanent Exhibition; CA 1990–1994; 1998-038.2; Box 13; Oral History. Emphasis in original.

96. Letter from Raye Farr to Ari Zev, 21 February 1995. USHMM; Institutional Archives; Records of Raye Farr Relating to the Segment Development of the Permanent Exhibition; CA 1990–1994; 1998-038.2; Box 13; Oral History.

97. Memorandum from Linda Kuzmack to Raye Farr, 2 August 1991. USHMM; Institutional Archives; Records of Raye Farr Relating to the Segment Development of the Permanent Exhibition; CA 1990–1994; 1998-038.2; Box 13; Oral History.

98. Memorandum from Linda Kuzmack to Raye Farr, re Question Guide, 14 June 1991. USHMM; Institutional Archives; Records of Raye Farr Relating to the Segment Development of the Permanent Exhibition; CA 1990–1994; 1998-038.2; Box 13; Oral History.

99. Ibid.

100. Ibid.

101. Ibid.

102. Ibid.

103. Ibid.

104. Procedures—United States Holocaust Memorial Museum—Instructions for Interviewers, 2 March 1992, p. 3. USHMM; Institutional Archives; Records of Raye Farr Relating to the Segment Development of the Permanent Exhibition; CA 1990–1994; 1998-038.2; Box 13; Oral History.

105. Correspondence and Analysis of Fortunoff Archive Testimonies from Lawrence Langer to Michael Berenbaum, 4 April 1991. USHMM; Institutional Archives; Research Institute; Subject Files of the Director Michael Berenbaum; 1989–1997; 1988-011; Box 20; Lawrence Langer. Emphasis in original.

106. Ibid.

107. See Langer, *Holocaust Testimonies,* 77; Correspondence and Analysis of Fortunoff Archive Testimonies from Lawrence Langer to Michael Berenbaum, 4 April 1991.

108. Ibid. (Correspondence). Emphasis in original.

109. Ibid.

110. Ibid.

111. Langer uses both sets of terms in his correspondence with Berenbaum.

112. Ibid.

113. Ibid. Emphasis in original.

114. Ibid.

115. "The United States Holocaust Memorial Museum," by Michael Berenbaum, undated, p. 1. U.S. Holocaust Memorial Museum; Institutional Archives; Records of Raye Farr Relating to the Segment Development of the Permanent Exhibition; CA 1990–1994; 1998-038.2; Box 13; Oral History.

116. Press Release, "Videotaped Oral Histories Will Preserve Holocaust Eyewitness Accounts in United States Holocaust Museum," by Dana Goldberg, undated 1989, p. 2. USHMM; Institutional Archives; Records of Raye Farr Relating to the Segment Development of the Permanent Exhibition; CA 1990–1994; 1998-038.2; Box 13; Oral History.

117. Raye Farr Agenda for Oral History Meeting, 31 March 1989. USHMM; Institutional Archives; Records of Raye Farr Relating to the Segment Development of the Permanent Exhibition; CA 1990–1994; 1998-038.2; Box 13; Oral History.

118. Memorandum from Martin Smith to Linda Kuzmack and Bonnie Durrance, Re: Oral History Interviews, 11 May 1989; USHMM; Institutional Archives; Records of Raye Farr Relating to the Segment Development of the Permanent Exhibition; CA 1990–1994; 1998-038.2; Box 13; Oral History.

119. Memorandum from Martin Smith to Linda Kuzmack, 24 July 1989. USHMM; Institutional Archives; Records of Raye Farr Relating to the Segment Development of the Permanent Exhibition; CA 1990–1994; 1998-038.2; Box 13; Oral History.

120. Memorandum from Martin Smith to Linda Kuzmack, 16 October 1989, p. 2.

121. Memorandum from Linda Kuzmack to Martin Smith, 18 October 1989, p. 1.

122. Susan Bachrach, Historian, Exhibitions Division, USHMM, interview by author, 8 February 2007, Washington, D.C., USHMM. In this interview, Bachrach conveyed these sentiments when I raised the prospect of using testimony, documentary footage, and other visual sources in a self-reflexive manner, juxtaposing them with more "traditional" representations of sources in order to draw out how they challenge, interrogate, and reinforce each other.

123. The Permanent Exhibition's segment pertaining to Jewish life in the Warsaw Ghetto includes a monitor displaying film footage recorded by Nazi filmmakers in the ghetto, but there is no captioning to indicate the source or the filmmakers. This footage, along with other material documented by members of the same film crew, would subsequently be examined in their context in *A Film Unfinished* (Yael Hersonski, 2010), which was produced independently of the Holocaust Museum.

124. Analysis of the "Tower of Faces" can also be found throughout both Andrea Liss, *Trespassing through Shadows: Memory, Photography, and the Holocaust* (Minneapolis: University of Minnesota Press, 1998); and Linenthal, *Preserving Memory*.

125. Yaffa Eliach, "The Ejszyszki Tower: The Tower of Faces," *The Jewish Studies Network* 5, no. 1 (Spring 1991): 4. USHMM; Institutional Archives; Research Institute; Subject Files of the Director Michael Berenbaum; 1989–1997; 1988-011; Box 13; Yaffa Eliach.

126. Letter from Yaffa Eliach to Raye Farr, 14 May 1991. USHMM; Institutional Archives; Research Institute; Subject Files of the Director Michael Berenbaum; 1989–1997; 1988-011; Box 13; Yaffa Eliach.

127. Raye Farr, interview by author, 29 March 2007.

128. Ibid.

129. Memorandum from Martin Smith to Shaike Weinberg, Re: "Testimony"—
A Rationale and an Appeal 7 May 1990, p. 1. USHMM; Institutional Archives; Records
of Raye Farr Relating to the Segment Development of the Permanent Exhibition; CA
1990–1994; 1998-038.2; Box 13; Oral History.

130. Ibid.

131. Ibid., 2. Although that more interactive, mosaic display of audiovisual testimonies was never installed at the United States Holocaust Memorial Museum, a similar
concept can now be found on display in the "Tree of Testimony" exhibit of the Los Angeles Museum of the Holocaust. The permanent exhibit is made up of seventy video
screens, each positioned on a wall, representing leaves interconnected by electronic
cables shaped in the form of tree branches. Each of the seventy screens displays separate Holocaust testimonies that are pulled from the entire cache of the Shoah Foundation's Visual History Archive.

132. Ibid.

133. Request for Proposal No. CX-1100-RFP-1020-Title: "Motion Picture on Testimony,"
issued 20 June 1991. This and other documents on the development of the *Testimony*
film were generously made available to me from the personal files of Raye Farr, formerly the USHMM Permanent Exhibition director.

134. Ibid.

135. Ibid.

136. Sandra Bradley, "Amendment to the Work Plan," Testimony film, 21 October
1991.

137. Ibid.

138. Ibid.

139. Farr's notes on *Testimony* screening held on 6 May 1992.

140. Ibid.

141. Farr's notes on *Testimony*, taken on 24 March 1992.

142. Farr's notes on *Testimony* screening held on 6 May 1992.

143. Linenthal, *Preserving Memory*, 253–254.

144. Opening caption for the film *Testimony*. Film directed by Sandy Bradley, 1993.
Screened within the USHMM Permanent Exhibition, Closing Segment.

145. Abraham M. segment in film *Testimony;* and Abraham M. Holocaust Testimony
(Videotape 50.030*0145), 10 May 1990. Collections Department, United States Holocaust
Memorial Museum, Washington, D.C.

146. Gerda K. has become a prominent Holocaust survivor figure, having been the
focus of the Academy Award-winning documentary *One Survivor Remembers*. VHS. Directed by Kary Antholis, VHS released 1999. She is also the author of her memoir *All But
My Life* (New York: Hill & Wang, 1957), in addition to being a recipient of a Presidential
Medal of Freedom in 2010. The latter recognizes the work of her and her husband Kurt
through founding the Gerda and Kurt Klein Foundation aimed at advancing tolerance
among youth through education and community work, http://www.whitehouse.gov
/medal-of-freedom (accessed 13 November 2014). Gerda has also appeared as a subject of

scholarly examination in works, including Margarete Myers Feinstein, "Absent Fathers, Present Mothers: Images of Parenthood in Holocaust Survivor Narratives," *Nashim: A Journal of Jewish Women's Studies & Gender Issues* 13 (Spring 2007): 155–182; and David Patterson, "Some Theological Aspects of Jewish Memory in the Holocaust Memoir," *Annals of the American Academy of Political and Social Science* 548, The Holocaust: Remembering for the Future (November 1996): 200–218.

147. Gerda K. Holocaust Testimony (Videotape 50.030*0105), 11 October 1990. Collections Department, United States Holocaust Memorial Museum, Washington, D.C.

148. Segment of Gerda K. and Kurt K. in film *Testimony*.

149. Segment of Kurt K. appearing in *Testimony*. Film directed by Sandy Bradley, 1993. Screened within the U.S. Holocaust Memorial Museum, Permanent Exhibition, Closing Segment; and in Kurt K. Holocaust Testimony (Videotape 50.030*0106), 11 October 1990. Collections Department, United States Holocaust Memorial Museum, Washington, D.C.

150. Kurt K. Holocaust Testimony (Videotape 50.030*0106), 11 October 1990. Collections Department, United States Holocaust Memorial Museum, Washington, D.C.

151. Ibid.

152. Helen W. Holocaust Testimony (Videotape 50.030*0246), 14 November 1989. Collections Department, United States Holocaust Memorial Museum, Washington, D.C.

153. Ibid.

154. Ibid.

155. Helen W. segment in *Testimony*.

156. Agnes A. Holocaust Testimony (Videotape 50.030*0003), 29 November 1990. Collections Department, United States Holocaust Memorial Museum, Washington, D.C.

157. Ibid.

158. James E. Young, "Toward a Received History of the Holocaust," 40.

159. Agnes A. segment in *Testimony;* Agnes A. Holocaust Testimony (Videotape 50.030*0003), 29 November 1990. Collections Department, United States Holocaust Memorial Museum, Washington, D.C.

160. Abe M. segment in *Testimony*.

161. Leo B. segment in *Testimony*.

162. Leo B. Holocaust Testimony (Videotape 50.030*0038), 28 September 1989 and 31 July 1989. Collections Department, United States Holocaust Memorial Museum, Washington, D.C.

163. Ibid.

164. The multiple testimonies of Leo B. are examined in Chapter 4.

165. Correspondence and Analysis of Fortunoff Archive Testimonies from Lawrence Langer to Michael Berenbaum, 4 April 1991. USHMM; Institutional Archives; Research Institute; Subject Files of the Director Michael Berenbaum; 1989–1997; 1988-011; Box 20; Lawrence Langer.

166. "The Learning Center: An Overview with Preliminary Budgets," 26 August 1988. USHMM; Institutional Archives; Research Institute; Subject Files of the Director Michael Berenbaum; 1989–1997; Box 20; 1988-011; Learning Center.

167. Ibid.

168. Ibid.

169. Summaries of Completed USHMM Oral Histories, undated. USHMM; Institutional Archives; Research Institute; Subject Files of the Director Michael Berenbaum; 1989–1997; 1988-011; Box 26; Oral History.

170. Nesse G. Holocaust Testimony (Videotape RG-50.030*0080), 8 May 1989. Collections Department, United States Holocaust Memorial Museum, Washington, D.C.

171. Memorandum from Martin Smith to Linda Kuzmack, 16 October 1989, p. 2. USHMM; Institutional Archives; Records of Raye Farr Relating to the Segment Development of the Permanent Exhibition; CA 1990–1994; 1998-038.2; Box 13; Oral History.

172. Simon Wiesenthal Center, "Holocaust Survivors in Three Cities Across North America Join Together to Confront Iran's Conference of Holocaust Deniers and Revisionists," Simon Wiesenthal Center press release, 11 December 2006, http://www .wiesenthal.com/site/apps/nlnet/content2.aspx?c=fwLYKnN8LzH&b=245494&ct =3287257 (accessed 20 December 2006).

173. United States Holocaust Memorial Museum, "United States Holocaust Memorial Museum Denounces Iranian Conference on the Holocaust," United States Holocaust Memorial Museum press release, 11 December 2006, http://www.ushmm.org /museum/press/archives/detail.php?category=07—general&content=2006—12—11 (accessed 20 December 2006).

174. Public Law 96–388, Enacted by the 96th United States Congress, 7 October 1980, cited in "Responding to the Future: Work Plan 2000," 3 May 2000. U.S. Holocaust Memorial Museum; Institutional Archives; Director's Office; Records of the Museum Director Jeshajahu "Shaike" Weinberg; 1979–1995; 1997-014; Box 22; Committee: Conscience.

175. Ibid. The responsibility for implementing the mission of the COC now rests largely with the Center for the Prevention of Genocide (which is under the umbrella of the COC and the Holocaust Museum).

176. *Our Walls Bear Witness*, U.S. Holocaust Memorial Museum, Washington, D.C., 20 November 2006.

177. Typed Transcripts of the Meeting of the Museum Concept Planning Committee; 6 November 1985, pp. 42–43. USHMM; Institutional Archives; Records of the Chairperson Elie Wiesel, 1978–1986; 1997-013; Box 21; Museum Concept Planning Committee Minutes, 6 November 1985.

178. *Our Walls Bear Witness*, 20 November 2006.

179. Bridget Conley-Zilkic, Project Director, Committee on Conscience, U.S. Holocaust Memorial Museum, interview by author, 23 February 2007, Washington, D.C., U.S. Holocaust Memorial Museum.

180. Ibid.

181. Ibid.

182. Transcript of the Meeting of Ad Hoc Exploratory Group on the Committee of Conscience, 24 May 1994, p. 7.

183. Nesse G. Holocaust Testimony (Videotape RG-50.030*0080), 8 May 1989. Collections Department, United States Holocaust Memorial Museum, Washington, D.C.

184. Janet Walker, *Trauma Cinema: Documenting Incest and the Holocaust*, xviii.

185. Ellen Blalock, Director, Survivors Affairs and Speakers Bureau, U.S. Holocaust Memorial Museum, interview by author, 26 March 2007, Washington, D.C., U.S. Holocaust Memorial Museum.

186. Correspondence and Analysis of Fortunoff Archive Testimonies from Lawrence Langer to Michael Berenbaum, 4 April 1991. USHMM; Institutional Archives; Research Institute; Subject Files of the Director Michael Berenbaum; 1989–1997; 1988-011; Box 20; Lawrence Langer.

187. Ibid.

188. Ibid.

189. Elie Wiesel speech, "The Holocaust: Beginning or End?" USHMM; Institutional Archives USHMM Council: Records of the Chairperson Elie Wiesel, 1978–1986; Box 27; 1997-013; Wiesel, Elie: Remarks [Various].

190. Linenthal, *Preserving Memory*, xiv.

3. The Cinematic Origins and the Digital Future of the Shoah Foundation

1. See David Bordwell, Janet Staiger, and Kristin Thompson, *The Classical Hollywood Cinema: Film Style and Mode of Production to 1960* (London: Routledge, 1985), 6; and Miriam Bratu Hansen, "*Schindler's List* Is Not *Shoah:* The Second Commandment, Popular Modernism, and Public Memory," in *The Historical Film: History and Memory in Media,* edited by Marcia Landy (New Brunswick, N.J.: Rutgers University Press, 2001), 212.

2. Janet Murray, *Hamlet on the Holodeck: The Future of Narrative in Cyberspace* (Cambridge, Mass.: MIT Press, 2001), 49. Murray discusses how an "imaginative product" such as a film can be experienced across multiple platforms. One such platform for the Shoah Foundation included the educational CD-ROM *Survivors: Testimonies of the Holocaust,* featuring the voices of Leonardo DiCaprio and Winona Ryder, published by the Survivors of the Shoah Visual History Foundation in 1999.

3. Interview Training Guidelines; Survivors of the Shoah Visual History Foundation, revised 15 February 1996, 1–2. USC Shoah Foundation, institutional archive. These and related materials were generously made available to me by Ari Zev, director of administration for the USC Shoah Foundation.

4. Ibid.

5. Survivors of the Shoah Visual History Foundation, Project Overview, Revised 5 February 1996, 1. USC Shoah Foundation, institutional archive.

6. Ibid.

7. Ibid.

8. Ibid.

9. Ibid.

10. Ibid.

11. Crispin Brooks, curator, Visual History Archive [hereafter VHA], USC Shoah Foundation, interview by author, 2 October 2006, Los Angeles.

12. Douglas Ballman, coordinator of on-site and scholarly access, USC Shoah Foundation, interview by author, 10 October 2006, University of Southern California [USC], Los Angeles.

13. USC Shoah Foundation website, Find an Access site near you. http://sfi.usc.edu/locator (accessed 13 June 2014).

14. Douglas Greenberg, executive director, USC Shoah Foundation, interview by author, 13 January 2006, USC, Los Angeles.

15. Douglas Greenberg, remarks made during meeting of affiliate institutions on Andrew W. Mellon Foundation grant, Survivors of the Shoah Visual History Foundation offices, 22 June 2005.

16. Ibid.

17. "An Invitation to Make History," undated invitation soliciting participants for interviews. USC Shoah Foundation, institutional archives.

18. Greenberg, interview by author, 23 September 2006, USC.

19. "Techniques for Effectively Applying Interview Methodology." Undated. USC Shoah Foundation, institutional archive. Emphasis in original.

20. Ibid. Emphasis in original.

21. "Videographer Guidelines," July 1997, 8–11. USC Shoah Foundation, institutional archive.

22. "Quality Assurance Self-Assessment Form," revised 6 September 1996. USC Shoah Foundation, institutional archive.

23. Quality Assurance Report, 11 February 1998. USC Shoah Foundation, institutional archive.

24. Untitled Interview Training Exercises (undated). USC Shoah Foundation, institutional archive.

25. "Quality Assurance Report," revised 13 September 1996. USC Shoah Foundation, institutional archive.

26. "Interviewer Guidelines, Domestic," revised 19 March 1997, 2. USC Shoah Foundation, institutional archive.

27. Each of the three archives featured in this book is similar in that respect.

28. "Interviewer Guidelines, Domestic," revised 19 March 1997, 3.

29. Ibid.

30. "Pre-Interview Questionnaire, Guidelines, Suggestions, and Tips (Draft)," 26 November 1996. USC Shoah Foundation Institute, institutional archive.

31. Ibid.

32. Ibid.

33. "Pre-Interview Questionnaire," 8 July 1996. USC Shoah Foundation, institutional archive.

34. Ibid.

35. "Interviewer Guidelines, Domestic," revised 19 March 1997," 5.

36. "Quality Assurance Reference Guide," 17 April 1997, 1. USC Shoah Foundation, institutional archive.

37. "Interviewer Guidelines, Domestic," revised 19 March 1997, 6.

38. "Tips and Reminders for Interviewers," 21 May 1996, 2. USC Shoah Foundation, institutional archive.

39. Ibid.

40. "Interviewer Guidelines, Domestic," revised 19 March 1997, 6.

41. Ibid.

42. "Interviewer Guidelines, Domestic," revised 19 March 1997, 7.

43. "Interviewer Guidelines, Domestic," revised 19 October 1995, 11–12.

44. "Interviewer Guidelines, Domestic," revised 15 February 1996, 7.

45. "Interviewer Guidelines, Domestic," revised 19 October 1995, 11–12.

46. Ibid.

47. Ibid.

48. "Tips and Reminders for Interviewers," 21 May 1996, 4.

49. Ibid.

50. "Interviewer Guidelines, Domestic," revised 19 March 1997, 8–9.

51. "Interviewer Guidelines, Domestic," revised 15 February 1996, 1–2.

52. Quality Assurance Guide, revised 13 September 1996, 3. Emphasis in the original.

53. "Tips and Reminders for Interviewers," 21 May 1996, 4.

54. "Videographer Guidelines," July 1997, 11.

55. Ibid.

56. "Interviewer Guidelines, Domestic," revised 19 March 1997, 6.

57. Ibid.

58. "Topical Questions," 23 June 1997, 2. USC Shoah Foundation, institutional archive.

59. Ibid., 3.

60. Ibid., 4.

61. Ibid.

62. Ibid.

63. Ibid.

64. "Interviewer Guidelines, Domestic," revised 19 March 1997, 8–9.

65. "Topical Questions," 23 June 1997, 8.

66. Ibid., 11.

67. Ibid., 21.

68. Ibid.

69. Ibid., 27.

70. Ibid.

71. I will explore such a moment in Chapter 4.

72. "Interviewer Guidelines, Domestic," revised 19 March 1997, 10.

73. "Videographer Guidelines," July 1997, 6.

74. Ibid., 2.

75. Ibid., 4.

76. Ibid., 6.

77. Ibid., 7. Emphasis in original.

78. Ibid., 8.

79. Douglas Ballman, interview by author, 10 October 2006, USC.

80. Ibid.

81. Ibid.

82. Crispin Brooks, interview by author, 2 October 2006, USC.

83. Ibid.

84. Survivor Release Agreement, revised 15 February 1996. USC Shoah Foundation, institutional archive.

85. I will discuss the pedagogical issues in greater detail later in this chapter.

86. Remarks made during my attendance at the meeting of affiliate institutions on Andrew W. Mellon Foundation grant, 22 June 2005, held at the Shoah Foundation offices then located on the backlot of Universal Studios in Universal City, Los Angeles.

87. "Mellon Foundation, Survivors of the Shoah Visual History Foundation, and Yale University Library Department of Manuscripts and Archives: Collaborative Project, Addendum to the Final Report," June 2005, 4.

88. Final Grant Report to the Andrew W. Mellon Foundation, "Pedagogical and Scholarly Implications of the Shoah Foundation Archive in Research Universities," September 2005, 4.

89. Ibid., 5.

90. Mellon Foundation, "Survivors of the Shoah Visual History Foundation, and Yale University Library Department of Manuscripts and Archives: Collaborative Project, Addendum to the Final Report," June 2005.

91. Remarks made during the meeting of affiliate institutions on the Andrew W. Mellon Foundation grant, Survivors of the Shoah Visual History Foundation offices, 22 June 2005. USC Shoah Foundation.

92. I want to reiterate that I utilize my own assessment protocols when evaluating interviews. The analytical rubrics that I employ are essential to navigating the overwhelming volume of material stored at the Shoah Foundation and other archives. Nonetheless, as tools of segmentation and categorization in their own right, they mirror to some extent the very instrumentalization that I reflect upon throughout this book.

93. Olga K. Holocaust Testimony (Videotape 3012), 4 June 1995. Visual History Archive, USC Shoah Foundation.

94. Richard K. Holocaust Testimony (Videotape 18752), 19 August 1996. Visual History Archive, USC Shoah Foundation.

95. Douglas Ballman, interview by author, 5 December 2008, USC.

96. Julia L. Holocaust Testimony (Videotape 5891), 12 November 1995. Visual History Archive, USC Shoah Foundation.

97. USC Shoah Foundation website, Living Histories (Julia Lentini), http://dornsife.usc.edu/vhi/education/livinghistories/lesson.php?nid=714 (accessed 1 February 2012).

98. Remarks made by Douglas Greenberg during the meeting of affiliate institutions on the Andrew W. Mellon Foundation grant. Survivors of the Shoah Visual History Foundation offices, 22 June 2005, USC Shoah Foundation.

99. Douglas Greenberg, interview by author, 13 January 2006, USC.

100. However, a relatively small sampling of the Shoah Foundation's interviews, including the one with Julia L. can be found on the Foundation's YouTube channel. https://www.youtube.com/user/USCShoahFoundation (accessed 28 June 2014).

101. This is a particularly topical issue insofar as the Shoah Foundation, in addition to consulting on other genocide documentation projects and housing a small collection of non-Holocaust testimonies within the VHA, announced in April of 2014 the creation of the Center for Advanced Genocide Research, housed at USC. I will discuss the creation of this center in more detail in the book's conclusion.

102. *Shoah: The Complete Text of the Acclaimed Holocaust Film by Claude Lanzmann* (New York: Da Capo Press, 1995), 59.

103. USC Shoah Foundation website, http://sfi.usc.edu/teach_and_learn/iwitness (accessed 1 April 2014).

104. Walter Reich, "Unwelcome Narratives: Listening to Suppressed Themes in American Holocaust Testimonies," *Poetics Today* 27, no. 2 (Summer 2006): 466.

4. Telling and Retelling Holocaust Testimonies

1. Müller, "Trauma, Historiography and Polyphony," 161.

2. For an analysis of my larger group of comparative testimonies, see "Embodied Memory" (Ph.D. diss.).

3. The literature on gender and the Holocaust is voluminous. For an insightful examination of gender in Holocaust testimonies in particular, see Waxman, "Unheard Testimony, Untold Stories."

4. Lily M. Holocaust Testimony (Videotape 50.030*0150), 16 October 1990. Collections Department, United States Holocaust Memorial Museum, Washington, D.C. Department, USHMM, Washington, D.C.

5. Ibid.

6. Ibid.

7. Ibid.

8. Ibid.

9. A particularly compelling examination of the role of song in Holocaust survivor testimony can be found in Leah Wolfson, "'Is there anything else you would like to add?': Visual Testimony Encounters the Lyric," *South Atlantic Review* 73, no. 3 (Summer 2008): 86–109.

10. Lily M. Holocaust Testimony (Videotape 50.030*0150), 16 October 1990.

11. Lily M. Holocaust Testimony (HVT-1711), 13 November 1990. Fortunoff Video Archive for Holocaust Testimonies, Yale University Library.

12. Lily M. Holocaust Testimony (Videotape 2420), 4 May 1995. Visual History Archive, USC Shoah Foundation.

13. Leo B. Holocaust Testimony (HVT-1217), 5 February 1989. Fortunoff Video Archive for Holocaust Testimonies, Yale University Library.

14. Leo B. Holocaust Testimony (Videotape 50.030*0038), 28 September 1989 and 31 July 1989. Collections Department, United States Holocaust Memorial Museum, Washington, D.C. (each session catalogued as part of the same interview).

15. For further analysis of the Holocaust Museum testimony of Leo B., particularly as it concerns the olfactory and other sensory aspects of his memory and the distinctions between his written and videotaped accounts of his escape, see Simone Gigliotti, "'Cattle Car Complexes': A Correspondence with Historical Captivity and Post-Holocaust Witnesses," *Holocaust and Genocide Studies* 20, no. 2 (2006): 268–269.

16. Leo B. Holocaust Testimony (Videotape 50.030*0038), 28 September 1989 and 31 July 1989.

17. Leo B. Holocaust Testimony (Videotape 8503), 9 November 1995. Visual History Archive, USC Shoah Foundation.

18. Letter from Anita Kassof to Max "Amichai" H., 29 November 1989. USHMM; Institutional Archives; Director's Office; Records of the Museum Director—Jeshajahu "Shaike" Weinberg; 1979–1995; 1997-014; Box 144; Smith, Martin.

19. Max H. and Johanna J. Holocaust Testimony (HVT-1329), 12 March 1989. Fortunoff Video Archive for Holocaust Testimonies, Yale University Library.

20. Max "Amichai" H. Holocaust Testimony (Videotape 50.030*0094), 1 February 1990. Collections Department, United States Holocaust Memorial Museum, Washington, D.C.

21. Max H. Holocaust Testimony (Videotape 7405), 6 October 1995. Visual History Archive, USC Shoah Foundation.

22. Chaim E. Holocaust Testimony (HVT-756), 12 May 1986. Fortunoff Video Archive for Holocaust Testimonies, Yale University Library.

23. Langer, *Holocaust Testimonies*, 61.

24. Correspondence and Analysis of Fortunoff Archive Testimonies from Lawrence Langer to Michael Berenbaum, 4 April 1991. USHMM; Institutional Archives; Research Institute; Subject Files of the Director Michael Berenbaum; 1989–1997; 1988-011; Box 20; Lawrence Langer. As was the case in my previous chapters citing correspondence between Langer and Berenbaum, I refer to both Langer's scholarly and archival consultation work in order to highlight how his perspectives have entered into conversation with academic discourses as well as archival and museological debates and practices.

25. Chaim E. Testimony (HVT-756). FVA, Yale University Library.

26. Correspondence and Analysis of Fortunoff Archive Testimonies from Lawrence Langer to Michael Berenbaum, 4 April 1991. USHMM; Institutional Archives.

27. Greene and Kumar eds., *Witness*, 220.

28. Chaim E. Holocaust Testimony (Videotape 50.030*0066), 16 July 1990. Collections Department, United States Holocaust Memorial Museum, Washington, D.C.

29. Chaim E. Holocaust Testimony (Videotape 7683), 18 October 1995 (first VHA interview). Visual History Archive, USC Shoah Foundation.

30. Chaim E. Holocaust Testimony (Videotape 7683), 16 October 1998 (second VHA interview). Visual History Archive, USC Shoah Foundation.

31. The oral historian Selma Leydesdorff has worked closely with Selma E., including on the "The Long Shadow of Sobibor" interview project, http://www.long shadowofsobibor.com/ (accessed 6 June 2014).

32. Selma E. Holocaust Testimony (HVT-42), 1 March 1980. Fortunoff Video Archive for Holocaust Testimonies, Yale University Library.

33. Selma E. Holocaust Testimony, Videotape 50.030*0067), 16 July 1990. Collections Department, United States Holocaust Memorial Museum, Washington, D.C.

34. Selma E. Holocaust Testimony (Videotape 7684), 18 October 1995 (first VHA interview). Visual History Archive, USC Shoah Foundation.

35. For further discussion of the challenges of addressing gender in testimony see Waxman, "Unheard Testimony, Untold Stories."

36. Selma E. Holocaust Testimony (Videotape 7684), 16 October 1998 (second VHA interview). Visual History Archive, USC Shoah Foundation.

37. Chaim E. Holocaust Testimony (Videotape 7683), 16 October 1998 (second VHA interview). Visual History Archive, USC Shoah Foundation.

38. Hirsch, "Surviving Images," 221.

39. Chaim E. Holocaust Testimony (Videotape 7683), 16 October 1998 (second VHA interview). Visual History Archive, USC Shoah Foundation.

40. Landsberg, *Prosthetic Memory*, 23–24.

Conclusion

1. As one example, in 2011, staff members of the Kigali Genocide Memorial Centre traveled to the Shoah Foundation's offices in Los Angeles to receive training on how to index the testimonies recorded in Kigali, http://sfi.usc.edu/collections/rwandan (accessed 13 April 2014). At the moment, the Shoah Foundation has integrated sixty-five testimonies of the Rwandan genocide into its Visual History Archive, http://sfi.usc.edu/what_is_the_vha (accessed 13 April 2014). I am currently conducting two research projects, one examining the Shoah Foundation's work with the Documentation Center of Cambodia, the other exploring its work with the Kigali Genocide Memorial Centre.

2. Ben Kiernan, *The Pol Pot Regime: Race, Power, and Genocide in Cambodia under the Khmer Rouge, 1975–1979*, 3rd ed. (New Haven, Conn: Yale University Press, 2008), ix.

3. http://www.d.dccam.org/Abouts/History/Histories.htm (accessed 30 July 2011).

4. Ibid.

5. Ibid.

6. http://sfi.usc.edu/witnessesforhumanity/cambodiangenocide/ (accessed 1 February 2013).

7. "Pre-Interview Questionnaire," developed for audiovisual testimonies of the DC-Cam. I am grateful to the USC Shoah Foundation for providing me with the Pre-Interview Questionnaire that they co-developed with the DC-Cam.

8. Ibid.

9. Michelle Caswell, "Using Classification to Convict the Khmer Rouge," *Journal of Documentation* 68, no. 2 (2012): 167.

10. Martha Minnow, *Between Vengeance and Forgiveness: Facing History after Genocide and Mass Violence* (Boston: Beacon Press Books, 1998), 70.

11. Such specialists include Alexander Laban Hinton, "The Dark Side of Modernity: Toward an Anthropology of Genocide," in *Annihilating Difference: The Anthropology of Genocide*, edited by Alexander Laban Hinton and Kenneth Roth (Berkeley: University of California Press, 2002), 1–40, and *Why Did They Kill: Cambodia in the Shadow of Genocide* (Berkeley: University of California Press, 2004); Ben Kiernan, *The Pol Pot Regime: Race, Power, and Genocide in Cambodia under the Khmer Rouge, 1975–1979*, 3rd ed. (New Haven, Conn.: Yale University Press, 2008); *How Pol Pot Came to Power: Colonialism, Nationalism, and Communism in Cambodia, 1930–1975*, 2nd ed. (New Haven, Conn.: Yale University Press, 2004); and David Chandler, *A History of Cambodia*, 4th ed. (Boulder, Colo.: Westview Press, 2007) and *Facing the Cambodian Past: Selected Essays 1971–1994* (North Sydney: Allen & Unwin, 1996).

12. Michael Rothberg, *Multidirectional Memory: Remembering the Holocaust in the Age of Decolonization* (Stanford, Calif.: Stanford University Press, 2009), 1–3.

13. Ibid., 2–3.

14. Ibid., 6–10.

15. Ibid.

16. See this book's introduction for detailed references to that body of scholarship.

17. https://sfi.usc.edu/cagr (accessed 21 June 2014).

18. I refer to the notion of the "baggage one carries" in scholarship on trauma and memory as explored by Diane Losche in her chapter "Bad Memories: The Poetics of Memory and the Difference of Culture," in *World Memory: Personal Trajectories in Global Time*, edited by Jill Bennett and Rosanne Kennedy (New York: Palgrave, 2003), 30–42. That volume as a whole addresses a diversity of challenges regarding the cultural specificity of memory and trauma, as well as issues regarding the paradigmatic status of the Holocaust in memory culture.

REFERENCES

Primary Sources

Archival Sources

This book is based on research in the following archives:

FORTUNOFF VIDEO ARCHIVE FOR HOLOCAUST TESTIMONIES (FVA).
YALE UNIVERSITY LIBRARY, NEW HAVEN, CONN.: INTERNAL PAPERS;
VIDEO TESTIMONY COLLECTION.

Abraham P. Holocaust Testimony (HVT-738), 13 August 1984. Fortunoff Video Archive for Holocaust Testimonies, Yale University Library.

Baruch G. Holocaust Testimony (HVT-295), 6 September 1984. Fortunoff Video Archive for Holocaust Testimonies, Yale University Library.

Benjamin M. Holocaust Testimony (HVT-194), 19 February 1983. Fortunoff Video Archive for Holocaust Testimonies, Yale University Library.

Chaim E. Holocaust Testimony (HVT-756), 12 May 1986. Fortunoff Video Archive for Holocaust Testimonies, Yale University Library.

Erwin B. Holocaust Testimony (HVT-2875), 18 January 1994. Fortunoff Video Archive for Holocaust Testimonies, Yale University Library.

Eva B. Holocaust Testimony (HVT-1 and HVT-1101), 2 May 1979 and 30 April 1988. Fortunoff Video Archive for Holocaust Testimonies, Yale University Library.

Fela W. Holocaust Testimony (HVT-3029), 16 December 1992. Fortunoff Video Archive for Holocaust Testimonies, Yale University Library.

Fred B. Holocaust Testimony (HVT-2047), 28 April 1992. Fortunoff Video Archive for Holocaust Testimonies, Yale University Library.

Fred O. Holocaust Testimony (HVT-943), 18 November 1987. Fortunoff Video Archive for Holocaust Testimonies, Yale University Library.

Frima L. Holocaust Testimony (HVT-2926), 13 March 1994. Fortunoff Video Archive for Holocaust Testimonies, Yale University Library.

Gerda H. Holocaust Testimony (HVT-1029), 9 July 1987. Fortunoff Video Archive for Holocaust Testimonies, Yale University Library.

Leo B. Holocaust Testimony (HVT-1217), 5 February 1989. Fortunoff Video Archive for Holocaust Testimonies, Yale University Library.

Liane R. Holocaust Testimony (HVT-1213), 17 April 1989. Fortunoff Video Archive for Holocaust Testimonies, Yale University Library.

Lily M. Holocaust Testimony (HVT-1711), 13 November 1990. Fortunoff Video Archive for Holocaust Testimonies, Yale University Library.

Max H. and Johanna J. Holocaust Testimony (HVT-1329), 12 March 1989. Fortunoff Video Archive for Holocaust Testimonies, Yale University Library.

Rochelle S. Holocaust Testimony (HVT-1473), 2 August 1988. Fortunoff Video Archive for Holocaust Testimonies, Yale University Library.

Selma E. Holocaust Testimony (HVT-42), 1 March 1980. Fortunoff Video Archive for Holocaust Testimonies, Yale University Library.

Thomas B. Holocaust Testimony (HVT-400), 19 June 1983. Fortunoff Video Archive for Holocaust Testimonies, Yale University Library.

UNITED STATES HOLOCAUST MEMORIAL MUSEUM (USHMM).
WASHINGTON, D.C.: INSTITUTIONAL ARCHIVES;
COLLECTIONS [ORAL HISTORY] DEPARTMENT.

Abraham M. Holocaust Testimony (Videotape 50.030*0145), 10 May 1990. Collections Department, United States Holocaust Memorial Museum, Washington, D.C.

Agnes A. Holocaust Testimony (Videotape 50.030*0003), 29 November 1990. Collections Department, United States Holocaust Memorial Museum, Washington, D.C.

Benjamin M. Holocaust Testimony (Videotape 50.030*0152), 1 March 1990. Collections Department, United States Holocaust Memorial Museum, Washington, D.C.

Cecilie K. P. Holocaust Testimony (Videotape 50.030*0107), 7 May 1990. Collections Department, United States Holocaust Memorial Museum, Washington, D.C.

Chaim E. Holocaust Testimony (Videotape 50.030*0066), 16 July 1990. Collections Department, United States Holocaust Memorial Museum, Washington, D.C.

Erwin B. Holocaust Testimony (Videotape 50.030*0016), 6 July 1994. Collections Department, United States Holocaust Memorial Museum, Washington, D.C.

Fela W. Holocaust Testimony (Videotape 50.030*0303), 9 February 1995, Collections Department, United States Holocaust Memorial Museum, Washington, D.C.

Frima Holocaust Testimony (Videotape 50.030*012), 30 April 1990. Collections Department, United States Holocaust Memorial Museum, Washington, D.C.

Gerda H. Holocaust Testimony (Videotape 50.030*0334), 12 June 1995. Collections Department, United States Holocaust Memorial Museum, Washington, D.C.

Gerda K. Holocaust Testimony (Videotape 50.030*0105), 11 October 1990. Collections Department, United States Holocaust Memorial Museum, Washington, D.C.

Helen W. Holocaust Testimony (Videotape 50.030*0246), 14 November 1989. Collections Department, United States Holocaust Memorial Museum, Washington, D.C.

Kurt K. Holocaust Testimony (Videotape 50.030*0106), 11 October 1990. Collections Department, United States Holocaust Memorial Museum, Washington, D.C.

Leo B. Holocaust Testimony (Videotape 50.030*0038), 28 September 1989 and 31 July 1989. Collections Department, United States Holocaust Memorial Museum, Washington, D.C.

Liane R. L. Holocaust Testimony (Videotape 50.030*0186), 24 October 1989. Collections Department, United States Holocaust Memorial Museum, Washington, D.C.

Lily M. Holocaust Testimony (Videotape 50.030*0150), 16 October 1990. Collections Department, United States Holocaust Memorial Museum, Washington, D.C.

Lilly M. Holocaust Testimony (Videotape 50.030*0146), 10 May 1990. Collections Department, United States Holocaust Memorial Museum, Washington, D.C.

Max "Amichai" H. Holocaust Testimony (Videotape 50.030*0094), 1 February 1990. Collections Department, United States Holocaust Memorial Museum, Washington, D.C.

Nesse G. Holocaust Testimony (Videotape RG-50.030*0080), 8 May 1989. Collections Department, United States Holocaust Memorial Museum, Washington, D.C.

Norman S. Holocaust Testimony (Videotape 50.030*0199), 15 May 1990. Collections Department, United States Holocaust Memorial Museum, Washington, D.C.

Rochelle S. Holocaust Testimony (Videotape 50.030*0216), 15 June 1990. Collections Department, United States Holocaust Memorial Museum, Washington, D.C.

Selma E. Holocaust Testimony, Videotape 50.030*0067), 16 July 1990. Collections Department, United States Holocaust Memorial Museum, Washington, D.C.

Thomas B. Holocaust Testimony (Videotape 50.030*0028), 6 September 1990. Collections Department, United States Holocaust Memorial Museum, Washington, D.C.

USC SHOAH FOUNDATION. LOS ANGELES, CA: INSTITUTIONAL ARCHIVE; INTERNAL PAPERS; VIDEO TESTIMONY COLLECTION (VHA).

Benjamin M. Holocaust Testimony (Videotape 50584), 5 August 1999. Visual History Archive, USC Shoah Foundation.

Chaim E. Holocaust Testimony (Videotape 7683), 18 October 1995 and 16 October 1998. Visual History Archive, USC Shoah Foundation.

Erwin B. Holocaust Testimony (Videotape 8001), 26 October 1995. Visual History Archive, USC Shoah Foundation.

Fred B. Holocaust Testimony (Videotape 1477), 14 March 1995. Visual History Archive, USC Shoah Foundation.

Frima L. Holocaust Testimony (Videotape 8705), 11 December 1995. Visual History Archive, USC Shoah Foundation.

Gerda H. Holocaust Testimony (Videotape 12976), 7 March 1996. Visual History Archive, USC Shoah Foundation.

Julia L. Holocaust Testimony (Videotape 5891), 12 November 1995. Visual History Archive, USC Shoah Foundation.

Leo B. Holocaust Testimony (Videotape 8503), 9 November 1995. Visual History Archive, USC Shoah Foundation.

Liane R. L. Holocaust Testimony (Videotape 13578), 30 April 1996. Visual History Archive, USC Shoah Foundation.

Lily M. Holocaust Testimony (Videotape 2420), 4 May 1995. Visual History Archive, USC Shoah Foundation.

Max H. Holocaust Testimony (Videotape 7405), 6 October 1995. Visual History Archive, USC Shoah Foundation.

Olga K. Holocaust Testimony (Videotape 3012), 4 June 1995. Visual History Archive, USC Shoah Foundation.

Richard K. Holocaust Testimony (Videotape 18752), 19 August 1996. Visual History Archive, USC Shoah Foundation.

Selma E. Holocaust Testimony (Videotape 7684), 18 October 1995 and 16 October 1998. Visual History Archive, USC Shoah Foundation.

Thomas B. Holocaust Testimony (Videotape 1873), 4 April 1995. Visual History Archive, USC Shoah Foundation.

Personal records

Ballman, Douglas (Coordinator, On-Site & Scholarly Access, USC Shoah Foundation).

Farr, Raye (Director, Film and Video, Collections Division, USHMM).

Rudof, Joanne (Archivist, FVA).

Interviews

Bachrach, Susan (Curator, Special Exhibitions, USHMM). Interview with author, Washington, D.C., February 8, 2007.

Ballman, Douglas (Manager, External Relations—Online Archive, Shoah Foundation). Interview with author, Los Angeles, 13 January and 10 October 2006; 5 December 2008.

Blalock, Ellen (Director, Survivors Affairs and Speakers Bureau, USHMM). Interview with author, Washington, D.C., 26 March 2007.

Brooks, Crispin (Curator, VHA). Interview with author, Los Angeles, 2 October 2006.

Conley-Zilkic, Bridget (Project Director, USHMM Committee on Conscience). Interview with author, Washington, D.C., 23 February 2007.

Farr, Raye (Director, Film and Video, Collections Division, USHMM). Interview with author, Washington, D.C., 20 December 2006; 8 February and 20 December 2007.

Friedberg, Edna (Historian, Education Department, USHMM). Interview with author, Washington, D.C., 26 March 2007.

Greenberg, Douglas (Executive Director, USC Shoah Foundation). Interview with author, Los Angeles, 13 January and 23 September 2006.

Jungblut, Karen (Director, Research & Documentation, Shoah Foundation). Interview with author, Los Angeles, 16 October 2006.

Millen, Ann (Historian, Education Department, USHMM). Interview with author, Washington, D.C., 26 March 2007.

Rudof, Joanne (Archivist, FVA). Interview with author. New Haven, Conn., 30 March, 22 August, and 15 December 2006; 10 July 2007. Email correspondence with author, 15 May 2014.

Secondary Sources

Assmann, Aleida. "History, Memory, and the Genre of Testimony." *Poetics Today* 27, no. 2 (Summer 2006): 261–273.

Beim, Aaron, and Gary Alan Fine. "Trust in Testimony: The Institutional Embeddedness of Holocaust Survivor Narratives." *European Journal of Sociology* 48, no. 1 (2007): 55–75.

Berenbaum, Michael. *After Tragedy and Triumph: Essays in Modern Jewish Thought and the American Experience.* Cambridge: Cambridge University Press, 2009.

Bolkosky, Sidney M. *Searching for Meaning in the Holocaust.* Westport, Conn.: Greenwood, 2002.

Bordwell, David, Janet Staiger, and Kristin Thompson. *The Classical Hollywood Cinema: Film Style and Mode of Production to 1960.* London: Routledge, 1985.

Browning, Christopher R. *Collected Memories: Holocaust History and Postwar Testimony.* Madison: University of Wisconsin Press, 2003.

———. *Remembering Survival: Inside a Nazi Slave-Labor Camp.* New York: W.W. Norton, 2010.

Caswell, Michelle. "Using Classification to Convict the Khmer Rouge." *Journal of Documentation* 68, no. 2 (2012): 162–184.

Chandler, David. *Facing the Cambodian Past: Selected Essays 1971–1994.* North Sydney: Allen & Unwin, 1996.

———. *A History of Cambodia.* 4th ed. Boulder, Colo.: Westview, 2007.

Cole, Tim. *Selling the Holocaust: From Auschwitz to Schindler; How History Is Bought, Packaged, and Sold.* New York: Routledge, 2000.

Dean, Carolyn. "Minimalism and Victim Testimony." *History and Theory,* Theme Issue 49 (December 2010): 85–99.

Diner, Hasia. *We Remember with Reverence and Love: American Jews and the Myth of Silence after the Holocaust, 1945–1962.* New York: New York University Press, 2009.

Felman, Shoshana, and Dori Laub. *Testimony: Crises of Witnessing in Literature, Psychoanalysis and History.* New York: Routledge, 1992.

Flanzbaum, Hilene, ed. *The Americanization of the Holocaust.* Baltimore: The Johns Hopkins University Press, 1999.

Friedländer, Saul. "Trauma, Memory, and Transference." In *Holocaust Remembrance: The Shapes of Memory,* edited by Geoffrey Hartman, 252–263. Oxford, UK and Cambridge, Mass.: Blackwell, 1993.

Frisch, Michael. *A Shared Authority: Essays on the Craft and Meaning of Oral History and Public History.* Albany: State University of New York Press, 1990.

Gigliotti, Simone. "'Cattle Car Complexes': A Correspondence with Historical Captivity and Post-Holocaust Witnesses." *Holocaust and Genocide Studies* 20, no. 2 (2006): 256–277.

Greene, Joshua M., and Shiva Kumar, eds. *Witness: Voices from the Holocaust.* New York: Touchstone, 2000.

Greenspan, Henry. *On Listening to Holocaust Survivors: Recounting and Life History.* Westport, Conn.: Praeger, 1998.

———. *On Listening to Holocaust Survivors: Beyond Testimony.* St. Paul, Minn.: Paragon House, 2010.

Greenspan, Henry, and Sidney Bolkosky. "When Is an Interview an Interview? Notes from Listening to Holocaust Survivors." *Poetics Today* 27, no. 2 (Summer 2006): 431–449.

Hansen, Miriam Bratu. "*Schindler's List* Is Not *Shoah:* The Second Commandment, Popular Modernism, and Public Memory." In *The Historical Film: History and Memory in Media,* edited by Marcia Landy, 201–217. New Brunswick, N.J.: Rutgers University Press, 2001.

Hartman, Geoffrey. *The Longest Shadow: In the Aftermath of the Holocaust.* New York: Palgrave Macmillan, 2002.

———. "About the Yale Archive." In *Witness: Voices from the Holocaust,* edited by Joshua M. Greene and Shiva Kumar, 251–255. New York: Touchstone, 2000.

———. "The Humanities of Testimony: An Introduction." *Poetics Today* 27, no. 2 (Summer 2006): 249–260.

High, Steven. "Telling Stories: A Reflection on Oral History and New Media." *Oral History* 38, no. 1 (2010): 101–112.

Hinton, Alexander Laban. "The Dark Side of Modernity: Toward an Anthropology of Genocide." In *Annihilating Difference: The Anthropology of Genocide,* edited by Alexander Laban Hinton and Kenneth Roth, 1–40. Berkeley: University of California Press, 2002.

———. *Why Did They Kill: Cambodia in the Shadow of Genocide.* Berkeley: University of California Press, 2004.

Hirsch, Marianne. "Surviving Images: Holocaust Photographs and the Work of Postmemory." In *Visual Culture and the Holocaust,* edited by Barbie Zelizer, 215–246. New Brunswick, N.J.: Rutgers University Press, 2001.

———. *The Generation of Postmemory: Writing and Visual Culture after the Holocaust.* New York: Columbia University Press, 2012.

Hirsch, Marianne, and Irene Kacandes, eds. *Teaching the Representation of the Holocaust.* New York: MLA, 2004.

Hirsch, Marianne, and Leo Spitzer. "The Witness in the Archive: Holocaust Studies/ Memory Studies." *Memory Studies* 2, no. 2 (2009): 151–170.

Jockusch, Laura. *Collect and Record! Jewish Holocaust Documentation in Early Postwar Europe.* Oxford: Oxford University Press, 2012.

Kiernan, Ben. *The Pol Pot Regime: Race, Power, and Genocide in Cambodia under the Khmer Rouge, 1975–1979.* 3rd ed. New Haven, Conn.: Yale University Press, 2008.

———. *How Pol Pot Came to Power: Colonialism, Nationalism, and Communism in Cambodia, 1930–1975,* 2nd ed. New Haven, Conn., Yale University Press, 2004.

Kushner, Tony. "Holocaust Testimony, Ethics, and the Problem of Representation." *Poetics Today* 27, no. 2 (Summer 2006): 275–295.

LaCapra, Dominick. *History and Memory after Auschwitz.* Ithaca, N.Y.: Cornell University Press, 1998.

Landsberg, Alison. *Prosthetic Memory: The Transformation of American Remembrance in the Age of Mass Culture.* New York: Columbia University Press, 2004.

Langer, Lawrence. *Holocaust Testimonies: The Ruins of Memory.* New Haven, Conn.: Yale University Press, 1991.

———. *Admitting the Holocaust: Collected Essays.* New York: Oxford University Press, 1995.

———. "Foreword" to *Witness: Voices from the Holocaust,* edited by Joshua M. Greene and Shiva Kumar, xi–xix. New York: Touchstone, 2000.

———. "Hearing the Holocaust." *Poetics Today* 27, no. 2 (Summer 2006): 297–309.

Lanzmann, Claude. *Shoah: The Complete Text of the Acclaimed Holocaust Film.* New York: Da Capo Press, 1995.

Linenthal, Edward. *Preserving Memory: The Struggle to Create America's Holocaust Museum.* New York: Columbia University Press, 2001.

Liss, Andrea. *Trespassing through Shadows: Memory, Photography, and the Holocaust.* Minneapolis: University of Minnesota Press, 1998.

Losche, Diane. "Bad Memories: The Poetics of Memory and the Difference of Culture." In *World Memory: Personal Trajectories in Global Time,* edited by Jill Bennett and Rosanne Kennedy, 30–42. New York: Palgrave, 2003.

Matthäus, Jurgen, ed. *Approaching an Auschwitz Survivor: Holocaust Testimony and Its Transformations.* New York: Oxford University Press, 2009.

Minnow, Martha. *Between Vengeance and Forgiveness: Facing History after Genocide and Mass Violence.* Boston: Beacon Press Books, 1998.

Mintz, Alan. *Popular Culture and the Shaping of Holocaust Memory in America.* Seattle: University of Washington Press, 2001.

Müller, Beate. "Trauma, Historiography and Polyphony: Adult Voices in the cjhc's Early Postwar Child Holocaust Testimonies." *History & Memory* 24, no. 2 (Fall/Winter 2012): 157–195.

Murray, Janet. *Hamlet on the Holodeck: The Future of Narrative in Cyberspace.* Cambridge, MA: MIT Press, 1998.

Myers Feinstein, Margarete. "Absent Fathers, Present Mothers: Images of Parenthood in Holocaust Survivor Narratives." *Nashim: A Journal of Jewish Women's Studies & Gender Issues,* no. 13 (Spring 2007): 155–182.

Novick, Peter. *The Holocaust in American Life.* New York: Houghton Mifflin, 1999.

Oral History Interview Guidelines. Washington, D.C.: United States Holocaust Memorial Museum, 2007.

Patterson, David. "Some Theological Aspects of Jewish Memory in the Holocaust Memoir." *Annals of the American Academy of Political and Social Science* 548, The Holocaust: Remembering for the Future (November 1996): 200–218.

Pinchevski, Amit. "The Audiovisual Unconscious: Media and Trauma in the Video Archive for Holocaust Testimonies." *Critical Inquiry* 39, no. 1 (Autumn 2012): 142–166.

Portelli, Alessandro. *The Death of Luigi Trastulli and Other Stories: Form and Meaning in Oral History.* Albany: State University of New York Press, 1991.

———. "Oral History as Genre." In *Narrative and Genre: Contexts and Types of Communication,* edited by Mary Chamberlain and Paul Thompson, 23–45. New Brunswick, N.J.: Transaction, 2009.

President's Commission on the Holocaust, Elie Wiesel, Chairman. Report to the President. Washington, D.C.: United States Holocaust Memorial Museum, 27 September 1979, USHMM, http://www.ushmm.org/research/library/faq/languages /en/06/01/commission/#principles.

Reich, Walter. "Unwelcome Narratives: Listening to Suppressed Themes in American Holocaust Testimonies." *Poetics Today* 27, no. 2 (Summer 2006): 463–472.

Renov, Michael. "Introduction: The Truth about Non-Fiction." In *Theorizing Documentary,* edited by Michael Renov, 1–11. New York: Routledge, 1993.

———. "The Work of Memory in the Age of Digital Reproduction." Paper presented at the Visible Evidence XI Conference, Bristol, UK, December 16–19, 2003.

Rosen, Alan. *The Wonder of Their Voices: The 1946 Holocaust Interviews of David Boder.* New York: Oxford University Press, 2010.

Rosenfeld, Alvin H. *The End of the Holocaust.* Bloomington: Indiana University Press, 2011.

Rothberg, Michael. *Multidirectional Memory: Remembering the Holocaust in the Age of Decolonization.* Stanford, Calif.: Stanford University Press, 2009.

Rothberg, Michael, and Jared Stark. "After the Witness: A Report from the Twentieth Anniversary Conference of the Fortunoff Video Archive for Holocaust Testimonies at Yale." *History and Memory* 15, no. 1 (Spring 2003): 85–96.

Rudof, Joanne Weiner. "Research Use of Holocaust Testimonies." *Poetics Today* 27, no. 2 (Summer 2006): 451–461.

———. "A Yale University and New Haven Community Project: From Local to Global." New Haven, Conn.: Fortunoff Video Archive for Holocaust Testimonies, October 2012, http://www.library.yale.edu/testimonies/publications/Local_to _Global.pdf.

Shandler, Jeffrey. "Holocaust Survivors on *Schindler's List;* or, Reading a Digital Archive against the Grain." *American Literature* 85, no. 4 (2013): 813–814; and the corresponding online Scalar project and accompanying PDF version at http://scalar .usc.edu/anvc/schindlers-list-on-vha/index (accessed 25 June 2014).

Shenker, Noah. "Embodied Memory: The Formation of Archived Audiovisual Holocaust Testimony in the United States." Ph.D. diss., University of Southern California, 2009.

———."Embodied Memory: The Institutional Mediation of Survivor Testimony in the United States Holocaust Memorial Museum." In *Documentary Testimonies: Global Archives of Suffering,* edited by Bhaskar Sarkar and Janet Walker, 35–58. New York: Routledge, 2009.

Simon Wiesenthal Center. "Holocaust Survivors in Three Cities across North America Join Together to Confront Iran's Conference of Holocaust Deniers and Revisionists." Press release, 11 December 2006, http://www.wiesenthal.com/site/apps/s /content.asp?c=lsKWLbPJLnF&b=4442915&ct=5849251.

Stier, Oren Baruch. *Committed to Memory: Cultural Mediations of the Holocaust.* Amherst: University of Massachusetts Press, 2003.

Stopford, Annie. "Turning a River of Blood into a River of Reconciliation: Cambodia's Catastrophe," in the DC-Cam publication, *Searching for the Truth* (October 2009),

http://www.genocidewatch.org/images/Cambodia_09_10_XX_Turning_a_river
_of_blood_into_a_river_of_reconciliation_Cambodia_s_catastrophe.doc (accessed 26 June 2014).

Trezise, Thomas. *Witnessing Witnessing: On the Reception of Holocaust Survivor Testimony.*
New York: Fordham University Press, 2013.

United States Holocaust Memorial Museum. "United States Holocaust Memorial Museum Denounces Iranian Conference on the Holocaust." USHMM press release, 11
December 2006, http://www.ushmm.org/museum/press/ archives/ detail
.php?category=07-general&content=2006-12-11.

Wake, Caroline. "Regarding the Recording: The Viewer of Video Testimony, the
Complexity of Copresence and the Possibility of Tertiary Witnessing." *History
and Memory* 25, no. 1 (Spring/Summer 2013): 111–144.

Walker, Janet. *Trauma Cinema: Documenting Incest and the Holocaust.* Berkeley: University of California Press, 2005.

Waxman, Zoë. "Unheard Testimony, Untold Stories: The Representation of Women's
Holocaust Experiences." *Women's History Review* 12, no. 4 (2003): 661–677.

———. *Writing the Holocaust: Identity, Testimony, Representation.* New York: Oxford
University Press, 2006.

———. "Testimonies as Sacred Texts: The Sanctification of Holocaust Writing." *Past
and Present* 206: suppl 5 (2010): 321–341.

Weissman, Gary. *Fantasies of Witnessing: Postwar Efforts to Experience the Holocaust.*
Ithaca, N.Y.: Cornell University Press, 2004.

Weissmann Klein, Gerda. *All But My Life.* New York: Hill & Wang, 1957.

Wiesel, Elie. "Trivializing the Holocaust: Semi-Fact and Semi-Fiction." *The New York
Times,* 16 April 1978.

Wieviorka, Annette. *The Era of the Witness.* Ithaca, N.Y.: Cornell University Press,
2006a.

———. "The Witness in History." *Poetics Today* 27, no. 2 (Summer 2006b): 385–397.

Wolfson, Leah. "'Is there anything else you would like to add?': Visual Testimony Encounters the Lyric." *South Atlantic Review* 73, no. 3 (Summer 2008): 86–109.

Yaeger, Patricia. "Testimony without Intimacy." *Poetics Today* 27, no. 2 (Summer 2006):
399–423.

Young, James E. *Writing and Rewriting the Holocaust: Narrative and the Consequences of Interpretation.* Bloomington: Indiana University Press, 1988.

———. *The Texture of Memory: Holocaust Memorials and Meaning.* New Haven, Conn.:
Yale University Press, 1993.

———. "Toward a Received History of the Holocaust." *History and Theory* 36, no. 4
(December 1997): 21–43.

———. "America's Holocaust: Memory and the Politics of Identity." In *The Americanization of the Holocaust,* edited by Hilene Flanzbaum, 68–82. Baltimore: Johns Hopkins University Press, 1999.

———. *At Memory's Edge: After-Images of the Holocaust in Contemporary Art and Architecture.* New Haven, Conn.: Yale University Press, 2000.

References   237

Film and Video Sources

Testimony. Film directed by Sandy Bradley, 1993. Screened within the USHMM Permanent Exhibition, Closing Segment.

Those Who Were There. VHS. Promotional video shown to the American Gathering of Holocaust Survivors, 1983.

Witness: Voices from the Holocaust. VHS. Directed by Joshua M. Greene and Shiva Kumar, 2000.

INDEX

Abe M. (witness), 100

Abraham M. (witness), 94

Abraham P. (witness), 39–40, 208n74

absent victims, giving voice to, 14, 155, 159

access to testimony: Fortunoff Archive, 15, 22, 33–34, 180, 206n13; Holocaust Museum, 135, 180; multidirectional memory, 196–197; Shoah Foundation, 114–115, 131–135, 147–150, 180, 197, 224n100

agency: concept of, 5–6, 110; Fortunoff Archive interviews, 15, 22, 33, 37, 47, 53, 158–159, 162; Holocaust Museum interviews, 84; Shoah Foundation interviews, 119

aging of survivors, 78, 140, 173, 185

Agnes A. (witness), 99–100, 106

All But My Life (Klein), 217n146

American Gathering of Jewish Holocaust Survivors, 20, 34, 58, 73

Americanization of the Holocaust, xi–xii, 8–9, 203n38

Andrew W. Mellon Foundation, 133, 147, 149

Anne Frank House (Amsterdam), 38

Anne Frank section (USHMM), 70

anti-memory, 9

Appelbaum, Ralph, 64

archives: versus exhibitions, 7, 76; proliferation of, x. *See also specific archives*

artifacts: Holocaust Museum, 62, 65–67, 71–72, 91, 93, 107; role of, 107, 110; in video testimonies, 100, 121, 123, 139–140, 142, 164–166, 177, 185–187

Assmann, Aleida, 6–7

attentive listening, 81

audience, for testimony, 15, 35–36, 63, 71, 119, 172, 192

audio content, extracted from videos, 79

Auschwitz-Birkenau: museum displays about, 66, 71, 78–79, 90; testimony about, 25, 39, 44, 49, 86, 98, 122, 137–138, 143–146

authenticity, standard of, 93, 110, 121, 130, 140, 144–146, 153, 166, 182, 195

autobiographical novels, 54

backdrops: Fortunoff Archive videos, 28, 41, 43, 45, 161, 169; Holocaust Museum videos, ix, 86, 91–92, 179; Shoah Foundation videos, 121, 130

Barbara T. (witness), 54

Baruch G. (witness), 47–53, 84

Berenbaum, Michael: on artifacts, 66, 72; on exemplary witnesses, 40, 51; on graphic representations, 70; on historical distance, 57; on interview methodology, 24–25, 82; on interviewee release form, 79–80; on Martin Smith, 64; on oral history collection, 73, 75; in role of testimony, 110; on *Testimony* film, 93

biographical information: comparative witnesses, 183, 185; DC-Cam interviews, 194–195; Fortunoff Archive videos, 48; Holocaust Museum videos, 81; Shoah Foundation videos, 124, 126–127, 139–140

Blalock, Ellen, 110

Bloch, Sam, 65–66

Bloomfield, Sara, 107

body language, 2, 13–14, 81, 124. *See also* gestures

Bolkosky, Sidney, 22–23, 39, 204n48, 204n50, 205n52

Bookbinder, Hyman, 109
boxcars: display of, 66, 71, 93, 107; testimony about, 156, 161–164
Bradley, Sandy, 91–95
Browning, Christopher, 10–11, 148

Cambodian genocide, 17, 193–195, 226n1
camera: frame (see framing); mobile documentary style of, 27
captions, 87–89, 108–109, 146
Carter, Jimmy, 8
Caswell, Michelle, 195
cataloguing system: DC-Cam, 195; Fortunoff Archive, 15, 33–34, 133, 180; Holocaust Museum, 154, 180; Shoah Foundation videos, 114, 131–135, 180
Center for Advanced Genocide Research (Shoah Foundation), 197, 224n100
Center for the Prevention of Genocide, 219n175
Chaim E. (witness), 169–177, 187
Charles H. Revson Foundation, 21
child Holocaust testimonies, 200n4
"choiceless choice," 23, 47, 84, 170
chronological approach. See narrative approach
circulating witnesses. See exemplary witnesses
Classical Hollywood Cinema, 112, 119, 125
close-ups: Fortunoff Archive videos, 27–28, 41, 170, 177; Holocaust Museum videos, 86, 92, 106, 173, 179; Shoah Foundation videos, 124, 130, 139, 140, 175
Cole, Tim, 203n38
collective memory, 10, 50; Fortunoff Archive, 158–159; Holocaust Museum, 62–63, 70–72, 76–77, 153–155, 181; versus individual expression, 10, 50, 70–72, 76–77, 102, 127, 153–159, 181–182; Shoah Foundation, 127
commercial use of testimony, 22, 64–65
Committee on Conscience (COC), 107–108, 219n175
common versus deep memory: comparative witnesses, 152–174; concept of, 5, 14, 23–25, 84; in Fortunoff Archive videos, 24–25, 42–45, 48–49, 84; in Holocaust Museum videos, 77, 84, 97–100; in Shoah Foundation videos, 128, 137
comparative witnesses, 12, 151–191
compartmentalization of memory, ix, 128–129
competitive memory, 196
Contribution of Oral Testimony to Holocaust and Genocide Studies, The (conference), 54, 202n25
copyright, 116, 132
counter-cinematic form, 4
cultural narrative, xi, 203n39, 227n18

Darfur genocide, 104, 108–109
death marches, testimony about, 79, 104–105, 153–154, 158, 160
deep memory. See common versus deep memory
Delbo, Charlotte, 5, 23
dialogic discourse, 10
digitization of testimony, 33–34, 115, 206n13
Documentation Center of Cambodia (DC-Cam), 17, 193–195, 226n1
Dori K. (witness), 25–26, 83
dramatization, in museum exhibitions, 69–72
dynamics of testimony, 5–7, 192; Fortunoff Archive videos, 25–26, 29–32, 40, 45, 48, 53–54, 172–173; Holocaust Museum videos, 76–77, 81, 83–84, 98–102, 152; interviewer's role, 11; Shoah Foundation videos, 114–115, 124–129, 135

editing of video: Fortunoff Archive, 27, 39–40; Holocaust Museum, 79–80, 90–104; Shoah Foundation, 124, 130, 143, 146–147, 149
educational use of testimony. See pedagogical use of testimony
Eichmann, Adolf, 8, 203n34
Ejszyszki shtetl (Lithuania), 88–90
Eliach, Yaffa, 88
Emanuel T. (witness), 93
embodied memory, 4, 201n14
emotional memory: concept of, 2, 6, 10; Fortunoff Archive videos, 21–22, 26,

46–47, 157, 178; frailty of, 109–110, 171–
172; Holocaust Museum videos, 82, 92,
95, 100, 104–106, 154; Shoah Foundation
videos, 117, 125–126, 129, 136, 159–160
English language, testimony in, xi, 83,
170–172, 174
Era of the Witness, The (Wieviorka), 203n34
European history, importation of, xi, 57,
59–60, 66, 87
Eva B. (witness), 41–47
evidence: standard of, 93, 110, 121, 140, 144–
146, 153, 166, 182, 195; testimony as, 11,
110, 123
exemplary witnesses, 12–13, 17; comparative testimonies, 12, 151–191; Fortunoff
Archive, 40–52; Holocaust Museum,
104–106; Shoah Foundation, 135–147.
See also specific witnesses
exhibitions: versus archives, 7, 76; experiential mode of, xi; Holocaust Museum, 60–72, 87–95
experiential learning, 72
experiential mode of exhibition, xi
explicit images, 69–72, 108–109
Extraordinary Chambers in the Courts of
Cambodia (ECCC), 193

Facing History and Ourselves (program), 22
Fagin, Helen, 72
family dynamics, 187–191; Fortunoff Archives videos, 50–51; Shoah Foundation videos, 117, 123, 129, 142
famous people, in testimonies, 122
fantasists, 93
Farr, Raye: on captions for photographs,
88–89; as director of exhibitions, 80;
on *Schindler's List,* 68–69; on *Testimony*
film, 93
finding aids, 33–34, 135, 180
Fortunoff, Alan A., 21
Fortunoff Video Archive for Holocaust
Testimonies, 14–15, 19; access points,
15, 22, 33–34, 133, 180, 206n13; circulation of testimonies, 15, 22, 33–40; collaboration with other archives, 20,
73–75, 113; comparative witnesses,
157–159, 161–162, 165–167, 169–173, 177–

179; compared to other archives, 21;
conceptual framework, 15, 21–23, 52–
55; conflict with Holocaust Museum,
75, 82–87; conflict with Shoah Foundation, 133; exemplary witnesses, 40–
52; interview assessment, 30–33; interview methodology, 15, 28–30, 37, 40,
43, 47–49, 76–77; Langer's influence
at, 23–26, 30, 76; library catalogue, 15,
33–34, 180; media specificity, 26–28,
54–55; origins of, 8, 20–21; pre-interviews, 29, 84; promotional activities,
28–29, 34–40; *Those Who Were There*
(video), 34–36; twentieth anniversary
event, 19; *Witness: Voices from the Holocaust* (book), 51–53, 173; *Witness: Voices
from the Holocaust* (documentary), 22,
36–40, 48, 173
frames of interpretation, 13–18
framing, 2–3; Fortunoff Archive videos,
27–28, 37, 41, 43, 45, 157, 161, 169, 177;
Holocaust Museum videos, 76–77, 81–
82, 85–86, 92, 106, 173–174, 179; Shoah
Foundation videos, 123, 124, 130, 137–
139, 143, 175, 183
Frank, Anne, 38, 70
Fred O. (witness), 31–32
Friedländer, Saul, 5
Frisch, Michael, 205n52
fugitive use of testimony, 147–149

gas chamber door, display of, 66
gender issues, 13, 152, 184–185, 205n51
generic film footage, 38–39, 87–88, 93,
216n123
genocides: Cambodian, 17, 193–195, 226n1;
Darfur, 104, 108–109; Holocaust as
paradigm for, 17–18, 109, 193, 227n18;
Holocaust Museum campaigns, 107–
111; Nanjing Massacre, 134; Rwanda,
108, 134, 226n1; Shoah Foundation archives, 116, 193–195
Gerda and Kurt Klein Foundation, 217n146
Gerda K. (witness), 93, 95–97, 217n146
gestures, 2, 13–14; Fortunoff Archive videos, 27–28, 157, 166–167, 170, 178; Holocaust Museum videos, 86, 105–106, 154,

163, 173–174, 179–180; Shoah Foundation videos, 138, 143–145, 159

Ginsberg, Ruth Bader, 68

Godin, Nesse, 104–106, 108, 109

Goldhagen, Erich, 34

graphic representation, 69–72, 108–109

Greenberg, Douglas, 116, 147

Greene, Joshua, 36, 39, 51, 53

Greenspan, Henry, 204n48, 204n50, 205n52

Greenwald, Alice, 70

hair, 72, 107, 213n63

Hansen, Miriam, 112

Hartman, Geoffrey: on agency, 53; on conceptual framework, 21, 22, 55; on counter-cinematic form, 4; on exemplary witnesses, 40; on frame conditions, 3; on popularization of Holocaust, 9

Hedlund, Elizabeth, ix

Helen W. (witness), 98

Hilberg, Raul, 64–65, 72, 148

Hirsch, Marianne, 3, 188

historical film footage, 38–39, 87–88, 93, 216n123

historical use of testimony, 6–7, 10–11; Fortunoff Archive, 26, 158; Holocaust Museum, 58–59, 65, 69–72, 76, 87–90, 103, 153–154; versus postmemory, 189; Shoah Foundation, 121, 125–127, 130, 148–149, 168–169, 175–176, 194–195

history: European, importation of, xi, 57, 59–60, 66, 87; postwar (see postwar history); received, 5, 100, 202n21

Hitler Youth, 38

Hochberg, Severin, 68

Hollywood cinematic conventions, 112, 119, 125

Holocaust (Shoah): Americanization of, xi–xii, 8–9, 203n38; denial of, 69, 87, 103, 106–107, 146; homogenization of, 22–23, 203n39; institutionalization of, xi–xii, 58, 94–95, 112; as paradigm, 17–18, 109, 193, 227n18; popular representations of, 8–9, 22–23, 59, 112, 149–150; trivialization of, 9, 53

Holocaust (TV miniseries), 22, 59

"Holocaust: A World Prospect" conference (Tehran), 106–107

Holocaust in American Life, The (Novick), 203n38

Holocaust Remembrance Day, 36

Holocaust Survivors Film Project, 20, 24–25

Holocaust Testimonies: The Ruins of Memory (Langer), 23, 30, 51, 82–83, 171, 208n70

homogenization of the Holocaust, 22–23, 203n39

Hopkins, Anthony, 113

"humiliated imagination," 51

indexing system. See cataloguing system

individual expression: versus collective memory, 10, 50, 70–72, 76–77, 102, 127, 153–159, 181–182; versus institutional protocol, 4, 7, 53–54, 94–97, 102, 111, 154; versus popular culture, 8–9, 22–23, 59, 112, 149–150

institutional protocols. See interview methodology

institutionalization of the Holocaust, xi–xii, 58, 94–95, 112

intergenerational dynamics, 187–191; Fortunoff Archives videos, 50–51; Shoah Foundation videos, 117, 123, 129

interview assessment, 13, 223n92; Fortunoff Archive, 30–33; Holocaust Museum, 79, 93, 103; Shoah Foundation, 120–121, 135

interview methodology: comparative witnesses, 151–191; Fortunoff Archive, 15, 28–30, 37, 40, 43, 47–49, 76–77; Holocaust Museum, 24, 63, 75–82, 85, 92; role of, 1–7; Shoah Foundation, 114–115, 118–120, 124–130, 135–147, 194; tension caused by, 4, 7, 53–54, 94–97, 102, 111, 138, 140, 160, 164, 182

interviewees. See witnesses; specific witnesses

interviewers: identification of, 45, 84–85, 157; mental health issues, 126, 129. See also specific interviewers

"Interviewing Holocaust Witnesses: Question Guide" (USHMM), 80–81 interviews: agency during (*see* agency); dynamic in (*see* dynamics of testimony); fragmenting nature of, 6; frames of interpretation, 13–18; number of, x, 11; post-interview recovery, 129; preparation for (*see* pre-interviews); questions during (*see* questions); release forms for, 79–80, 123, 132; sample scenario, ix–x; time limits for, 30, 77–78, 81, 122, 125, 152, 182; training for (*see* training of interviewers). *See also* testimony

Irene W. (witness), 24

Ismail, Omer, 108

"IWitness" (online resource), 149

John S. (witness), 38, 208n70

Joseph W. (witness), 38

Julia L. (witness), 143–147, 224n100

Katz, Alte, 90

Katz, Yitzhak Uri, 90

Ken Burns effect, 130, 139

"Khmer Rouge Regime Survivor Questionnaire" (DC-CAM), 194

Kigali Genocide Memorial Centre, 226n1

Kline, Dana, 30, 40, 48

Kristallnacht, 97

Kumar, Shiva, 36, 51

Kurt K. (witness), 96–97, 141, 217n146

Kushner, Tony, 202n20

Kuzmack, Linda: interview assessment, 79; interview methodology, 76–78, 80–81, 84–85, 106, 183; on interviewee release form, 79–80; as oral history department director, 74–75

labor of testimony, 2, 13–15, 205n52; comparative witnesses, 151, 159, 161–162; Fortunoff Archive videos, 26–33, 43, 50–51; Holocaust Museum videos, 83, 94–95, 110; Shoah Foundation videos, 129

Landsberg, Alison, 71–72, 189–190, 211n31

Langer, Lawrence: on anti-redemptive testimony, 6, 23–26, 42, 52, 84; forward to *Witness* (book), 51–52; Holocaust

Museum work, 76, 82–84, 169; on limits of testimony, 171–172; on media specificity, 54; on memory, 5, 23–25; re-interviews by, 40, 45–47, 51, 84, 171–173; on role of testimony, 110; on witness-interviewer bond, 102

language barriers, xi, 83, 170–172

Lanzmann, Claude, 91, 148

Laub, Dori: on interview methodology, 29–30, 35; on interviewer's role, 11; re-interviews by, 40, 41, 45–47; testimony of, 20

leading questions, 141, 184–185

Learning Center (USHMM), 102–104

Leo B. (witness), 101–102, 161–165

Leo G. (witness), 25

Leo Rosner Foundation, 135

Levy, Marvin, 68

Leydesdorff, Selma, 225n31

library catalogue. *See* cataloguing system

lighting setup, 2; Fortunoff Archive videos, 28; Holocaust Museum videos, 77, 86; Shoah Foundation videos, 123, 130, 183

Lily M. (witness), 152–160

Linenthal, Edward, 64, 70, 94, 111, 205n53

linguistic barriers, 174

literalist approach, 10

"Long Shadow of Sobibor, The" (interview project), 225n31

Los Angeles Museum of the Holocaust, 217n131

Losche, Diane, 227n18

Majdanek death camp (Poland), 57, 66

Max "Amichai" H. (witness), 67, 165–169

media specificity of testimony, 1–7, 26–28, 54–55, 85–86, 148

Meed, Benjamin, 58, 62, 73

Meed, Vladka, 58

Mellon Foundation, 133, 147, 149

memory: beyond survivor testimony (*see* postmemory); beyond wartime era (*see* postwar history); collective (*see* collective memory); common (*see* common versus deep memory); compartmentalization of, ix, 128–129;

competitive, 196; deep (*see* common versus deep memory); embodied, 4, 201n14; emotional (*see* emotional memory); history integrated with, 6–7, 10–11; multidirectional, 196–197; politics of, 54–55; prosthetic, 71–72, 190, 192, 211n31; sensory, 156–158, 161–163, 165; "stay with you all the time," ix

memory culture, 227n18

meta-discursive elements of testimony, 45–47

Minow, Martha, 195

Müller, Beate, 151, 200n4

multidirectional memory, 196–197

multisensory memory, 156–158, 161–163, 165

Museum of Jewish Heritage (New York), 113

Museum of the Diaspora (Israel), 63

museums: versus archives, 7; Holocaust (*See* United States Holocaust Memorial Museum)

Nanjing Massacre (1937–38), 134

narration (in film), 94, 100–101

narrative approach: versus deep memory, 24–25, 84, 101–102; Holocaust Museum, 65–69, 75, 81, 84, 87–90, 101–102, 153–154, 163–164; Shoah Foundation, 118–120, 124–129, 135–147, 160, 168–169, 185–187

national identity, xi, 197

National Registry of Holocaust Survivors, 58, 73

Natsios, Andrew, 108

Nazi rallies (Nuremberg) film footage, 87

New Haven Jewish Federation (Connecticut), 20

note-taking approach, ix, 131

novels, 54

Novick, Peter, 203n38

object survivors, 62, 67, 107. *See also* artifacts

obligation to remember, 50–52, 73, 159–160, 177, 187

off-camera dimensions of testimony, 14; Fortunoff Archive videos, 162; Holocaust Museum videos, 96, 98–100, 104, 163–164, 183

Olga K. (witness), 136–140

Olympic games (1936) film footage, 87

On Listening to Holocaust Survivors (Greenspan), 204n50

One Survivor Remembers (documentary), 217n146

Oral History Interviewee Release Form (USHMM), 79–80

Our Walls Bear Witness: Darfur: Who Will Survive Today? (photo installation), 108–109

paradigm, Holocaust as, 17–18, 109, 193, 227n18

"Peanut Butter Theory," 103

pedagogical use of testimony, 9, 12; Fortunoff Archive videos, 22, 36–40, 44; Holocaust Museum, 60–65, 69–72, 100–106; Shoah Foundation, 117, 146–147

performance of testimony, x, 2, 10–14; comparative witnesses, 155, 158, 162, 178; Holocaust Museum videos, 98–102, 105–106; limitations of, 171–172, 174, 176; Shoah Foundation videos, 135

Peter C. (witness), 32

Pfefferkorn, Eli, 60

photographs: captions for, 87–89, 108–109; "Tower of Faces" exhibition (USHMM), 88–90; in video testimonies, 100, 121, 123, 139–140, 142, 165–166, 177, 185–187

physical gestures. *See* gestures

poems, 155

politics of memory, 54–55

popular representations of Holocaust, 8–9, 22–23, 59, 112, 149–150

Portelli, Allesandro, 10

post-interview recovery, 129

postmemory: concept of, 3, 192; Fortunoff Archives videos, 50–51; media specificity and, 54–55, 148; role of testimony in, 58–59, 61–62; Shoah Foundation videos, 117, 123, 129, 147–150, 177, 189–190; transmission of, 187–191 postwar history, ix; comparative witnesses, 166–169, 179, 182–184; Fortunoff Archive videos, 51; Holocaust Museum videos, 84, 101; Shoah Foundation videos, 128

pre-interviews: DC-Cam, 194–195, 226n7; Fortunoff Archive, 29, 84; Holocaust Museum, 77, 96; Shoah Foundation, 118, 121–123, 131, 184, 194

Preserving Memory: The Struggle to Create America's Holocaust Museum (Linenthal), 205n53

President's Commission on the Holocaust, 8, 57

promotional activities: Fortunoff Archive, 28–29, 34–40; Shoah Foundation, 114–115, 117

proprietary issues: Holocaust Museum, 58, 79–80, 86; Shoah Foundation, 116, 117, 132–133, 147–150

prosthetic memory, 71–72, 190, 192, 211n31

"Quality Assurance Self-Assessment Form" (Shoah Foundation), 120

questions: depth and nature of, 2; Fortunoff Archive interviews, 32, 41–42, 48–49; Holocaust Museum interviews, 76, 80–81; leading, 141, 184–185; Shoah Foundation videos, 118–120, 122–123, 126–129, 141–142, 148, 183–185

"quiet empathy" approach, 76, 80, 163

"reading against the grain" of testimony, 202n21

received history, 5, 100, 202n21

"Red Book" (USHMM), 61

redemption: anti-redemptive testimony, 6–7, 9, 23–26, 42, 50–54, 84, 111; Fortunoff Archive, 44, 52–54; Holocaust Museum, 84, 111; Shoah Foundation, 128–129, 142, 149–150, 184–185

reenactments. *See* performance of testimony

Reich, Walter, 149

release forms, 79–80, 123

Renov, Michael, 4, 143, 201n14

"Representations of the Holocaust" (seminar), 143

Richard K. (witness), 140–142

Ringelheim, Joan, ix

Robert S. (witness), 38

Romani witness, 143–147

Rosen, Alan, 203n34

Rosensaft, Hadassah, 71–72

Rothberg, Michael, 196

Rudof, Joanne: as archivist, 21, 29; on exemplary witnesses, 40, 48; on interview assessment, 30; on *Schindler's List,* 22; on value of archives, 26

Rwandan genocide (1994), 108, 134, 226n1

Schindler, Oskar, 22, 67, 112

Schindler's List (film), 8–9, 22–23, 67–69, 112–113, 118, 149–150

Selma E. (witness), 177–187, 225n31

sensory memory, 156–158, 161–163, 165

shared authority, 205n52

Shoah. *See* Holocaust

Shoah (documentary), 91, 148

Shoah Foundation, 16–17, 112–114; access points, 114–115, 131–135, 147–150, 180, 197, 224n100; Center for Advanced Genocide Research, 197, 224n100; collaboration with other archives, 20, 113–115; comparative witnesses, 159–160, 164–165, 168–169, 175–177, 183–187; compared to other archives, 21; conceptual framework, 117–118; development of, 115–116; editing of video, 124, 130, 143, 146–147, 149; exemplary witnesses, 135–147; genocide archives, 116, 193–195; interview assessment, 120–121, 135; interview methodology, 114–115, 118–120, 124–130, 135–147, 194; limits and potential of archive, 147–150, 189–190; mission, 117, 132; pre-interviews, 118, 121–123, 131, 184, 194; promotional activities, 114–115, 117; proprietary issues, 116, 117, 132–133, 147–150; technical specifications, 130–131

shoes, display of, 66–67

silence, during interviews, 2, 76, 84, 104, 119, 124, 152

"silent empathy" approach, 76, 80, 163
Simon Wiesenthal Center, 107, 113
Singley, Katherine, 66
Sinti witness, 143–147
Smith, Martin: as director of exhibitions, 64; on exhibition displays, 67, 75, 79, 90–91; on interview methodology, 75–77, 79, 86, 106
Smith, Stephen, 116
Sobibor death camp (Poland), 169–187, 225n31
social constructivist approach, 10
social history, testimony as, 123, 126–127, 183, 185, 190, 194–195
songs, 44, 156–160, 224n9
Spielberg, Steven, 8–9, 22, 67–69, 112–113
Steven Spielberg Film and Video Archive (USHMM), 68
Stier, Oren, 199n1
storytelling approach: versus deep memory, 24–25, 84, 100–101; Holocaust Museum, 65–69, 75–76, 81, 84, 87–90, 100–101, 153–154, 163–164; Shoah Foundation, 118–120, 124–129, 135–147, 160, 168–169, 185–187
subjectivity, 10
subtexts of witness narratives, 46–47, 111, 151
Survivor Release Form (Shoah Foundation), 123, 132
survivors. See witnesses; specific witnesses
Survivors of the Shoah Visual History Foundation, 8–9
Survivors: Testimonies of the Holocaust (CD-ROM), 220n2

"talking heads" approach, 39, 100–101
tattoos, 49–50, 86, 144
technical conversation, 14; Fortunoff Archive videos, 162; Holocaust Museum videos, 95, 98–100, 104, 162–164, 183
"Techniques for Effectively Applying Interview Methodology" (Shoah Foundation), 118
testimonial literacy, 2, 111, 151, 192

testimony: access to (see access to testimony); anti-redemptive aspects of (see redemption); assessment of (see interview assessment); audience for, 15, 35–36, 63, 71, 119, 172, 192; body language during, 2, 13–14, 81, 124 (see also gestures); commercial use of, 22, 64–65; comparative, 12, 151–191; contradictions and gaps in, 202n20; dynamics of (see dynamics of testimony); educational use of (see pedagogical use of testimony); fugitive use of, 147–149; as history (see historical use of testimony); intertwined, 169–187; labor of (see labor of testimony); limitations of, 171–172, 174–176, 196–197; meaning of, 204n48; media specificity of, 1–7, 26–28, 54–55, 85–86, 148; meta-discursive elements of, 45–47; obligation to deliver, 50–52, 73, 159–160, 177, 187; performance of (see performance of testimony); popular representations of Holocaust and, 8–9, 22–23, 59, 112, 149–150; preparation for (see pre-interviews). See also interviews; witnesses; specific witnesses
Testimony (film), 91–102
"Testimony Amphitheater" (USHMM), 86, 90–95
Those Who Were There (video), 34–36
time limits for interviews, 30, 77–78, 81, 122, 125, 152, 182
"To Bear Witness, to Remember, and to Learn: A Confidential Report on Museum Planning" (USHMM), 61
topography of terror, xi
"Toward an Understanding of Media-Based Testimony" (training document), 26
"Tower of Faces" exhibition (USHMM), 88–90
training of interviewers: Fortunoff Archive, 26–32, 51, 169; Holocaust Museum, 80–81; Shoah Foundation, 118, 120–121, 126, 176, 194
transcripts, 135, 180

transference, 126, 129
translation, 83
traumatic memory. *See* emotional memory
"Tree of Testimony" exhibit (Los Angeles Museum), 217n131
trivialization of the Holocaust, 9, 53

United States, Holocaust commemoration in, x–xi, 8–9, 20, 203n38
United States Holocaust Memorial Council, 57, 64
United States Holocaust Memorial Museum (USHMM), 15–16, 56–57; artifacts in, 62, 65–67, 71–72, 91, 93, 107; Center for the Prevention of Genocide, 219n175; collaboration with other archives, 20, 57, 73–75, 113, 115; Committee on Conscience (COC), 107–108, 219n175; comparative witnesses, 152–156, 162–164, 167–168, 173–175, 179–183; compared to other archives, 21; conceptual framework, 87–90; as conceptual museum, 69–72, 211n31; conflict with Fortunoff Archive, 75, 82–87; Content Committee, 58–60, 62, 64–66, 69–72; Department of Oral History, ix–x, 16, 72–75; development of, 8, 20, 57–65, 205n53; editing of video by, 79–80, 90–104; exemplary witnesses, 104–106; experiential mode of exhibition, xi; Holocaust denial response, 106–107; interview assessment, 79, 93, 103; interview methodology, 24, 63, 75–82, 85, 92; Learning Center, 102–104; mission, 16, 56, 65, 90; Museum Concept Planning Committee, 60; Permanent Exhibition, 58–72, 86–95; pre-interviews, 77, 96; proprietary issues, 58, 79–80, 86; research library, 115; *Schindler's List* and, 67–69; Steven Spielberg Film and Video Archive, 68; as storytelling site, 65–69, 75–76, 87–90; *Testimony* (film), 91–102; "Testimony Amphitheater," 86, 90–95; "Tower of Faces" exhibition (USHMM), 88–90; transcripts, 135; "Voices from Auschwitz" segment, 78–79, 90
Universal Studios, 68–69, 115
University of Southern California (USC)—Institute for Visual History and Education. *See* Shoah Foundation

veteran interviewees, 204n50
Visual History Archive (VHA). *See* Shoah Foundation
Vlock, Laurel, 20, 41, 178
voice-overs, 94, 100–101
"Voices from Auschwitz" segment (USHMM), 78–79, 90
voyeurism, 111

Walker, Janet, 10, 109
Wallenberg, Raoul, 99
Wamariya, Clementine, 108
Warsaw Ghetto film footage, 88, 93, 216n123
Waxman, Zoë, 200n3, 203n34, 203n39, 205n51
Weinberg, Jeshajahu "Shaike," 62–63, 65, 68–69, 73, 75, 93
Wiesel, Elie, 31, 35–36, 57, 59, 61, 64, 111
Wieviorka, Annette, 8, 203n34
"Witness to the Truth" (videoconference), 107
Witness: Voices from the Holocaust (book), 51–53, 173
Witness: Voices from the Holocaust (documentary), 22, 36–40, 48, 173
witnesses: agency of (*see* agency); aging of, 78–79, 140, 173, 185; categories of, 11–13, 17; comparative, 12, 151–191; exemplary (*see* exemplary witnesses); family of (*see* family dynamics); interviews with (*see* interviews); obligation to remember, 50–52, 73, 159–160, 177, 187; passing of, x, 1, 150; selection of, 78; survivor community, 8–9, 35, 57–59, 77; testimony by (*see* testimony). *See also* specific witnesses
Witnesses for Humanity Project, 116
WNH-TV, 20

Wonder of Their Voices, The (Rosen), 203n34
"Working Response to the Question of
    Explicit Imagery, A" (USHMM), 69–70
Writing the Holocaust (Waxman), 203n34,
    203n39

Yad Vashem (Jerusalem), 113, 204n50
Yaeger, Patricia, 6, 202n25
"Yale Method," 76

Yale University: on access to Shoah Foun-
    dation archives, 133; archive at (*see*
    Fortunoff Video Archive for Holo-
    caust Testimonies)
Young, James, xi, 100, 202n21

zero-degree style, 28
zoom technique. *See* close-ups
Zwelling, Shomer, 70

NOAH SHENKER earned a doctorate in critical studies from the School of Cinematic Arts at the University of Southern California in 2009. While completing his doctoral work he was the recipient of the Charles H. Revson Fellowship for Archival Research at the Jack, Joseph, and Morton Mandel Center for Advanced Holocaust Studies of the United States Holocaust Memorial Museum. Following his graduate work he held a position as a postdoctoral fellow at McMaster University in Hamilton, Ontario. He is currently the 6a Foundation Lecturer in Holocaust and Genocide Studies within the Australian Centre for Jewish Civilisation at Monash University in Melbourne, Australia, where his research and teaching focus on representations of the Holocaust, genocide, and trauma more broadly in testimonies, film, and visual culture.

CPSIA information can be obtained at www.ICGtesting.com
Printed in the USA
LVOW06s2124040116

469073LV00002B/135/P